FANTASTIC
JOURNEYS

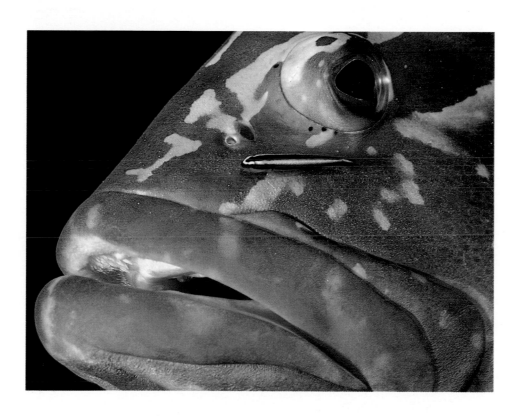

FANTASTIC JOURNEYS

FOG CITY PRESS

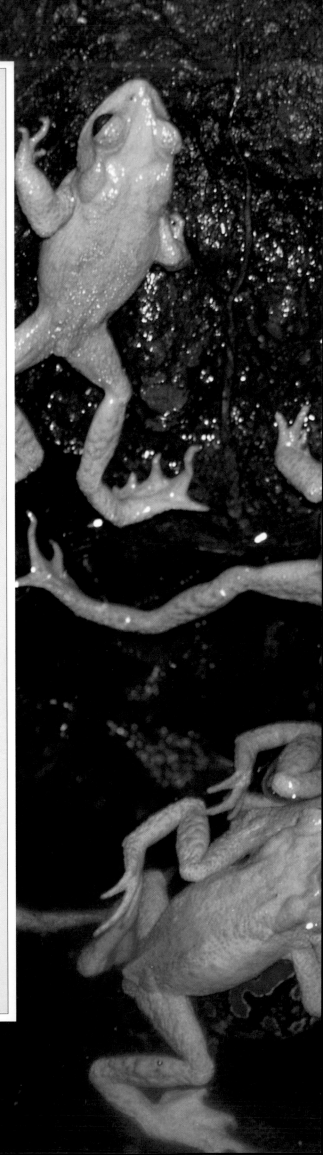

Published by Fog City Press
814 Montgomery Street
San Francisco, CA 94133 USA

CEO: John Owen
President: Terry Newell
Publisher: Sheena Coupe
Project Coordinator: Vanessa Finney
Picture Editor: Jenny Mills
Captions: Terence Lindsey
Design: Di Quick
Maps: Stan Lamond
Life Cycle Illustrations: Alistair Barnard, Frank Knight
Illustrations and Diagrams: Tony Pyrzakowski
Production Manager: Helen Creeke
Production Assistant: Kylie Lawson
Business Manager: Emily Jahn
Vice President, International Sales: Stuart Laurence

ISBN 1 875137 97 1

Printed by Kyodo Printing Co. (S'pore) Pte Ltd
Printed in Singapore

A WELDON OWEN PRODUCTION

Page 1: A Nassau grouper is cleaned by a goby. Photo by Marty Snyderman.
Pages 2–3: Pintado Petrels feeding on a lake. Photo by Doug Allan, Oxford Scientific Films.
Pages 4–5: Males compete for access to females at a spawning aggregation of golden toads in Costa Rica. Photo by Michael Fogden, Bruce Coleman Ltd.
Pages 6–7: Elephants on the move in Kenya. Photo by Yann Arthus Bertrand, Auscape.
Pages 8–9: From left to right; green turtle, photo by Ron & Valerie Taylor, A.N.T. Photo Library; aphid on a lupin, photo by Steve Littlewood, Oxford Scientific Films; blue-footed booby, photo by J.F. Carlyon, Aquila; blue-cheeked lemonfish, photo by Mike Neumann, Photo Researchers Inc.; caribou, photo by Michio Hoshino, Animals & Earth; Daubenton's bat, photo by Frank Greenaway, Bruce Coleman Ltd.
Pages 10–11: A hyena chasing flamingos on Lake Magadi, Tanzania.
Pages 12–13: Walruses basking on Round Island, Alaska. Photo by Jeff Foott, Auscape.
Pages 44–45: Mexican free-tailed bats. Photo by S. Krasemann, NHPA.
Pages 104–105: Schooling scalloped hammerhead sharks. Photo by Marty Snyderman.
Pages 168–169: Wildebeest crossing a river. Photo by Jonathon Scott, Planet Earth Pictures.

CONTENTS

INTRODUCTION

Dr R. Robin Baker

*Reader in Zoology
Department of Environmental
Biology, University of
Manchester, UK*

1 THE MYSTERIES OF MIGRATION

2 AERIAL EPICS

CONTENTS

INTRODUCTION

R. Robin Baker

All over the world—day and night and at all seasons—animals are on the move, migrating from one home or feeding place to another.

In the air are minute spiders, showy insects, frenetic bats, and noisy but graceful flocks of birds. Some are flying determinedly to some distant goal. Others are floating effortlessly through the air on threads of gossamer, while yet others are hitchhikers, gaining free transport by clinging to the legs of insects or the feathers of birds. Some migrants are traveling only a few meters or kilometers. Others are moving in true aerial epics from one end of the earth to the other.

As these aeronauts range over the earth's surface, their migration tracks crisscross those of other migrants traveling more slowly over the land beneath. Butterflies migrating over the plains of Africa fly through and over magnificent herds of wildebeest and zebra. Geese and ducks from the Canadian Arctic cross prairies that were once blackened by migrating herds of bison. Unseen in the surrounding grass are snakes, frogs, and toads, some exploring for new homes, others traveling between familiar summer and winter sites.

As shorebirds migrate along continental coasts, large adult salmon and tiny eels gather in the estuaries below before beginning their tiring migration upstream to breeding and feeding areas. On the rocky shores there are seals and sea lions hauled out to molt, mate, or give birth. In the tropics, shorebirds fly over sandy beaches on which marine turtles have emerged to dig holes and lay eggs. Birds migrating from northern Asia to Australasia may pass the occasional adventurous crocodile setting out to sea on an exploration that could lead to the colonization of new islands.

Even over the open ocean the skies are not empty of animal migrants. Albatrosses wander all over the Southern Ocean, mutton birds cross the Pacific from Australasia to Alaska, and terns fly annually from the Arctic to the Antarctic and back. Beneath these winged travelers the seas conceal a myriad of animals, ranging in size from the smallest plankton to the largest whales, all migrating on invisible tracks through the water. Shoals of fish travel the seas' highways on huge migration circuits, feeding on planktonic plants and animals which themselves migrate up and down through the water in daily and seasonal migration cycles. Whales swim languorously in family parties or herds en route between polar and tropical waters. Crisscrossing the paths of all of these are those same species of salmon, eels, turtles, and seals that from time to time appear in the estuaries and on shore as part of their own migration cycles.

Humans have always been part of, aware of, and fascinated by animal migrations. Inheriting the migration

patterns of his primate ancestors, *Homo sapiens* has in many ways been the most migratory of all animals. From humankind's African cradle, subsequent migrations have covered virtually every centimeter of the earth and even moved out into the solar system.

There is hardly an animal alive whose migrations do not cross the path of a human at some point. As hunters, humans have long been keenly aware of the local and seasonal abundances of migrating prey animals. The hunting of deer is depicted in cave paintings and the killing of animals on migration is described in ancient texts such as the Bible. At times and in places where the migrations of fish or whales brought them close to shore, whole human communities have grown and flourished on their exploitation.

It is not only as a hunter that humans' interest in animal migration has been predatory. Farmers in many parts of the world have for thousands of years feared the arrival of migrating swarms of locusts and the total destruction of their crops. They have also waged war against those large mammals whose migration tracks take them through cultivated fields.

However, interest in animal migration has not been exclusively predatory. Those animals whose migrations cause them to appear and disappear at particular times of year have for millenia been part of the human calendar, marking the procession of the seasons. Since the time of Aristotle, humans have offered explanations and interpretations of seasonal changes in the animals around them.

Always, it seems, an air of mystery has surrounded animal migration. No longer, of course, do we believe as did our ancestors from the Middle Ages that swallows hibernate in the mud at the bottom of ponds, eels grow from horse hairs that drop into water, or that barnacle geese grow from barnacles. Nor do we believe, as biologists did only a decade or so ago, that animals can be divided into migrants and nonmigrants. Every gradation can now be seen between the travels of an earthworm a few centimeters up and down in the soil or the flight of a sparrow from the roof of a house onto the lawn on the one hand, and the interpolar journeys of Arctic terns on the other.

All animals are born in a place determined for them by their mother, and die at a place determined by their own migrations. Between these two events and places, each individual animal traces a path through time and space that is its lifetime track. Essentially, the study of animal migration is the study of lifetime tracks. Now that superstitions have been overturned and scientific misconceptions cleared up, we appear to have a high and intellectually satisfying level of understanding of lifetime tracks. We are even beginning to understand the sophisticated mechanisms of orientation and navigation by which animals manage to find their way.

In a strange way, the more the veneer of mystery is stripped away from the phenomenon of migration, the more fascinating it becomes and the more fantastic animal journeys appear to be. Perhaps, too, the more fascinated we become by these fantastic journeys and the more we understand them, the easier we may make the transition from predator to conserver.

Part 1

THE MYSTERIES OF MIGRATION

At all times, and in all seasons, animals are migrating
somewhere. Some move only short distances but others cross
half the globe, sometimes year after year. The powerful forces
that underlie migration are still quite mysterious, but answers
are slowly beginning to emerge.

THE URGE TO MOVE

Those animals that migrate do so spontaneously, and often en
masse. What triggers such dramatic behavior? The explanations
are complex and various.

TYPES OF MIGRATION

The best known migrations are the cyclical ones undertaken by
many birds. But there are also once-only, one-way migrations,
and some animals seem to merely wander.

THE RIDDLE OF PATHFINDING

How do animals find their way over great distances, often to
small and specific sites? Orientation and pathfinding can be as
complex as the urge to move was in the first place.

WHEN TWO WORLDS COLLIDE

Migration is always a hazardous undertaking. When humans
interfere, or take advantage of it, the cost of migration may
well be extinction.

THE URGE TO MOVE

Peter Berthold

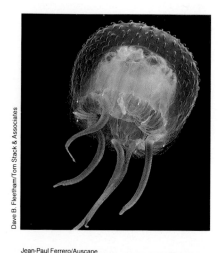

What is it that suddenly prompts an animal to embark on a marathon journey, in some cases across oceans and continents? Is it need or an inherited response? The answers are complex and various.

Without a doubt, the most favorable way of life for any animal is a settled one within a limited home area. This means that any kind of movement is ultimately due to some shortage of food or habitat, or to other selective pressures, such as competition from other species or adverse living conditions. Only within the tropics can we find utopian conditions, in which food in abundance at all times of year and continuously attractive climatic conditions allow a large group of animals to lead a completely sedentary existence. Toward higher latitudes, exclusively resident species become progressively more scarce.

There may be hundreds of individual causes that trigger those movements that we call migration. Ultimately, however, all of

these journeys have evolved in order to provide sufficient food for individuals or their offspring, to guarantee living space where the level of predatory pressure is, at worst, tolerable, or to reproduce. To meet these necessities of life, marine and freshwater plankton organisms and various fishes, for instance, undertake daily and seasonal vertical migratory movements to reach water levels where the food, light, temperature, and oxygen conditions are suitable for reproduction and resting. In order to reach adequate breeding areas, marine crustaceans may walk several hundred kilometers, sea turtles may swim several thousand kilometers, and butterflies may fly up to 4,000 kilometers (2,500 miles). Some large marine mammals and birds cover tens of thousands of kilometers in their migrations.

Of these, birds are a paramount example

of migration. And as such they provide the most comprehensive answers to the question, "Why migrate?" Not only do birds regularly commute between breeding and wintering areas, but they have also evolved specific migration behaviors. "Avoidance migration" behavior may help them overcome ice, snow, or food shortages. "Follow-up migration systems" allow tropical species in particular to keep in touch with mobile food sources, such as army ants, or to take advantage of events like bushfires that provide escaping and injured prey and promote particular plant growth. Specific "molt migration systems" can direct individual birds to safe and nutrient-rich molting places for periods of flightlessness. And special lifetime "nomadic movement systems" enable some species to localize favorable breeding conditions within areas of unpredictable environmental conditions.

◀ (Opposite page, top) Some small jellyfish take part in the daily vertical migrations of plankton between the surface and the depths of the water column.

▶ (Following pages) The distances traveled by migrating animals are as varied as the animals themselves. On land, some toads and snakes crawl several kilometers to breeding or hibernation sites. Black bears (*Ursus americanus*) may travel up to 200 kilometers (125 miles) while exploring for a place to live. But the longest migrations take place in the air and sea. The record is held by the Arctic tern (*Sterna paradisea*), which each year flies the 20,000 kilometers (12,400 miles) from the Arctic to the Antarctic.

▼ Humpback whales (*Megaptera novaengliae*) normally travel in groups, traversing shallow coastal waters in their annual migrations between polar regions and winter breeding areas in the tropics.

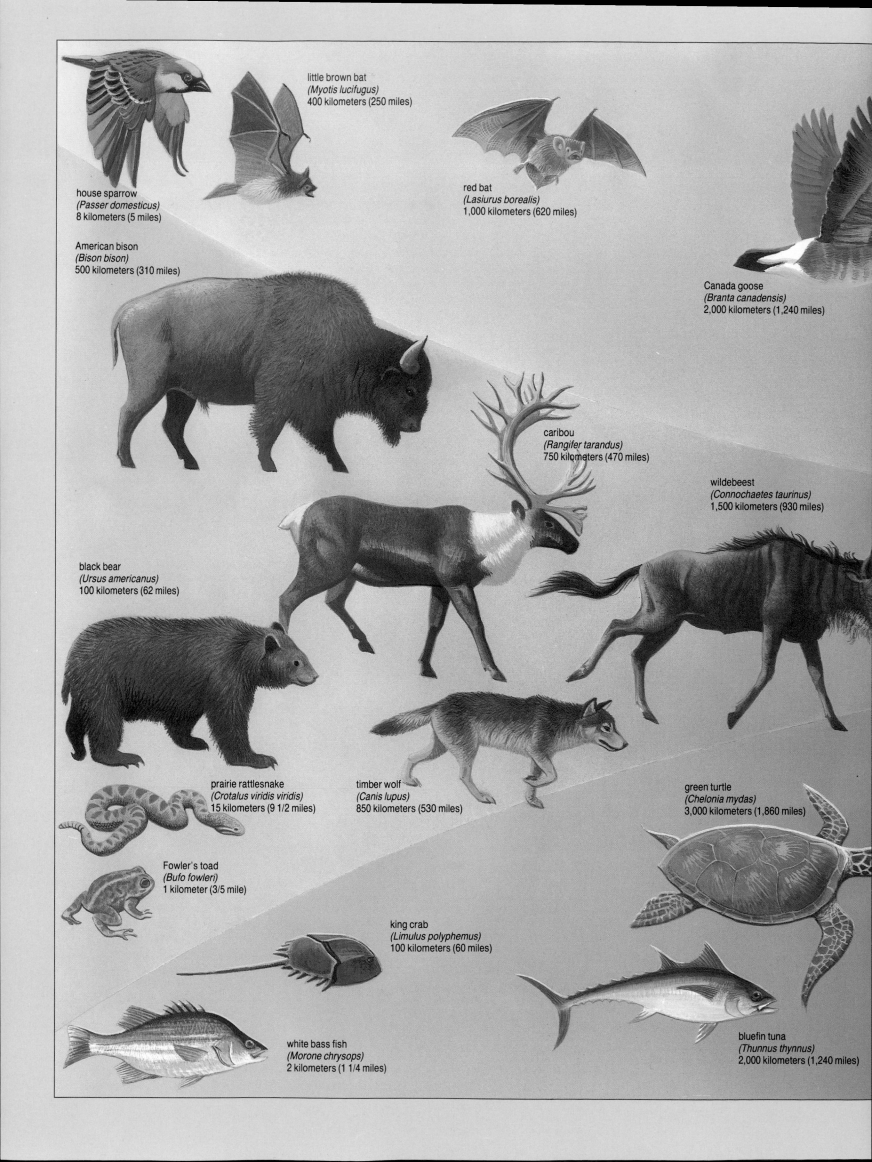

house sparrow
(*Passer domesticus*)
8 kilometers (5 miles)

little brown bat
(*Myotis lucifugus*)
400 kilometers (250 miles)

red bat
(*Lasiurus borealis*)
1,000 kilometers (620 miles)

American bison
(*Bison bison*)
500 kilometers (310 miles)

Canada goose
(*Branta canadensis*)
2,000 kilometers (1,240 miles)

caribou
(*Rangifer tarandus*)
750 kilometers (470 miles)

wildebeest
(*Connochaetes taurinus*)
1,500 kilometers (930 miles)

black bear
(*Ursus americanus*)
100 kilometers (62 miles)

prairie rattlesnake
(*Crotalus viridis viridis*)
15 kilometers (9 1/2 miles)

timber wolf
(*Canis lupus*)
850 kilometers (530 miles)

green turtle
(*Chelonia mydas*)
3,000 kilometers (1,860 miles)

Fowler's toad
(*Bufo fowleri*)
1 kilometer (3/5 mile)

king crab
(*Limulus polyphemus*)
100 kilometers (60 miles)

white bass fish
(*Morone chrysops*)
2 kilometers (1 1/4 miles)

bluefin tuna
(*Thunnus thynnus*)
2,000 kilometers (1,240 miles)

rufous hummingbird
(*Selasphorus rufus*)
3,000 kilometers (1,860 miles)

Arctic tern
(*Sterna paradisaea*)
20,000 kilometers (12,400 miles)

monarch butterfly
(*Danaus plexippus*)
4,000 kilometers (2,480 miles)

desert locust
(*Schistocerca gregaria*)
3,000 kilometers (1,860 miles)

barn swallow
(*Hirundo rustica*)
10,000 kilometers (6,200 miles)

wandering albatross
(*Diomedea exulans*)
15,000 kilometers (9,300 miles)

sockeye salmon
(*Oncorhynchus nerka*)
3,500 kilometers (2,200 miles)

eel larva
(*Anguilla anguilla*)
3,000 kilometers (1,860 miles)

humpback whale
(*Megaptera novaeangliae*)
7,000 kilometers (4,350 miles)

northern fur seal
(*Callorhinus ursinus*)
5,000 kilometers (3,100 miles)

HOW DO ANIMALS KNOW WHEN TO MIGRATE?

The capacity for spontaneous migratory movement has probably evolved in all groups of animals. This is, above all, a safety precaution that allows for rapid place changes when living conditions deteriorate. In caged birds of various species, for instance, removal of their food immediately results in a substantial increase in movement. This "hunger restlessness" in free-living members of the same species would quickly motivate them to explore nearby areas for better feeding conditions. In contrast to this opportunistic and exploratory type of migration, more regular forms like seasonal migration require exact timing and reliable periodic stimuli.

Two basic questions need to be asked here. These involve timing and decision-making. Long-distance migrants are normally extremely precise with respect to departure, time spent en route, and arrival. It is with good reason then, that many long-distance migratory bird species in northern latitudes were called calendar birds: such animals must know when to begin their migratory flight practically to the day. The question is, who, or what, tells them when to leave? On the other hand, some populations are only partially migratory. Individuals either stay regularly in the breeding area or regularly migrate. Those who leave must know when to do so, but all members of the population must already know whether to stay or leave in the first place. Here the question is, who, or what, tells them how to decide?

Recent studies of insects, fishes, and birds, and to a lesser extent of small mammals, have yielded the first insights into the control mechanisms underlying both decision-making and the exact timing of migration. Basic to these mechanisms are genetic determinants. These include inherited behavioral traits, innate physiological time programs, and the ability to respond to the annual changes in day length as an environmental timing cue.

When blackcaps (*Sylvia atricapilla*) resident on the Cape Verde Islands were experimentally crossbred with exclusively seasonal migrants of the same species from central Europe, 40 percent of the hybrid birds in the first generation were seasonally migratory. Thus the urge to migrate can be genetically transmitted immediately into the offspring of a resident animal population. In addition, even the specific north–south orientation behavior of the migrants was inherited by the offspring.

Corresponding results were also obtained from a selective breeding experiment using blackcaps from southern Europe. These birds belong to a partially migratory population. Pairs which normally migrated south in autumn were separated from the general population and bred together, as were pairs which normally did not migrate south. The results showed that within four to six generations the offspring were, respectively, either exclusively migratory or almost wholly resident. In other words, parental behavior

S. Nielsen/DRK Photo

rapidly becomes the norm for the offspring. The urge to migrate is once more shown to be highly heritable.

The timing of migration is also genetically controlled. Among American milkweed bugs (*Oncopeltus fasciatus*), the timing of migratory flights appears to be related to the timing of oviposition—the laying of eggs. By selectively breeding individuals which delayed their flight for several days, a population of late-flying individuals in which oviposition was also delayed was rapidly produced.

In seasonally migratory species that live at least a few years an amazing system has evolved for determining the exact timing of annual events in general and of seasonal migration in particular. Endogenous (or innate) annual rhythms are synchronized by external stimuli. Such "internal calendars" are known as "circannual rhythms" (from the Latin *circa* meaning "about" and *annum* for "year") have evolved in many organisms, ranging from coelenterata ("plant animals") to mammals. They appear to be a common

▲ Three mallards (*Anas platyrhyncos*) take flight. In many parts of the world wildfowl have come to represent the very essence of the urge to migrate.

MIGRATION—WHAT DOES IT MEAN?

When a couple of songbirds scour the forest searching for food for their offspring in the nest, or when a group of deer in the mountains leave a thicket at dusk to graze in a nearby alpine pasture, few people would say these animals "migrate." But when the same songbirds and their fledged nestling leave the breeding territory a few weeks later, and when the deer move downhill to lowland feeding areas as winter approaches, then most biologists would agree that these animals are carrying out some type of migration.

However, this level of agreement does not mean that there is an accepted definition of migration that is convenient and at the same time comprehensive. Migration-like behaviors are too diverse to allow that, and they are exhibited, sometimes regularly and sometimes once only, by organisms ranging from bacteria and primitive algae to humans.

Some scientists propose a broad but somewhat abstract definition of migration, describing it as the act of moving from one "spatial unit" to another. The term "spatial unit" may refer to anything from a breeding place or a seasonal feeding ground to a staging area (that is, a place of assembly prior to an exodus).

Others, including ornithologists in particular, concentrate their definitions more on regular annual or seasonal movements. The best known of such journeys are those undertaken by migratory bird species between breeding grounds and wintering areas. Unfortunately, this commonly used definition fails to take into account more irregular movements such as population explosions (for example, of migratory locusts), range expansions, or lifetime movements (for example, of many insects).

To cover so many forms and patterns of migratory movements amongst living beings, and to help understand their various causes and control mechanisms, a broad definition appears to be more appropriate. Thus a creature can be classified as migratory when it moves at least beyond the boundary of its normally inhabited home range.

▼ Migrating wildebeest (*Connochaetes taurinus*) hasten across a river in East Africa. Migrating animals often have to contend with such perilous obstacles.

Jonathan Scott/Planet Earth Pictures

base for regular seasonal migration.

Internal calendars can easily be demonstrated. When animals are kept in constant experimental conditions—that is, without exposure to any seasonal changes of perceptible environmental factors—they nevertheless produce fairly accurate patterns of seasonal behaviors. Furthermore, they do so in the correct sequence, and at approximately the appropriate time of year. When animals are kept in such conditions for longer than a year it becomes obvious that their endogenous rhythms deviate from the calendar year, usually by about two months. This deviation demonstrates the "circa"—or approximate—characteristic of these rhythms in relation to the year, proves their truly innate origin, and establishes their independence from environmental annual cycles. In free-living animals, however, these circa rhythms are synchronized exactly to the calendar year by so-called *zeitgebers* (or time-giving cues), of which the most important is photoperoid— that is, the annual changes in day length. The endogenous component, originating from various physiological processes that have not yet been fully explained, prepares the animal for an annual event such as the onset of seasonal migration. Photoperiod, which is the most reliable and predictive of all environmental cues, then sychronizes this preparedness with the exact day when migration is required.

These endogenous and inherited species-specific rhythms are the key factor in determining when to show seasonal migration. This has been shown in a comparative study with 19 seasonally migratory bird species comprising early- , intermediate- , and late-departing forms. The exact dates of the onset of autumn migration in these birds were noted at a large bird tagging station. At the same time, the onset of migratory activity was measured under controlled conditions in caged individuals of the same populations. The dates for the caged and the free-living birds were practically identical. This indicates that the endogenous factors that trigger seasonal migratory activity in caged individuals under controlled conditions are also essentially responsible for the population-specific migratory patterns found in the wild.

As a worldwide phenomenon and a characteristic of almost all evolutionary stages of creatures, migration is all but immeasurable in its enormous diversity. Nevertheless, intensive research, especially during recent decades, has elucidated a number of underlying principles and basic control mechanisms.

Migration is surely not an "amusing enterprize" as was once believed, but is alway some form of evasive movement ultimately related to food, reproduction, or living space. Irregular types of migration may be triggered by environmental factors

Frans Lanting/Minden Pictures

including food shortages, population density, or cold spells. Most of the more regular forms of migration—for instance, biannual commuting between breeding grounds and wintering areas, dispersal of juveniles, or specifically partial migration—all appear to be controlled to a considerable extent by inherited endogenous programs. In intensively studied long-distance migratory bird species, genetically determined programs for the time course of migration and for direction finding appear to be of primary importance.

▲ An Antarctic fur seal (*Arctocephalus gazella*) pup. Baby fur seals are weaned at about 10 or 11 months and accompany their mothers when they leave the breeding colony to go to sea.

TYPES OF MIGRATION

Hugh Dingle

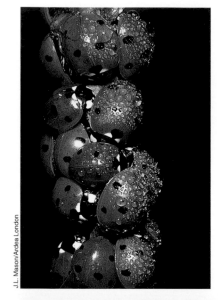

Animal migration can take many forms—a one-way journey to a new habitat, a regular return journey according to seasonal changes, or a full circle to complete the life cycle. In some cases, animals just wander about.

THE VARIETY OF MIGRATION

To all but the most casual observers of nature, evidence of animal migration is clear, and sometimes abundant. In the temperate regions, each spring millions of birds return from wintering areas to breed. Their often sudden appearance and their tuneful songs remind us of both animal movements and the cycle of the seasons. In the tropics, forests fill with bird migrants from temperate zone winters, while changes between wet and dry seasons also promote animal movements, sometimes on a very large scale. The migrations of huge herds of hoofed mammals about the Serengeti Plains of East Africa or the mass flights of locusts in Africa or Australia are amongst the best known of such tropical journeys.

Migrating animals have profoundly affected the livelihood of many people who live in their paths, or who even follow them. Locust plagues are mentioned as destroyers of crops in the Bible (for example, in Exodus and Psalms), the northern Inuit and Lapps

have depended on the seasonal appearance of marine or terrestrial mammals (and may themselves follow their prey), coastal Amerindians still fish for migrating salmon, and African tribes like the Masai follow the wet and dry season migrations of hoofed mammals. Nor have human responses to migrations been restricted to practical ones. The sheer beauty of birds, butterflies, dolphins, and other animals, and their often spectacular mass movements, have excited their share of curiosity and wonder. Bird migrations were known to Homer and Aristotle, and these and other migrations have been celebrated in literature from the Elizabethan period to the present.

Although we are most familiar with a few spectacular long-distance movements, a closer look at migration reveals its extent and its variety. While blue whales (*Balaenoptera musculus*) or Arctic terns (*Sterna paradisaea*) undertake round-trip journeys of thousands of kilometers, the Caspian tern (*S. caspia*) and Risso's dolphin

Clark Stede/G & J Fotoservice

(*Grampus griseus*) on the Pacific coast of North America may move only a few hundred kilometers over an annual cycle. Monarch butterflies (*Danaus plexippus*) may fly thousands of kilometers between breeding areas and overwintering sites or not migrate at all, while small insects, including many true bugs (Hemiptera) and certain ladybird beetles (Coccinellidae), sometimes move only a few kilometers or even meters, either between the places where they breed and overwinter, or to seek refuge during a dry season or a wet one.

In many species some individuals migrate while others do not, a situation called partial migration. A good example is the vermilion flycatcher (*Pyrocephalus rubinus*) of Mexico and the southwestern United States. This bright red and black bird is largely resident in cottonwood tree canyons and other streamside areas of Mexico, but some birds migrate north to breed in the American southwest, from southern California eastward to southern Texas.

Even among migrants like the monarch butterfly there is great variety in its patterns of migration, and some populations do not migrate at all. In eastern North America these orange and black beauties migrate from the northern states to central Mexico to overwinter in mountain pine forests. In the west they overwinter in clusters at a few protected sites along the Californian coast. Some individuals move very little to breed; others migrate inland to the east and north in spring and summer, their offspring returning to the coastal overwintering sites in the autumn. The monarch butterfly extends all the way to Argentina where it is also a migrant, but in Central America and on Caribbean islands populations are sedentary. In the last century it was introduced into Hawaii, where it is also sedentary, and into Australia, where it is called the "wanderer" and has evolved a migration cycle of northward movement to overwinter and southward movement to breed in the austral spring and summer.

However, migrants are more truly characterized by the way they behave, or by their behavior changes, than by the distances they travel. For instance, a young migratory adult black bean aphid (*Aphis fabae*) displays a distinct series of behaviors. First it climbs to the top of a plant and takes off. At this time it is sensitive to blue light from the sky and is not attracted to fresh young leaves as these aphids usually are. Once airborne, the direction of the flight is controlled by the wind, but its duration is

◀ (Opposite page, top) Ladybird beetles pass the winter in sheltered places packed together in a torpid state.

◀ (Opposite page, bottom) Once Amerindians followed bison across the western prairies of North America, and Masai tribespeople followed zebra and wildebeest in their journeys over the plains of East Africa. Both are instances of early humans migrating to ensure a reliable food supply. Some human populations continue such migrations to this day.

▶ (Following page) White-chinned petrels (*Procellaria aequinoctialis*) squabbling at their nesting burrow.

23

Frans Lanting/Minden Pictures

determined by the aphid. After an hour or so of flight it becomes insensitive to blue light, but is instead attracted to yellow wave-lengths that are most likely to be reflected from the young leaves of potential host plants. It then descends to settle, begin feeding, and give birth to its live-born young.

Young spiderlings display very similar behavior. Like the black bean aphids, they climb to the top of plants or other suitable objects, but once there the spiderlings spin out ballooning threads that allow the breeze to transport them. Their flights also demonstrate that the changeover to behavior that will end a migration is not simply due to fatigue. Because they ride their own silk parachutes, the spiderlings are not expending any energy, but they still reel in their threads and descend after a programed period of airborne transport.

The swimming larvae of many bottom-dwelling marine organisms have also evolved variations to behavior that ensure they can colonize new sites. This involves becoming temporarily pelagic—that is, living near the surface. When the time comes to migrate to a new area, usually at hatching or in one of the early stages of life, these larvae are photopositive and swim upward toward the light. After a period of time that varies between species and conditions they become photonegative—that is, they are repelled by light—and return to the depths where they eventually metamorphose into adults.

As a final instance of behavioral alterations that can accompany migration, many birds that are usually active only during the day fly at night when they migrate between breeding and non-breeding ranges. This altered behavior is evident even in the laboratory, where birds that usually sleep at night hop and flutter about their cages, displaying "migratory restlessness" that ceases only when their species' seasonal migration time has ended.

These examples from a range of animals show that migratory behavior consists not only of movement, but also of other responses that succeed in taking the organism to its correct destination, be it nearby or distant. These responses produce migrants noticeable for the undistractibility with which they pursue their courses.

ONE-WAY MIGRATIONS

Most one-way migrations serve to colonize new areas, often in an attempt to escape deteriorating habitats. Perhaps the best known of these are the swarming migrations of honeybees (*Apis mellifera*). When a hive

becomes large enough to divide, and conditions are right, usually in late spring or early summer, one queen and a large group of worker bees leave the hive in an exodus that can take them over several kilometers. The swarm then clusters in a sheltered site or on a tree branch while scout bees explore for a hollow tree or hole in the ground suitable for establishing a new hive. When a site is found, the swarm enters it, and this migratory phase is concluded as the new honeybee colony is founded.

Ants and termites are also social insects that form large colonies and undertake one-way migrations. All individuals in a colony are wingless and in ants only a queen, or in the termites a king and queen, are reproductive. In the spring, or at the beginning of the rains in the tropics, winged reproductives are formed. These leave the colony and fly out to found new ones. The swarms of flying ants and termites can be an impressive sight and may attract both bird and insect predators. After landing, the flying reproductives break off their wings along suture lines and, if they are lucky,

found a new colony. A pair of termites serve as founders, while a single foundress queen is the rule amongst ants, although sometimes two or more queens may cooperate to establish the new nest.

Among the driver ants of Africa and army ants of tropical America, the whole colony

▲ In winter the Arctic fox (*Alopex lagopus*) ranges vast distances across frozen polar wastes in search of food.

▼ A greater horseshoe bat (*Rhinolophus ferrumequinum*) chases a moth. Some bats travel great distances to congregate at caves where they spend the winter.

Stephen Dalton/Oxford Scientific Films

▲ A column of driver ants (*Eciton* species) raids a wasps' nest. These formidable ants alternate between a static stage, during which the queen lays eggs and workers are raised, and a migratory stage, when the ants march through the forest in columns carrying eggs, grubs, and their queen with them, in search of new foraging grounds.

will leave a nest site if conditions become unfavorable. The colony, which may number in the hundreds of thousands, then moves off in columns, carrying the eggs and helpless larvae and attending the queen as they go. They glean the forest floor of prey in the form of insects or helpless young birds or

lizards, and bivouac each night. The relentless marching of the ants is an impressive display of migratory behavior. Eventually a new colony site is found and the population settles once again.

Many wingless insects other than ants and termites also produce winged migrants under various conditions that lead to the need for migration over distances that could not be walked. Asexual aphid females, for example, are wingless and produce wingless daughters. But when aphid populations become crowded they produce winged offspring that migrate to new host plants. Pond skaters or water striders vary in the proportion of winged and wingless individuals, according to their location. On large permanent lakes they are likely to be entirely wingless, putting all their energy into reproduction. Those pond skaters living in temporary ponds, however, divert a good deal of their energy into growing wings and wing muscles which will enable them to migrate to new ponds when their ponds dry up.

The swimming larvae of many crabs and shrimp must colonize new areas of the substrate on which they live, but in doing so they also face a problem. These creatures live primarily in estuaries, and need to migrate within the estuary while avoiding being swept out to sea. The key to accomplishing this lies in the larvae synchronizing their movements with the tidal cycle. They move off the bottom and up the water column on the incoming tide and return to the bottom when the tide recedes, thus remaining in the estuary. Adherence to this tidal rhythm is controlled by an internal clock, which can be demonstrated in the laboratory, where the rhythm is maintained in the absence of tides. The remarkable nature of this feat is emphasized when one realizes that the rhythm shifts 50 minutes each day to match the tidal cycle!

MIGRATIONS TO AND FRO

To and fro migrations are the ones with which most people are familiar. This is largely because they are often spectacularly long range and are undertaken by many of the most conspicuous and colorful of birds.

Because it usually takes a relatively long life for round trips to be completed, these migrations are most frequent in long-lived organisms such as birds, mammals, and fish that live from one to several years. However, round-trip migrations are not exclusive to long-lived animals. Many insects, amongst them some ladybird beetles and the European small milkweed bug (*Lygaeus equestris*), migrate to hibernation sites in rock crevices, wood or trash piles, or even in old buildings. They then return to their usual habitats to breed in the spring.

Nor is it the case that an animal will migrate over long distances just because it is long-lived. The yellow-eyed junco (*Junco*

phaeonotus) is a small sparrow-like bird from Arizona whose life expectancy is measured in years. But it migrates only a few kilometers up and down mountains, wintering at lower altitudes.

Because they are so often driven by the seasons, to and fro migrations usually follow north–south routes. In birds and large terrestrial mammals movement is generally into temperate or Arctic zones to breed, taking advantage of the explosive summer bloom of plants and insects, followed by a return to lower latitudes for the winter. Thus many wood warblers of North America breed in northern coniferous forest zones and winter in Central America and the Caribbean. The barren ground caribou (*Rangifer tarandus*) migrates north of the tree line in the summer but returns southward to the forests to winter. Marine mammals, such as the gray whale (*Eschrichtius robustus*) of western North America, calve in warmer waters and return to higher latitudes in summer to feed on the rich marine life in colder seas. (Cold waters dissolve more carbon dioxide and hence support a higher density of the microscopic plants that form the base of marine food chains.)

Not all to and fro migrations are north to south, however. Some populations of the blackcap warbler (*Sylvia atricapilla*) in Europe have recently established a new migration route flying northwest to overwinter in southern Britain and Ireland before returning southeast to breed in southern Germany. Overwintering in Britain is apparently sustained by food put out in gardens, which is especially important in late winter when fruiting shrubs have been stripped so bare that they cannot sustain the birds.

In the aquatic realm one of the best known east–west migrants is the Atlantic salmon (*Salmo salar*). This fish begins life in freshwater streams and migrates to the sea for up to three or four years of feeding in the open ocean. The adults then return to rivers on both sides of the Atlantic to breed. At the conclusion of breeding adults return to the sea, but they enter streams and rivers to breed once more the following year. Long-lived individuals may make the journey several times.

MIGRATION CIRCUITS

For other animals, the pattern of migration is a circuit rather than a one-way or to and fro journey. For some, this migratory circuit is repeated within their lives. For two well-known marine to freshwater migrants,

ONE-WAY MIGRATION

Movement from one breeding site to another to escape deteriorating habitats and colonize new ones. Dotted lines indicate that several alternative directions are possible.

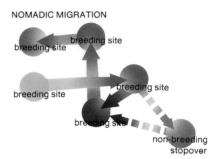

NOMADIC MIGRATION

Similar in some ways to one-way migration (both are removal migrations), in nomadic migrations some individuals may breed at several places during their lifetimes. There may also be temporary non-breeding stopovers for the winter or dry season.

RETURN MIGRATION

To and fro (return) migrations are often seasonal. Movement is between breeding and winter or dry season areas. Sometimes different routes are followed on the return journey (dotted line).

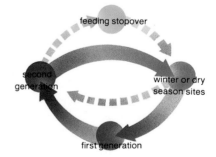

MIGRATION CIRCUITS

A to and fro migration with stopovers. Circuits include return migrations where the return includes a generation of breeding before final return to the original site by the next generation. In addition to winter or dry season areas, there may be stops at feeding areas by juveniles or adults. Also included are closed circuits where the animals die after breeding.

Andrew Henley/Biofotos

▲ Australian plague locust (*Chornocetes terminifera*) hoppers (juveniles) warming in the sun. Locusts are nomadic, but their movements are not random. Their responses are predictable and fixed, but are tied to largely unpredictable environmental factors such as rainfall and patterns of prevailing winds.

however, the circuit takes some years to complete, but it is a closed one. Both the Pacific salmon (*Oncorhynchus* species) and the Atlantic eels (*Anguilla anguilla* and *A. rostrata*) breed only once and then die.

Like their Atlantic cousins, Pacific salmon are anadromous, meaning that they are born in fresh water and migrate to the sea, where they spend several years. Adults then return to their natal rivers and streams. While migrating upstream they undergo a remarkable transformation, changing the shape of the jaw, especially in males, until they are unable to feed but can fight for breeding territories. After spawning the salmon are totally exhausted and soon die. There are no to and fro movements.

A similar circuit occurs in Atlantic eels, except that they are catadromous (that is, they are born at sea and migrate to fresh water). They are spawned in deep water somewhere in the Sargasso Sea off Bermuda, but even after years of study no one knows precisely where. The elvers enter streams and lakes on both sides of the Atlantic, where the eels mature for several years before returning to the sea to breed and die.

Many important marine fisheries depend on species which undertake migratory

circuits within the sea. Fishes like the herring, cod, and plaice in the North Atlantic have separate areas where they spawn, where the young mature (nursery areas), and where the adults feed. The separation of the life cycles among areas joined in a migration circuit probably allows exploitation of more resources and accounts for the abundance of these fishes and for the fisheries dependent on them.

Migration circuits also occur on land. Wildebeest (*Connochaetes taurinus*) of the Serengeti Plains of East Africa occupy southerly grasslands in the wet season, move to wetter scrubland at the beginning of the dry season, then travel northward to where earlier rains arrive, and finally move back to the original grasslands. There is much annual variation in the route depending on the timing of the rains.

The red-billed quelea (*Quelea quelea*), also of East Africa, displays a similar sort of migratory circuit to take advantage of the rains. At the beginning of the wet season these birds migrate to areas where the rains occurred some weeks earlier and breed there. During the return from this migration aggregations stop to breed at suitable locations and so produce successive broods during the same season at several sites far apart. Eventually the circuit is complete with a return to dry season areas.

Perhaps the best known of all insect migrants, the African desert locust (*Shistocerca gregaria*) also has a migration circuit that is tied to wind and rain. Under favorable conditions large swarms build up and migrate on the winds. In the areas where they occur in tropical and subtropical regions, winds from the two hemispheres meet along the Inter-Tropical Convergence Zone, and where convergence occurs so does rain. By migrating with the winds, the locusts arrive where rains have fallen and the flush of new plant growth promotes reproduction and survival.

NOMADS

Some migratory organisms have no fixed place of breeding and their movements are nomadic. Such migrations are especially likely in environments with cyclic fluctuations in food abundance and long intervals between good years for breeding in any one place. Deserts and boreal (far northern) regions are examples.

Even though they migrate more or less in circuits, as described above, desert locusts are also, in a sense, nomads. It may be many years before they breed again in an area they left as a migrating swarm. Northern birds such as waxwings (*Bombycilla garrulus*) or crossbills (*Loxia curvirostra* and *L. leucoptera*) are also nomadic because the

Marty Snyderman

fruit and seeds on which they rely for food undergo great fluctuations in abundance.

Especially notable nomads are birds of the Australian desert such as budgerigars (*Melopsittacus undulatus*), zebra finches (*Taeniopygia guttata*), and grey teals (*Anas gibberifrons*). These species may be absent from a breeding ground for long periods, but suddenly reappear in numbers to breed when it rains. Their gonadal cycles are keyed to the rains so that when conditions are right, the gonads reach reproductive condition within a few days and breeding takes place before the habitat dries out.

▲ Some migratory animals such as this remora solve their transport problems by hitchhiking. The remora is equipped with a suction disk (actually a highly modified first dorsal fin) on the top of its head, with which it attaches itself to the underside of some larger fish. It can detach itself at will, dashing forward for scraps as the host fish feeds.

▼ An elephant herd at a waterhole. Elephants are browsers and feed mainly on the foliage of trees. Their foraging behavior is so destructive that they must remain forever on the move and give the vegetation an opportunity to recover before they return that way again.

THE RIDDLE OF PATHFINDING

Verner P. Bingman

Surely the most exceptional aspect of migration is the variety of mechanisms that allow animals to actually find their way—in some cases across oceans and continents. It has fascinated observers for centuries and scientists are now coming up with some intriguing explanations.

▲ Footprints in stone. Scientists suspect that some dinosaurs may have migrated between different home ranges.

▼ When salmon return from the sea to spawn in huge numbers in the upper reaches of rivers and streams, grizzly bears (*Ursus arctos*) congregate from far around to share in this fleeting abundance of food. Flocks of glaucous-winged gulls (*Larus glaucescens*) hang around for scraps.

Virtually from the beginning of life on earth, organisms have been capable of self-generated movement, and even among primitive life forms there were almost certainly inheritable differences in the way they oriented in space. Given three and a half billion years of evolution by natural selection, it is not surprising that animals today, from simple bacteria to humans, possess sophisticated capacities to guide their movements through space. Under strong pressure from natural selection, there has most likely been a rapid accumulation of changes in spatial behavior that have permitted individuals to better use their environment by locating critical resources such as food, shelter, and mates.

However, the complex spatial behavior mechanisms that control animal migrations are not necessarily recent in evolutionary terms. Fossil evidence suggests that individuals of some dinosaur species living more than 100 million years ago migrated to communal egg-laying sites. Then as now, migratory species must have used particular environmental stimuli or cues in order to orient their journeys.

A SENSE OF DIRECTION: ORIENTATION

Orientation refers to a directed movement through space, or the direction of the body's axis, in relation to external reference points. For humans, orientation is typically discussed in terms of compass directions using the sun, stars, moon, or earth's magnetic field as references. Other environmental cues can also serve as reference points. For example, movement away from a factory whistle or driving to one side of a building are both oriented movements, with the whistle and building serving as references.

Among environmental stimuli that serve as orientation cues for animals, the sun is

probably the most widely used. Under some conditions, the sun's position in the sky is used by animals retracing their steps after a foraging trip. A number of species of ants do this, and if one were to screen off the sun as the animals returned, they would no longer be able to find their way home. Placing a mirror to shift the apparent position of the sun also causes a corresponding shift in the orientation of the ants.

However, there is one important factor that complicates the sun's use as an orientation cue. The sun appears to move across the sky at a rate of approximately 15 degrees per hour. For one species of ant (*Lasius niger*) this could create a major problem, since it does not compensate for the sun's apparent movement. Assume that as an individual of this species leaves its nest to forage it maintains an angle of 45 degrees clockwise to the sun. To return home, the ant reverses its direction and now moves 135 degrees counterclockwise with respect to the sun. If the ant is intercepted during the return journey, placed in a box, and later released at the capture location, it will immediately resume its earlier bearing. This means that if the ant is held in the box for three hours it will then move off in a direction 45 degrees away from home. Fortunately, the foraging period of these ants is normally relatively short and they rarely experience lengthy delays in nature.

Not surprisingly, those species that travel for extended periods of time can compensate for the sun's apparent movement. In contrast to the ant species described above, a desert ant (*Cataglyphis bicolor*) held in a box will return straight home after release. Honeybees (*Apis mellifera*) also use the sun for orientation and compensate for its changing position in the sky. If such bees are trained to a food source to the southeast late in the day, they will correctly pick up that bearing the next morning and continue traveling in that direction.

For many animals that live along shorelines, a critical piece of spatial information involves knowing the directional axis perpendicular to the shoreline. In other words, the direction that would enable an animal to cover the shortest distance when moving from land to water or water to land. Orientation along such an axis allows animals to escape from danger as quickly and efficiently as possible. Talitrid amphipods, or beachhoppers, are small crustaceans that generally inhabit a narrow strip of beach associated with the crest of high tide. When disturbed during the day by

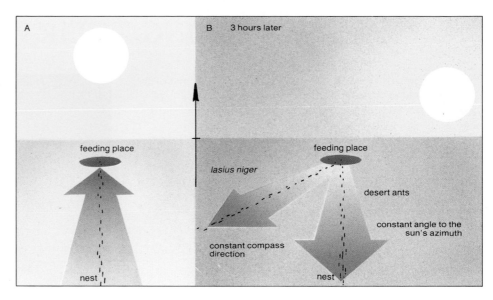

a potential predator, they use this method of orientation to minimize the distance and time taken to find the safety of water. This response is under strong hereditary control, and individual beachhoppers are born displaying the orientation response appropriate to the directional axis of their population's natal shoreline. But recent evidence shows that beachhoppers are also capable of learning new orientation responses, based on the sun, when they are moved to a new location. A number of amphibian species that live along shorelines,

▲ In an experiment designed test for time-compensated, sun-compass orientation in ants, desert ants and ants of the species *Lasius niger* were captured on arrival at their feeding grounds (A), and held for 3 hours. On release (B), *Lasius niger* ants simply reversed their direction with respect to the sun, but because the sun had moved across the horizon, did not arrive back at the nest. Desert ants, on the other hand, compensated for the apparent movement of the sun across the sky and returned to their nest site.

▼ A Belding's ground squirrel (*Spermophilus beldingi*) with its young.

FOLLOWING THEIR NOSES

Odors seem to be just as important as visual landmarks in helping some animals locate goal areas. Harvester ants (*Pogonomyrmex badius*) leave a scent trail on their way out to forage and follow the trail back to their nest. The ability of salmon to return and breed in their natal freshwater stream following a migration of thousands of kilometers in seemingly tractless ocean is one of nature's great navigational feats and remains a mystery. But once they are close to their natal stream it seems that salmon use odor as a cue to location and recognition of the stream.

In one experiment, young coho salmon (*Oncorhynchus kisutch*) were taken from a state hatchery and placed in a tank in which a specific odorant had also been placed. The fish were marked and later released into Lake Michigan, while the odorant was placed at the mouth of just one stream. Some time later, as the fish began to enter streams for breeding, the marked fish were more likely to enter the stream where the odorant had been placed.

Newts (*Taricha rivularis*) migrate seasonally from mountain woodlands to breeding ponds along streams. Individuals, displaced up to 10 kilometers (6 1/4 miles) from their breeding pools, have been seen to orient back to the pools following release and to succeed in returning there. Their navigational ability seems to be based on odors, as those newts that were deprived of their ability to smell were much less successful than normal ones. Spotted salamanders (*Ambystoma maculatum*) use specialized behaviors, such as tapping their chin and nose on the ground, to aid in the perception of odors and are able to recognize the odor of their own pond.

The ability of homing pigeons to navigate home from a distance of several hundred kilometers is another mystery

Stephen Dalton/NHPA

▲ An axolotl (*Ambystoma mexicanus*), a species of salamander. Experiments with newts and salamanders indicate that they use odors to guide them on their annual journeys from their woodland homes to the ponds and streams in which they breed.

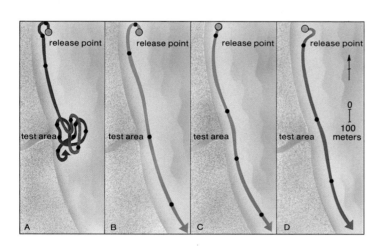

▲ To assess the role of smell in orientation by salmon, a number of fish were released through a test area that had been scented with either morpholine or a different chemical. A shows the behavior of fish who had been imprinted with morpholine when young when they were released through the test site where morpholine was present: they prefered to stay. B shows the behavior of salmon imprinted with morpholine when the chemical was no longer found in the test area. Fish in C had also been exposed to morpholine when young, but were uninterested in the test area when a different chemical was present. Fish in D had not been imprinted with morpholine when young and showed no interest in the test area when morpholine was present.

whose solution may lie in the perception of odors. As with newts, homing pigeons deprived of their ability to smell are often less successful than normal animals in returning home from distant locations. It is thought that pigeons build up a landmark map made up of distinctive odors carried by winds from different directions. North winds, for example, would carry specific odorous substances from perhaps several hundred kilometers away. If a pigeon is later released from a site where those odors normally perceived with north winds are particularly strong, the bird could assume its location to be north of home.

By associating specific odors with wind directions that carry them to its loft, a pigeon could construct a landmark map based on odors that extended for hundreds of kilometers, and do so without ever leaving its loft! Starlings navigating to roost sites may also rely on odors.

such as some frogs and salamanders, also learn an orientation response perpendicular to the shoreline using the sun.

It has been known for a long time that birds that migrate during the day use the sun for orientation. When starlings (*Sturnus vulgaris*) are placed in a cage during the migratory season, they are generally very active and their activity is oriented in the direction of migration. If mirrors are used to shift the apparent position of the sun, the starlings show a corresponding shift in the orientation of their cage activity. Recently, it has been shown that the sun is also important for birds that migrate at night. The savanna sparrow (*Passerculus sandwichensis*) of North America is thought to orient its migration by referring to the position of the sun at sunset.

Such orientation by the sun focuses specifically on directional information provided by the disc of the sun itself. However, the sun is also the source of another important orientation cue, known as skylight polarization.

Light from the sun is scattered by air molecules and other particles as it enters the earth's atmosphere. As a result, skylight is polarized, the percentage of polarization differing from one portion of the sky to another depending on the position of the sun. The principal plane of skylight polarization, or that part of the sky where light is most polarized, is referred to as the e-vector. At sunrise and sunset, the e-vector is a band of light that runs north–south through the top of the sky. Although it is very difficult for humans to see, it is perceived by a number of animals and used for orientation. The advantage of this is that the e-vector can be seen under partly cloudy skies when the sun itself might not be visible. The major disadvantage, at least in the way some animals use it, is that it provides axial directional information without distinguishing one end of the orientation response from the other. In other words, it does not tell you east from west. Fortunately, animals usually view the e-vector in combination with a number of other directional cues that allow them to distinguish its two ends. Virtually every species of animal that has been shown to use the sun for orientation has also been shown to use skylight polarization.

Use of the sun for orientation depends on light energy that emanates directly from it. Orientation responses not directly linked to the sun, but based on the asymmetrical distribution of light energy in the

environment, have also been identified. The most dramatic example of this comes from the behavior of sea turtle hatchlings, which emerge from their underground beach nests at night and immediately make a rapid dash for the sea, where they will begin their migration to localized feeding areas. Green turtles (*Chelonia mydas*) that hatch on Ascension Island migrate to feeding areas along the coast of Brazil. How do these hatchling turtles find the sea? They seem to be guided by the dim glow of light reflected off the ocean, which makes the seaward direction brighter than the landward one.

During the day, the sun is the dominant celestial cue to orientation. At night, the stars and the moon are the conspicuous celestial stimuli. The best example of stellar orientation comes from those birds that migrate by night. During spring and autumn, radar screens at airports around the world light up with the well-directed movements of nocturnally migrant birds. Using the seasonally oriented activity of captured migrant birds in a cage above which stars are projected on a planetarium dome, a number of Old World species such as warblers and New World species such as the indigo bunting (*Passerina cyanea*) have been shown to use the stars to guide their nocturnal migratory flights.

At night, beachhoppers, whose sun orientation was discussed earlier, rely on the moon to orient their activity. In fact, they

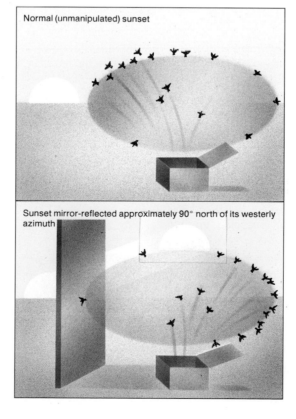

Normal (unmanipulated) sunset

Sunset mirror-reflected approximately 90° north of its westerly azimuth

◄ Savanna sparrows are thought to orient their migration by referring to the position of the sun at sunset (top). This has been shown experimentally by using mirrors to apparently shift the position of the sun (bottom). When tested, both groups of birds oriented their activity at the same angle to the sun's perceived azimuth.

▲ A European sparrowhawk at its nest. Juveniles on their first southward migration use a simple compass bearing in probable combination with an internal cue that tells them when to stop traveling ("compass-oriented" migration), but adults can modify their orientation if necessary in returning to their wintering area ("goal-oriented" migration).

even compensate for the moon's apparent movement across the sky. This indicates that they have two separate timing mechanisms: one for the sun, which has a period of 24 hours; and another for the moon, which has a period closer to 25 hours.

Other sources of potential orientation information include the earth's magnetic field and the physical medium in which the animal may find itself. Most prominent among the physical-medium cues are water currents and the wind. Many species of fish living in streams and rivers are known to orient with respect to water current. Current can be detected through a variety of sensory channels, including electric fields generated by the water movement. Migratory spiny lobsters (*Panulirus argus*) orient with respect to water current and water movements that occur on the sea bottom to guide their seasonal journey from shallow to deeper oceanic water. It has been suggested that migratory salmon in the North Pacific Ocean

orient in some way using ocean currents and that hatchling sea turtles, once in the ocean, seem to maintain their offshore direction by relying on oceanic swells and waves.

Desert locusts (*Schistocera gregaria*) appear to simply fly downwind to orient their African odyssey. However, by also timing their movements to coincide with favorable winds, they succeed in moving to regions where they are likely to find fresh vegetation for feeding. In some regions of North America, nocturnal migrant birds consistently orient their movements downwind. Particularly in the southeastern United States, migrants seemingly ignore other sources of directional information once they are aloft and fly with the wind, even if it takes them in an inappropriate direction. Like the desert locusts, however, birds are selective concerning the conditions in which they fly, preferring to migrate when the direction the wind is blowing is similar to their preferred migratory direction.

A SENSE OF LOCATION: PILOTING AND TRUE NAVIGATION

Orientation involves relating direction to an external reference, like using a compass. However, the selection and maintenance of a compass bearing does not necessarily mean that an animal has a sense of where it is in relation to other locations. A camper lost in the woods with a compass can identify where north is, but that knowledge won't help find the camp site unless he also knows his location. To determine its location with respect to some goal, an animal needs something like a map. Researchers divide navigation mechanisms that permit an animal to orient to a specific goal location into two categories; piloting and true navigation. Piloting occurs when an animal relies on familiar landmarks to specify the direction of a goal. True navigation occurs when an animal is beyond sensory contact with any familiar landmark and relies on some other source of information to specify the direction of a goal.

Before discussing mechanisms of pilotage and true navigation, let us clarify the difference between simple compass orientation and goal orientation.

A number of European sparrowhawks (*Accipter nisus*) were captured on a North Sea island during their migration. These birds typically fly southwest through this region to reach their winter homes on the northern coast of France. The captured adult and first-year birds were then transported 600 kilometers (370 miles) east to Poland, where they were released and their flights were monitored. First-year birds were primarily recovered southwest of the release location, even though resuming their earlier migratory direction no longer brought them close to their winter home in France. Adult birds, in contrast, were recovered primarily to the west-southwest—an orientation that brought them reasonably close to their winter home. That is to say, the first-year birds displayed compass orientation, but lacked the adult sparrowhawks' ability to determine the approximate location of their winter home and display goal orientation to it. Similar experiments with European starlings have also demonstrated compass orientation in first-year birds and goal orientation in adults.

When one thinks of navigation through space using familiar landmarks, one generally thinks of visible ones. Foraging honeybees use visual landmarks to navigate to a reliable food source or to return to their hive. In fact, it has been suggested that bees

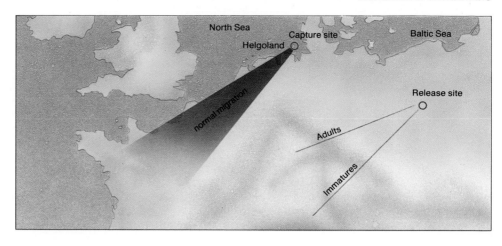

have something like a landmark map coded in their nervous system that enables them to compute the most direct path to a goal area. Coral reef fish including grunts and butterfly fish seem to rely on visual cues to navigate to and recognize feeding and home areas, while painted turtles (*Chrysemys picta*) may rely on such landmarks to return home following displacement. Birds such as homing pigeons and swallows also seem to rely on familiar visual landmarks to navigate to their loft or roosting site.

It is suspected that experienced migrant birds returning to previous breeding and wintering areas also navigate by familiar landmarks once they are close to their goal. In contrast, migrants on their first migration, such as sparrowhawk and starling young, are thought to arrive at their wintering areas using a mechanism of compass orientation coupled with an inherited sense of time or distance that tells them when they should stop. Using such a strategy, young birds would not need to have any sense of location to arrive at their wintering area for the first time.

▲ In an experiment designed to test the uses of goal and compass orientation in birds, European sparrowhawks were collected during migration on a North Sea island and released in Poland. Experienced, adult migrants flew a course more likely to bring them to their normal destinations than the younger birds that flew an inappropriate course, parallel to their original one.

▼ Bizarre and colorful, spiny lobsters orient themselves to patterns of ocean currents and wave movements in their migrations.

Mike Osmond/Auscape

▲ A humpback whale (*Megaptera novaeangliae*) sounding. It is thought that the possession of a magnetic sense, perhaps related to deposits of magnetite in the tissues surrounding the brain, permits whales to use the earth's geomagnetic map to navigate.

shearwater may well have been out of sensory contact with any familiar landmarks. If that is the case, the animal may have used a mechanism of true navigation.

Homing pigeons display goal orientation so far beyond the range of familiar landmarks it could require an explanation based on true navigation. Migrant birds might also use a mechanism of true navigation, and the success of adult sparrowhawks and starlings in orienting to their normal wintering areas following displacement to possibly unfamiliar regions might be explained in this way. However, it should be noted that even migrations of 10,000 kilometers (6,200 miles) or more to specific areas can be explained by assuming that birds use simple compass orientation and a sense of time or distance, combined with landmark navigation as they near their goal areas.

If true navigation exists, the mystery of its sensory basis remains unsolved. The most favored explanation, however, continues to lie in information derived from the earth's magnetic field, which has already been discussed as a compass cue.

There are a number of parameters that define the earth's magnetic field, such as its strength and the angle geomagnetic lines of force make with the surface of the earth, which vary predictably as one changes geographic location. A migrant bird, for example, could use some part of this information to locate its position practically anywhere on earth and then use it to determine its location with respect to a particular goal.

True navigation based on geomagnetism has yet to be experimentally demonstrated, although salmon during the open ocean phase of their migration have been theorized to use geomagnetism to navigate a goal-oriented course to the mouth of their natal river system. Newts (*Notophthalmus viridescens*) have also been reported to have two independent geomagnetic processing mechanisms, one for compass orientation and the other possibly for true navigation.

The most intriguing, albeit indirect, evidence for a geomagnetic map comes from homing pigeons, whose goal-oriented behavior is affected by naturally occurring magnetic disturbances, such as magnetic storms, and by experimentally induced magnetic fluctuations. Since some of these effects are difficult to interpret as effects on the birds' magnetic compass, they could suggest the existence of a separate geomagnetic map used for true navigation.

Many animals display piloting goal orientation techniques. Experiments with laboratory rats and gerbils demonstrate the use of visual landmarks in navigation and in recognizing the location of food and shelter. Migratory bats are apparently also dependent on visual landmarks for navigation, while some animals take advantage of other senses, especially that of smell. More intriguing still is true navigation, the identification of location without the possession of any information based on familiarity or collected during the outward journey.

Several years ago, a manx shearwater (*Puffinus puffinus*) was taken from its home on the coast of Wales and released from Boston 5,000 kilometers (3,100 miles) across the ocean. In 12 days, the bird was back home. It is difficult to explain the rapid return of this bird except in terms of goal-oriented behavior, but at such a distance and an ocean away from home, the

GUIDED BY THE EARTH'S MAGNETIC FIELD

Many animals are sensitive to the earth's north–south magnetic field and use it for orientation.

Some species of aquatic bacteria have even been found to contain little pieces of iron that act as a kind of compass needle, leading the organisms to align their body axes parallel to the force lines of the earth's magnetic field. Since the lines of force of the geomagnetic field at the earth's surface actually dip into the ground at an angle (except at the magnetic equator), these bacteria generally orient themselves at an angle to the earth's surface. This is a highly adaptive response, since the bacteria can then arrive at their preferred mud bottom habitat by simply swimming downward.

Because water is a good conductor of electrical current and there is a reciprocal relationship between electrical current and magnetic fields, aquatic environments are well suited to geomagnetic orientation. The electric current generated by an animal moving through water will vary depending on the animal's orientation. As a result, the ability to sense electric fields can be used to indirectly detect one's orientation to the earth's magnetic field. An example demonstrating this comes from an experiment in which round stingrays (*Urolophus hallerri*) were placed in an experimental pool and trained to enter an enclosure, the direction of entry being defined by the ambient magnetic field. When the magnetic field around the animals was altered the stingrays detected the changed orientation indirectly, by using their electrical sense to perceive changes in the electric field induced by their movement, and altered their directional choices. The orientation of European eels (*Anguilla anguilla*) and of sockeye salmon fry (*Oncorhynchus nerka*) have also changed in experiments in which the magnetic field around them was shifted.

Although air is not a good conductor of electricity, use of the earth's magnetic field is nonetheless common among

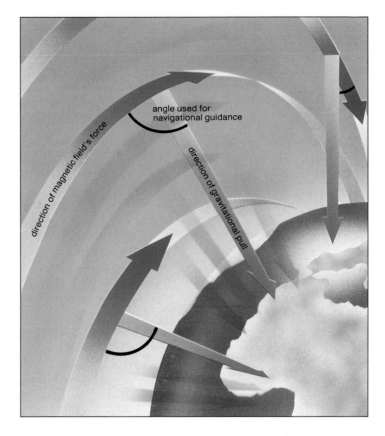

▲ Like most, if not all, animals, the compass takes advantage of the fact that the earth has a magnetic field, oriented approximately parallel to the earth's axis of spin. This field generates lines of force that are parallel at all points, like lines of longitude. Although a compass measures the field's polarity only in a horizontal plane, animal "compasses" might also sense dip (angle to the earth's surface) and its change with latitude, the direction of maximum dip (a measure for north or south), or the intensity of the field, which becomes greater with increasing latitude.

In the figure: *direction of magnetic field's force*, *angle used for navigational guidance*, *direction of gravitational pull*

terrestrial species. The orientation behavior of newts (*Notophthalmus viridescens*), toads (*Bufo bufo*), North American box turtles (*Terrapene carolina*), wood mice (*Apodemus sylvaticus*), white-footed mice (*Peromyscus leucopus*), and even humans has been reported to be influenced by changes in the ambient magnetic field.

Perhaps the most dramatic example of orientation by a migratory animal comes from birds. Several Old and New World species, as well as homing pigeons, rely on the earth's magnetic field for orientation. Several species that do so, including the indigo bunting (*Passerina cyanea*), also use the sun or stars.

To demonstrate magnetic orientation in migratory birds, they are placed in cages surrounded with electric coils and the magnetic field around them is then altered. Under some conditions, migrant birds show shifts in the orientation of their activity that correspond with the shifts manufactured in the ambient magnetic field.

H. Rivarola/Bruce Coleman Ltd.

◄ Experiments with indigo buntings have confirmed that these nocturnal migrants are sensitive to the earth's magnetic field and can use it, as well as the stars, to orient themselves. The birds breed in North America and overwinter in southern Mexico and Central America.

WHEN TWO WORLDS COLLIDE

G.V.T. Matthews

▲ Scene in a Japanese fish market. Commercial fisheries are depleting fish populations to such an extent that fish farming may ultimately prove to be the only practical solution.

Migration is a hazardous process in itself, but when humans interfere with migrating animals or their habitats it can lead to extinction. Only a true change of heart will save some surviving species.

Exodus tells us that the Israelites were saved from starvation by the Lord providing manna and quails (*Coturnix coturnix*). From Numbers we can deduce that the quails were migrating with a following wind, flying vulnerably low, and landing over a wide area. The Israelites killed birds for two days and a night and "he that gathered the least gathered ten homers," that is 10 ass-loads or about 2 cubic meters (3 cubic yards) of quails. Such wanton destruction of migratory animals has frequently disgraced mankind. However, in this case "while the flesh was yet between their teeth, ere it was chewed, the Lord was kindled against the people, and the Lord smote the people with a very great plague." Such swift divine retribution upon those who slaughter migratory animals to excess has been sadly lacking in recent centuries.

Hunters need not be senseless destroyers. Prey populations produce an excess of young that do not survive to breeding age. Hunters taking less than the surplus will have "sustainable yield." The need for such responsible conservation is more obvious when hunters and hunted remain throughout the year in the same area. If too many prey are killed their diminution rapidly becomes apparent. Hunters can redress the balance by killing less, protecting breeding animals, improving habitat, or even rearing animals artificially to add to the wild stock.

If both hunters and prey are seasonal migrants a balance may still evolve. Such was the case with those Amerindians who were wholly dependent on the prairie bison (*Bison bison*) for food, clothing, and shelter. Their folklore and taboos ensured that they preyed on the beasts with circumspection, indeed with respect. It was the European settlers, with their greater destructive power and attempted genocide on the Indians, who nearly eliminated the bison. "You take my life/ When you do take the means whereby I live," to quote Shakespeare. In Scandinavia, the Lapps likewise became integrated with

reindeer (*Rangifer tarandus*), following them on their migrations, protecting them from other predators, and eventually semi-domesticating them.

No such sustainable relationship between man and beast developed in the case of the whales. For centuries they were attacked as they passed coastal settlements, without serious losses. Then knowledge of whale migration grew and they were pursued continually and remorselessly as boats became larger, faster, and independent of wind power. Finally, the explosive harpoon and the factory ship drove the whales almost to extinction. Only a moratorium on whaling in 1986, when returns had diminished to the point of non-viability, may have saved the day. Yet some "civilized" nations are again calling for the butchery.

As knowledge of fish migrations improved, they too were harried incessantly and many populations stripped down to a remnant. Coastal countries extended their territorial waters, in which they could then enforce restrictions. They also entered into agreements with other fishing nations to limit catches on the high seas. Even so, fish-farming may be the only long-term solution to the problem of overfishing. Moreover, not only fish populations suffer from overfishing. Seabird young have died in their thousands of malnutrition and millions of auks have drowned through entanglement in the near-invisible nets.

Itinerant (migratory) humans have also brought disaster to sedentary animal populations. When passing sailors landed on islands in search of fresh meat, the animals there were frequently indifferent to human approach and were slaughtered out of hand. The most famous victim was the flightless dodo (*Raphus cucullatus*) whose name is now synonymous with extinction. Dozens of other species have been eliminated. If they were not killed directly by man, his fellow-travelers such as rats, cats, dogs, and pigs completed the job. Introduced grazing

National Museums of Scotland

animals have also rendered some habitats unsuitable for native species. These seafarers also struck at more mobile species.

Seabirds and small marine mammals, at little risk from humans when dispersed, become highly vulnerable when breeding brings them ashore in great congregations to lay their eggs or drop their pups. Penguins were boiled down for oil and seals skinned for their fur: millions were slaughtered and entire colonies exterminated. Fortunately, in some cases there were survivors and in a more enlightened age these have begun to increase when afforded protection.

Mass breeding colonies can be relatively easily protected. Much more difficult to conserve are those species that scatter over vast areas to breed, but which gather in great numbers before and during migration or when overwintering. Such concentrations are attacked by local hunters as a seasonal source of food or sport. For example, when the Europeans arrived in North America there may have been 3,000 million passenger pigeons (*Ectopistes migratorius*); certainly

Jonathan Gordon/Planet Earth Pictures

▲ An icon of extinction, the dodo inhabited the island of Mauritius in the Indian Ocean, and was exterminated during the early waves of European exploration in the sixteenth and seventeenth centuries.

This 1601 drawing of daily life on an island having its first experience of humans is the earliest known illustration of a dodo, shown stalking out of the frame on the left.

◀ Whales have been hunted with lances and boats since at least the ninth century and in some parts of the world, such as the Azores, whaling is still conducted in this way. Even this primitive method affects whale stocks, at least locally, but it was the advent of the explosive harpoon and the factory ship in the mid-nineteenth century that quickly drove whales to the point of global extinction.

UPI/Bettmann

▲ High society in British India. In one of the most conspicuous of sporting excesses, it was fashionable in this era to attend morning wildfowl shoots, given by the local maharaja and attended by British administrators and other notables. Large numbers of local villagers served as beaters, driving ducks and other birds to the waiting guns of the guests. Hundreds of ducks were killed in a single morning, as in this photograph of one such shoot conducted by the Maharaja of Bharatpur in 1927.

many millions still lived when one game dealer alone handled three million of their corpses in 1878. Sober observers wrote of the skies darkened by the passing hordes, yet 40 years later the passenger pigeon was extinct, put under pressure by habitat changes but exterminated by market hunters. Waterfowl and waders were also slaughtered as they massed on the wetlands.

Sickened by the killings for meat and for feathers to decorate hats, the Americans outlawed market hunting for birds early this century. Then, in 1916, the United States and Canada signed the Treaty on Migratory Birds. This established the principles that such birds are a shared resource and that there must be an equitable distribution of any "harvest" over the whole migratory range. Since then, the size of bird harvests has become more and more realistically related to a given populations' size and annual production, as determined by surveys on the northern breeding grounds.

In Europe, wars and social upheavals delayed the emergence of continent-wide agreements. National measures were enacted, however. Great Britain, for instance, passed a

Peter Davey/Bruce Coleman Ltd.

comprehensive Bird Protection Act in 1954, embodying another important principle; that all birds were protected except named huntable species (afforded closed seasons when breeding) and "pest" species. Not until 1979 did the 9 (now 12) countries of the European Economic Community agree on a Directive incorporating this principle and requiring member states to bring their domestic legislation on bird conservation into line.

To make laws is one thing, to enforce them quite another. Thus Bewick's swans (*Cygnus columbianus bewickii*) have for years been totally protected in every country they live in or pass through, from Siberia to Ireland. Yet, when several hundred were X-rayed, one-third were found to have gunshot in their flesh, embedded there by out-of-range hunters. Again, education and a real change of heart are needed before hunters cease to blast protected birds out of the sky.

Truly worldwide treaties for the protection of long-distance migrants have long been the dream of conservationists, and in Bonn an "umbrella" Convention on the Conservation of Migratory Species of Wild Animals was concluded in 1979. Global in coverage, it included the oceans, the Arctic, and Antarctic, but therein lay the seeds of its diminished effectiveness. Large countries

B & C. Alexander/Bruce Coleman Ltd

▲ Inuit peoples have long hunted the polar bear, especially valuing its fur for outer clothing. But it is a formidable opponent and traditional hunting methods often favored the bear rather than the human hunter, so that comparatively few bears were killed each year. This changed with the proliferation of motorized sleds and high-powered rifles in the Arctic and the polar bear is now seriously endangered.

◄ The remains of an elephant slaughtered by poachers for its ivory tusks.

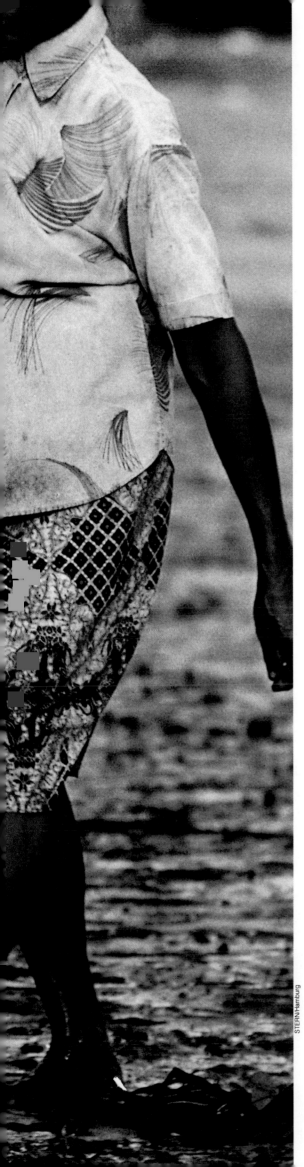

with commercial interests in those areas, such as Australia, Canada, the Soviet Union, and the United States, have not yet ratified the Convention to which only a couple of dozen disparate countries are Parties. The intention was that Agreements on particular species or groups would put flesh on the skeleton. So far no Agreement has been ratified, though there is some progress in one on western palearctic waterfowl to parallel long-existing arrangements in North America.

The Convention on International Trade in Endangered Species of Wild Fauna and Flora, concluded in Washington in 1973, reduces exploitation of some migrants, such as sea turtles, and many countries are Parties. But as long as any major trading nation remains outside the Convention, a loophole will remain for activities that are illegal on the territories of the Parties.

One global convention that does not suffer from this all-or-nothing requirement is the oldest. The Convention on Wetlands of International Importance, Especially as Waterfowl Habitat, was concluded in Ramsar, Iran, in 1971. It grasped the fact that species must have suitable habitat wherever they go on their migrations and that wetlands, those most fragile and easily destroyed habitats, are vital to traveling waterfowl. Sixty countries have acceded to the Ramsar Convention, each setting aside, for perpetual conservation, one or more wetlands that meet agreed criteria of international importance. Over 500 wetlands have been designated, covering more than 30 million hectares (75 million acres). Each Party also undertakes to formulate land-use programs in a way that ensures all its wetlands are wisely used. This is of great benefit to waterfowl, and also to humans, but much remains to be done.

The groundswell of "green" public opinion came too late to save some remarkable migrants. From now on the elimination of market hunting, strong restrictions on sport hunting, and proper care for the natural environment can together ensure the survival of those that are left. No longer can hunters justify mass slaughter by pleading ignorance of the numbers of their prey or whence they come. Gone are the days when people could believe that barnacle geese (*Branta leucopsis*) were produced from the goose barnacles (*Lepas antifera*) encrusting rocky shores, and were thus inexhaustible. Migration is a hazardous enough process when only natural dangers are encountered. Let humankind's additional impacts, direct and indirect, be reduced to an acceptable minimum.

◀ Indonesian villagers returning from a turtle hunt. Traditional hunting by indigenous peoples has seldom had a severe impact on wild populations, especially in the case of more migratory animals. Pollution, habitat destruction, and high-tech over-exploitation usually pose a far graver threat.

STERN/Hamburg

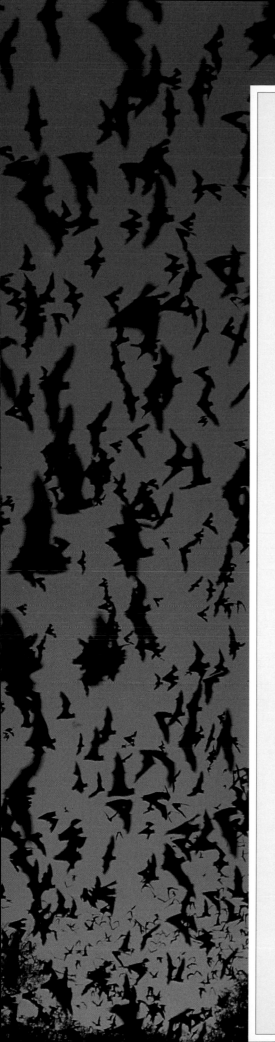

Part 2

AERIAL EPICS

The air teems with creatures on their way to more hospitable environments, whether as colonists or seasonal visitors.

BUTTERFLIES AND MOTHS

The fluttering behavior of butterflies and moths may appear aimless, but it is part of a complex and clearly defined life cycle.

LOCUSTS

Locusts are often solitary, but when they swarm their combined weight can be measured in thousands of tonnes and their destructiveness is legendary.

OTHER INSECTS

Amongst flying insects, migrations are usually brief periods between the larval and breeding stage, but many non-flying insects are constantly on the move.

AMERICAN BIRDS

The flights of American birds, from large areas to concentrated tropical ones and then back again, are among the most spectacular and urgent of migrations.

EUROPEAN AND AFRICAN BIRDS

The migratory paths of European and African birds are considerably longer than was once believed, and more elaborate.

ASIAN AND AUSTRALIAN BIRDS

The Asia–Pacific flyway stretches from the Arctic tundra to Australia, but its length does not prevent many shorebirds from flying half this distance nonstop.

SEABIRDS

Seabirds forage over huge areas, and some migrate from polar ice to polar ice. But there is much variation and irregularity in their behavior.

BATS

Many bats appear to migrate, but much evidence is anecdotal and many questions central to bat migration have still to be answered.

BUTTERFLIES AND MOTHS

R. Robin Baker

The migration of butterflies and moths is often inconspicuous, although some swarm in their millions and their journeys may take on epic proportions, in some cases taking several generations to complete the migratory circuit.

▲ In North America some populations of the monarch butterfly (*Danaus plexippus*) migrate thousands of kilometers to spend the winter in the southern United States and Mexico. Here they suspend breeding and most other activities and, especially on cold days, spend much of their time clustered on the trunks of trees.

TEMPERATE ZONE BUTTERFLIES

The migrations of temperate butterflies are seldom conspicuous, let alone spectacular. In fact, only very careful observation has revealed that migrations are taking place at all. Yet, for many of the more common temperate butterflies, migration is neither infrequent nor sporadic, but a normal episode of life.

Choose a large grassy field well-grazed by sheep or cattle anywhere in the world's temperate zones. The grass is short and there are few flowers from which adult butterflies can feed. Every so often, on any sunny summer day, a butterfly will appear over one edge of the field, fly straight across, and disappear over the other edge. The chances are, in North America, western Europe, or even Australia, that the butterfly will be a small cabbage white (*Pieris rapae*) and that it is just passing through the field on migration.

For many years entomologists thought that only those butterflies seen flying across country were migrants, and that butterflies seen flitting around within gardens and other favored habitats were residents. This view has now been discarded. Observers fit and agile enough to run across fields at a steady 10 kilometers (6 miles) per hour, jump gates, and crawl through fences can prove this for themselves. As soon as the small cabbage white encounters a field of cabbages or flowers, it changes its behavior. It stops flying in a straight line and behaves as if it lives there. Perhaps it will feed from flowers. A male may search for females, court them, and may even succeed in copulation. A female may lay eggs. Eventually, however, after a time of between a few minutes and several days, the butterfly will leave the cabbage field, and the direction in which it departs will not be random. If our fit and agile observers have managed to keep an eye on the same individual small white from the moment it entered the cabbage field, they will find that it flies off in a straight line

and in more or less its original compass direction. It appears that for a butterfly such as the small white its lifetime track—that is, the track in space made by each individual animal from its place of birth to its place of death—is a fairly straight line in a particular compass direction.

In western Europe, in spring and summer, more small white butterflies fly north and west than fly east and south. The most common flight direction is north-northwest but by no means do all individuals fly in this direction. In Britain, 42 percent of small whites fly across country to the north-northwest, compared to 21 percent which fly to the west-southwest, 21 percent to the east-northeast, and 16 percent to the south-southeast.

Throughout the north temperate zone the mean migration direction of butterflies in spring and summer is to the north. In the south temperate zone it is to the south. The general rule, just as for temperate birds, seems to be that, in spring, temperate butterflies fly toward the poles and away from the tropics.

Also, just like birds, temperate butterflies change their direction of migration in late summer or early autumn. In western Europe, second generation small whites that emerge in July and early August at first continue to migrate to the north-northwest. After a certain date in middle to late August, however, mean direction changes to due south. At any one location, the change in direction takes only two to three days, but occurs later farther south. In northeast England, for example, small whites change direction from north to south around 12 August. In southern England the change-round date is about 26 August, and in the Alsace region of France the date is about 2 September. Experiments have shown that it is the length and temperature of the autumn nights, rather than the days, that triggers this change in direction.

How do butterflies recognize compass

Collobert/Jacana

direction? A clue is provided by comparing mid-morning and mid-afternoon flight directions. In western Europe, in spring and summer, the mean direction of several species of butterflies shifts from west-northwest to north-northeast during the day. Detailed study has shown that this shift in mean direction occurs because the preferred direction of each individual changes during the day at the same rate as the sun's azimuth (the point on the horizon directly below the sun's disc) moves across the horizon. Butterflies migrate only during the warmest part of the day and only then if the sun is shining. It seems, then, that each individual butterfly flies along maintaining a preferred angle to the sun's azimuth. This gives them a rough, but usable, sense of compass direction.

Insofar as they judge compass direction by the sun, the orientation of temperate butterflies during migration is the same as that of day-migrant birds. Unlike such birds,

however, temperate butterflies do not correct for the apparent movement of the sun's azimuth across the horizon. As a result, their angle to the azimuth stays constant while their geographical direction changes by about 15 degrees per hour.

Our final picture of the lifetime track of a temperate zone butterfly is that of an individual gradually working its way across country. As it flies from one suitable habitat to another, it maintains a relatively constant geographical direction by orienting at a fixed angle to the sun. Little is known, however, about how far such butterflies fly on their journey across country from birth to death. The life span of most temperate butterflies is usually no longer than three or four weeks and may be much less. Calculations based on the observed rate of cross-country migration of butterflies such as the small white suggest that over land most individuals have a lifetime track of no more than 200 kilometers (125 miles) in length.

▲ A small cabbage white butterfly prepares to land. The caterpillars of this species develop on cabbages and related plants. They are widely cultivated plants and the small cabbage white has spread with them from its original home in Eurasia across much of North America, Australia, and elsewhere.

THE LIFE CYCLE OF THE SMALL WHITE BUTTERFLY

The male small white butterfly (*Peiris rapae*) hovers briefly above a potential mate, beating his wings. A receptive female joins in the courtship flight and the pair alight to mate, the female closing her wings while the male curves his abdomen and holds her with his genital claspers.

The female deposits her eggs one at a time, glueing them carefully to the leaves of cabbages or similar plants so that the larvae will have food close at hand on hatching.

Hatching takes place within a week or so, the larva chewing its way out of the tough shell. On emergence, the caterpillar first unfolds and inflates itself by gulping air.

An adult maintains a preferred direction throughout its life, deviating only when it encounters obstacles such as houses or fences. It flies around these and resumes its previous direction. The butterfly travels briskly over unsuitable ground, but lingers to rest, feed, or seek a mate wherever it encounters a patch of suitable habitat.

Eventually the fully formed butterfly is ready to emerge, a delicate process lasting an hour or so. Once free, the adult is limp and soft, and usually perches in the sun while body fluids are pumped into its wings, stiffening and hardening them until the butterfly is finally ready for flight.

The caterpillar does little else but eat, quickly outgrowing its external skin. Ultimately, it stops feeding and seeks a place to pupate. There it deposits a pad of silk, spins a silken girdle, and sheds its skin for a fifth and last time. Now it is called a pupa or chrysalis. Within, the caterpillar enters a quiescent stage while its internal tissues are re-organized for full adulthood.

THE MAGNIFICENT MONARCH

A major exception to the above rule is the monarch or milkweed butterfly (*Danaus plexippus*) of North America. This is perhaps the most famous of all migrant butterflies. Female monarchs lay their eggs on the underside of milkweed leaves, the principal food of the caterpillars. Each autumn, these North American monarchs (there is another American population south of the Amazon basin) migrate south in masses of many thousands. So predictable is this movement with respect to direction, time of year, and the vast numbers involved, that many towns along the monarchs' flight path celebrate the butterflies' arrival with festivals and carnivals. Pacific Grove, California, even calls itself "Butterfly City, USA."

To entomologists, however, monarch migration is all the more interesting and spectacular since it produces a lifetime track far longer than that of more typical temperate zone butterflies, such as the small white. Experiments using tagged butterflies suggest that approximately two-thirds of the monarchs that emerge in the vicinity of the Great Lakes of North America in late summer and early autumn migrate distances of between 2,000 and 3,000 kilometers (1,240 and 1,865 miles) to overwintering sites along the coast of the Gulf of Mexico or inland in Texas or Mexico. The fate of the other one-third that appear to remain in northern States is still unclear. One theory is that they perish with the first frosts of winter. The other is that they hibernate in hollow trees or under loose bark and are the individuals that first appear in the north early the next spring. Monarchs that develop west of the Rockies fly south and west to the coast of southern California.

The winter behavior of this autumn generation of migrants depends largely on how far south they travel. Those to the east of the Rockies that reach Florida, Georgia, or Louisiana, and those to the west that reach coastal California before being overtaken by cold winter air from the north, form the spectacular and legendary "butterfly trees." As the polar weather front moves back and forth over these trees during the winter months, the monarchs leave their trees on warm days to feed but return to roost at night. On cold days they remain in the trees. These monarchs do not begin to mate until the polar front starts to retreat some time toward the end of February.

The monarchs that manage to reach Texas and Mexico in autumn and thus escape the polar front altogether either climb the

Michael Fogden/DRK Photo

Mexican highlands and join butterfly trees like those on the coasts farther north, or spend the winter as free-flying butterflies.

From the beginning of March, the majority of overwintered monarchs fly north, mating and laying eggs as they go. The rate of migration in spring, up to 15 kilometers (9 1/2 miles) per day, is much slower than in autumn and compares with that of most other temperate butterflies. Even so, as monarchs may live for four or five months after leaving their overwintering sites, some may travel more than 1,000 kilometers (620 miles) before dying. The majority, though, do not travel so far. Even those that fly fastest and farthest are unlikely to return to the Great Lakes region from the Gulf Coast or Mexico, at least not before July.

▲ Monarch butterfly caterpillars develop on many species of milkweeds, genus *Asclepias*. These plants are abundant in tropical and temperate regions, have attractive flowers, and are widely cultivated. Here a monarch caterpillar browses on a blood flower in Costa Rica.

49

Frans Lanting/Bruce Coleman Ltd.

One important fact about the autumn generation of the monarch is that, although adult, individuals are reproductively inactive. They do not begin to produce sperm and eggs until spring of the following year. In autumn, therefore, monarch butterflies do not have to invest time and energy in courting or laying eggs; they need only to feed and rest. In consequence, much more time and energy is available for migration. Perhaps the evolution of reproductive inactivity and the long adult life associated with it (many monarchs live nearly 12 months as adults) makes possible the long-distance migration to warmer latitudes for the winter.

There is some support for this view from the fact that other temperate species with a reproductively inactive autumn generation are also thought to migrate long distances. In western Europe and North America, for example, the red admiral butterfly (*Vanessa atalanta*) and the painted lady, or thistle, butterfly (*Cynthia cardui*) produce an autumn generation, some members of which may migrate southward for up to 3,000 kilometers (1,865 miles). In western Europe these migrants may reach the Mediterranean region or even North Africa for the winter.

◀ Many wintering sites of monarch butterflies, like this one in the highlands of Mexico, are traditional and are used year after year. Millions of monarchs may congregate in groves of trees at these sites.

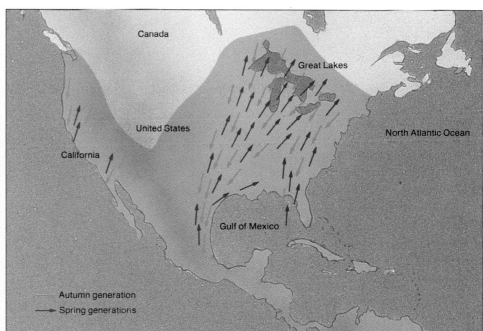

Autumn generation
Spring generations

These long-distance migrants have clearly evolved a form of autumn migration different from that of other temperate butterflies. When a monarch butterfly emerges in autumn as an adult, its major concern is to travel south as fast and as economically as possible. For autumn monarchs, straight-line distance traveled is more important than efficient searching of any one area.

▲ Major trends of monarch butterfly migrations in North America. In spring the butterflies move northward, laying eggs as they go, at a rate of about 15 kilometers (9 1/2 miles) per day. Subsequent generations returning southward in autumn fly much farther and faster and do not breed.

51

▶ The brown-veined white is one of the most conspicuous butterfly migrants of Africa. Closely related to the small cabbage white, it inhabits savanna and cultivated land. These butterflies are in a sleeping cluster at night.

Anthony Bannister/NHPA

▼ Many butterfly migrations in Africa seem more closely related to rainfall than to temperature. South Saharan populations of the butterfly *Catopsilia florella*, for example, migrate towards high rainfall areas in the Congo Basin between December and February, while populations in southern Africa tend to move eastward to the moist coastal belt between March and May.

TROPICAL BUTTERFLIES

Imagine a hot, dusty road stretching ahead across the arid scrublands of East Africa. As you drive past grazing herds of zebra and wildebeest, browsing groups of giraffe, and an occasional pride of lions, large white or yellow butterflies begin to appear. At first you see one at a time. Then several are in view at once. You notice that each butterfly is flying, apparently purposefully, in the same fixed compass direction. Soon there are butterflies everywhere, still all flying in the same direction. Their squashed bodies clog the radiator grille of your vehicle and the mixture of blood and dust on your windscreen makes driving difficult. Every so often you have to stop, wash the windscreen, and unblock the radiator. For tens of kilometers along the track these migrating butterflies are everywhere. Then,

gradually, they become less abundant, until finally they have gone and once more the air is empty.

In its own way, the migration of tropical butterflies can be as awe-inspiring and exciting as the migrations of wildebeest and zebra over which they fly. Migrating swarms may be vast. In Kenya, migrations have sometimes involved tens of millions of individuals. As well, nearly all the tropical migrants fly in the same direction. Surprisingly, however, little is known of the migration of tropical butterflies.

In a sense the function of the migration—a search for food—is the same in the tropics as in temperate regions. In the tropics, however, the underlying factor is rainfall. Near the equator, rainfall is heavy but often restricted to certain times of the year. Over large areas, the result is luxurious, fast-growing vegetation for part of the year and dry nutritionless remnants for the remainder. The insect populations in these regions depend for their food on the green vegetation produced by the rains. The rest of the time they can choose between lying dormant while they wait for the rains to return, or migrating to where the rain is falling. Those that migrate provide one of the natural world's great spectacles.

These mass tropical migrations are confined largely to the grassland and semi-arid regions of southern Africa, South America, and Asia, where rain falls either irregularly or for only a short time each year. For example, the brown-veined white (*Belenois aurota*), an African migrant, feeds as a larva on caper, a bush that occurs in arid districts. Sometimes, during a really heavy migration, a caper bush standing in a particularly favorable position can be smothered with countless numbers of eggs. In South Africa, Botswana, and Zimbabwe, a regular seasonal migration of this species occurs in December and January. This migration is always to the east, toward an area of higher rainfall. Mysteriously, no clear return migration has so far been observed.

The phenomenon of an apparently one-way migration is not uncommon among migrant tropical insects. The reason seems to be that an observer at any point along the route sees only one leg of a migration circuit. In order to keep pace with the rainfall as it moves from place to place, one generation of a species may need to migrate hundreds or thousands of kilometers to the east. The next generation may need to migrate a similar distance to the north, the next to the west, and the next to the south,

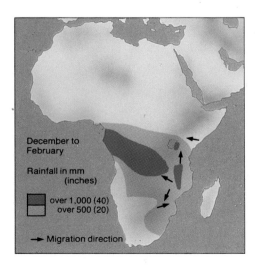

December to February

Rainfall in mm (inches)

▨ over 1,000 (40)
☐ over 500 (20)

→ Migration direction

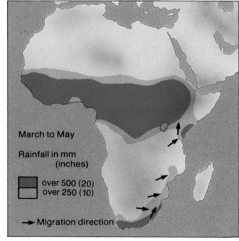

March to May

Rainfall in mm (inches)

▨ over 500 (20)
☐ over 250 (10)

→ Migration direction

so completing the circuit. Such migration circuits, already known to occur with locusts, have yet to be demonstrated for any tropical butterfly.

In one sense, arid zone tropical butterflies are faced with a situation similar to that faced by the autumn generation of monarch butterflies in the northern United States and Canada. Optimum migration behavior takes the butterfly by the shortest and most economical route possible from the place it has been born to a place suitable for breeding and laying eggs. In the case of arid zone butterflies, the place to be is the general area in which rainfall is most likely.

Unlike temperate migrants, therefore, except perhaps for autumn monarchs and

their ilk, tropical migrants should compensate for the movement of the sun's azimuth across the horizon so that they fly in a straight line. To date, however, no major study has been carried out to test these expectations. All that is known is that tropical butterflies, unlike temperate species, do not change their migration direction during the day. An individual flying east in the morning is still flying east by late afternoon. If such butterflies orient by the sun, they must also be compensating for its movement across the sky during the day. Such apparently sophisticated behavior is not beyond the capabilities of an insect. Honey bees, for example, are known to do just this during their foraging trips.

▲ Almost worldwide in distribution, the painted lady (*Vanessa cardui*) is an active migrant wherever it occurs, in both temperate and tropical regions. Specimens have been seen in the mid-Atlantic and in the Indian Ocean, more than 800 kilometers (500 miles) from the nearest land.

▲ The migratory behavior of moths is difficult to investigate because of their nocturnal habits. One tagging study on the oriental armyworm moth revealed that alternate generations move considerable distances northward in spring and southward in autumn.

MOTHS

As far as is known, moths migrate in much the same way as butterflies. Because most moths migrate at night, however, information has been very difficult to obtain. Radar has been used, primarily in the arid tropical and subtropical regions of Africa and Australia, and the majority of large nocturnal insects observed take to the air about an hour after sunset. The insects then climb quite fast, over 30 centimeters (1 foot) per second, to an average height of about 400 meters (1,300 feet) and a ceiling, limited by temperature, of about 1,500 meters (5,000 feet). This rapid "dusk ascent" is followed by a gradual descent over one to four hours. How long individual moths remain in the air and the distances they cover is still unknown. Depending on the

condition of the night, insects as a whole can be in the air from 1 to 12 hours, and travel at a ground speed of between 10 and 80 kilometers (6 and 50 miles) per hour, depending on wind speed. Such large nocturnal insects, mainly moths and solitary locusts in the areas studied, usually travel downwind, but only because their preferred direction invariably coincides with the direction of the wind. If the wind shifts slightly, the insects adjust their orientation to travel to one side of downwind.

Only one major marking experiment has been carried out on moths. It took place in China in 1964 and involved the oriental armyworm moth (*Pseudaletia separata*). Many of China's entomologists took part and between March and September many thousands of moths were marked and released. Only a few were recaptured, but these showed that in spring and early summer the moths migrate at least 1,400 kilometers (870 miles) to the north. In autumn they may fly up to 800 kilometers (500 miles) to the south. Successive generations seem to migrate north in spring and summer and south in the autumn. The rate of migration seems to be about 150 to 200 kilometers (95 to 125 miles) per day during the first three to four days after emergence, and thereafter about 30 to 50 kilometers (20 to 30 miles) per night. During those first few days the moths are still reproductively inactive and they may migrate by day as well as by night.

In its general pattern the armyworm moth is perhaps the nocturnal, oriental equivalent of the monarch, red admiral, and painted lady butterflies. Perhaps also similar is the

▶ The large yellow underwing is a widespread Eurasian moth that feeds on nectar. Experiments have shown that it orients during migration by the moon, but that it does not correct for the moon's changing position through the night.

silver-Y moth (*Plusia gamma*) of western
Europe, which, just like the monarch, has an
autumn generation that delays the onset of
sexual maturity and migrates to the south to
warmer latitudes. In common with the
oriental armyworm moth, the silver-Y
migrates day and night for the first few days
of adult life. Thereafter, it migrates only
at night.

Like butterflies, moths have a sense of
compass direction. Except when migrating
over the sea at night, silver-Y moths
maintain a preferred compass direction
(north-northwest in spring and summer,
south in autumn) irrespective of wind
direction. A variety of experiments have now
shown that, when it is shining, the major

compass cue for migrating moths is the
moon. On starlit nights, in the absence of
the moon, moths seem to orient by the stars.
At least one species of temperate moth, the
large yellow underwing (*Noctua pronuba*),
has been shown, like the small white
butterfly with the daytime sun, not to
correct for the shift in direction of celestial
cues during the course of the night.

On overcast nights, however, moths judge
compass direction from the earth's magnetic
field. As yet, there is no evidence for a
similar magnetic sense in butterflies. Recent
experiments on moth orientation suggest that
they begin each night orienting magnetically
but then transfer their orientation to the
moon or stars if these are visible.

▲ An oak hawk-moth (*Marumba quercus*)
at rest on an oak leaf. Like most moths,
males are probably greater travelers than
females. Both sexes are likely to orient by
the stars and the earth's magnetic field on
nights when the moon is not visible.

LOCUSTS

Cliff Ashall

A voracious appetite and the capacity to move rapidly over great distances have made locusts, in many parts of the world, the most dreaded pest since people began growing crops 10,000 years ago. The arrival of a locust swarm—the sky dark with millions of flying insects consuming crops in their path—frequently spells economic ruin for the farmer, and starvation for the community.

▲ A medieval French illuminated manuscript showing a plague of locusts inflicted upon the Pharaoh of Egypt to compel the release of Moses and his people from slavery.
▶ A swarm of locusts in northern Ethiopia.
▼ A simplified diagram to show the relationship between swarming locusts and wind speed and direction. Most swarms are clustered within 10 degrees on either side of the wind direction.

The wind-borne appearance and disappearance of locusts has long been documented. In Exodus it tells how "the Lord brought an east wind upon the land all that day, and all that night; and when it was morning the east wind brought the locusts." Further on it recounts how "the Lord turned a mighty strong west wind which took away the locusts and cast them into the Red Sea."

Since biblical times, too, there has been much speculation as to the origin of locust swarms. Thought of as a punishment sent by angry gods, some believed that they came from caves or from the mouths of fishes. It was not until the early twentieth century that work by Boris Uvarov, a scientist working in Russia, began to unravel the mystery of these devastating plagues.

There are about a dozen species of locusts, members of the large Acrididae family, the short-horned grasshoppers, and at least one species is found on all continents except Antarctica. The desert locust (*Schistocerca gregaria*), the locust mentioned in the Bible, is the most widespread, and the one that has caused the greatest destruction. It is found throughout northern Africa, south to Tanzania, and in all of Arabia, westward to Pakistan and northern India. It has probably been studied more than any other insect in the world.

Locusts have developed a remarkable ability that distinguishes them from grasshoppers. They respond to changes in population density by changing their phase. When they are uncrowded they are known as solitary; under crowded conditions they change into the gregarious phase, their shape, color, physiology, and behavior altering. At low density gregarious locusts revert to being solitary once more.

The degree to which locust species show phase difference varies considerably, but the desert locust provides a good example of the sorts of changes that take place. Solitary hoppers are green, sometimes with a few dark markings; gregarious hoppers are yellow or orange, with heavy dark patterning. Solitary hoppers move no more than a few meters per day, whereas gregarious ones form highly mobile bands and travel as much as 1.6 kilometers (1 mile) per day. Solitary adults form groups that are always small and short-lived: they fly by day only when disturbed, although they frequently fly by night. Gregarious adults form swarms and fly spontaneously, mainly by day.

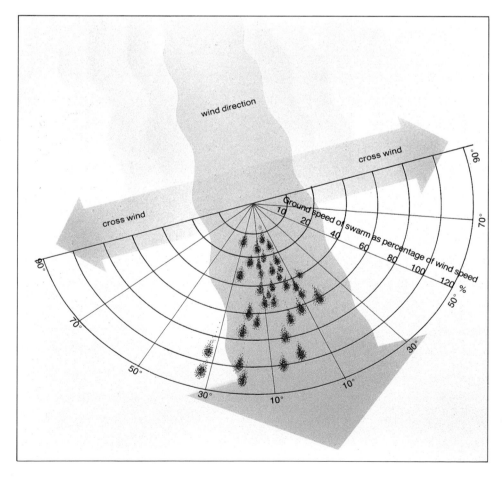

Kathie Atkinson/Auscape

In eastern Ethiopia, in October 1958, one of the largest swarms ever recorded covered some 1,000 square kilometers (400 square miles). It was estimated to comprise 40,000 million locusts. A swarm this size would weigh about 80,000 tonnes (176 million pounds). One swarm locust can consume its own weight in food every day, which gives some indication of the devastation caused by these devouring clouds. (And a regional invasion can consist of many such swarms.) Ethiopia's 1958 swarm had traveled around 3,000 kilometers (2,000 miles) from hatching grounds in northern Ethiopia and the Sudan. A large number of the locusts managed to fly right across Somalia to die finally in the Indian Ocean. Smaller numbers remained in eastern Ethiopia to breed again.

In some species the females lay their eggs after rain has fallen; in others they lay their eggs in dry soil, but they will not hatch until there has been rain. This means there is food for the hoppers when they hatch. If large numbers of hoppers hatch, and crowding takes place then swarm behavior begins. The work of Reg Rainey and Zena Waloff has shown that migration ties in with weather frontal systems and seasonal rainfall patterns. Swarms travel with the winds, journeys downwind eventually carrying the locusts to fronts where rain is likely to fall, making it possible to breed again. A swarm stays together because the gregarious locusts turn in when they reach the edge of the swarm. Depending on the amount of air turbulence, swarms tend to resemble cumulus clouds in shape, with the topmost locusts reaching a height of 1,500 to 2,000 meters (5,000 to 6,500 feet).

Locusts have muscles capable of 10 to 20 times as much work as those of a human, and they fly at a speed of between 16 and 19 kilometers (10 and 12 miles) per hour. A fuel supply of fat enables them to fly continuously for up to 20 hours. During longer journeys the locusts use gliding as well as flapping flight. Swarms generally move more slowly than the wind speed because they have a rolling movement— there are always some locusts settled beneath the swarm that take off once again as soon as others pass over them.

Sea crossings by desert locusts are common, insects appearing on ships far from land. There are travelers' tales of locusts alighting and taking off from platforms of floating masses of locusts, but there is no scientific evidence of this. Cannibalism may provide food on such trips. In October 1988 the desert locust set a new record, specimens from West Africa being picked up in the West Indies, a journey of some 5,000 kilometers (3,000 miles) in five days or less.

Marking and recapture and radar observations have shown that solitary locusts also migrate over long distances, but they generally travel by night. They certainly travel distances of up to 250 kilometers (150 miles), and over a season many travel much farther than this.

Since 1943, monthly summaries and forecasts combining locust and weather information have been issued for regions threatened by locust plagues. This work was initially done by the Anti-Locust Research Centre in London and since 1973 has been carried out by the Food and Agriculture Organization of the United Nations in Rome. These summaries and forecasts, which now make use of satellite weather data, have been useful both in planning control operations and in encouraging the provision of information for further research, but infestations continue to occur. Plague prevention is possible, but only through the best efforts of a centralized intelligence and forecasting system, and extensive international cooperation.

◀ An Australian plague locust. Though widely associated with countries of the Middle East and north Africa, locusts are found on all continents except Antarctica.

Stephen Dalton/NHPA

◀ A young desert locust just completing its molt from the fifth (and final) juvenile stage to the adult form. The abandoned skin can be seen at the bottom of the picture. The wings take about twenty minutes to unfurl and harden, but the insect will not fly for several days.

THE LIFE CYCLE OF THE DESERT LOCUST

The female locust lays between 50 and 70 eggs at a time in pods, thrusting her extended abdomen about 10 centimeters (4 inches) deep into moist soil.

Roughly the size and shape of a grain of rice, each egg must absorb its own weight of water — ideally within the first five days — in order to hatch.

The young emerge in about two weeks, but this varies with conditions. Known as nymphs or "hoppers," they soon shed their white skin. The young of swarming parents are darker than the young green nymphs of solitary parents.

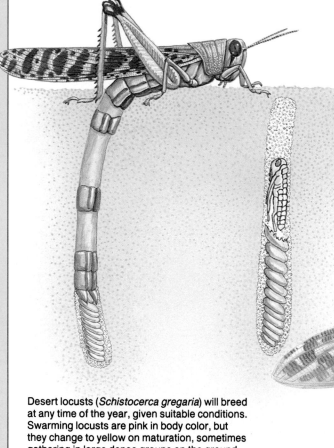

Desert locusts (*Schistocerca gregaria*) will breed at any time of the year, given suitable conditions. Swarming locusts are pink in body color, but they change to yellow on maturation, sometimes gathering in large dense groups on the ground to mate.

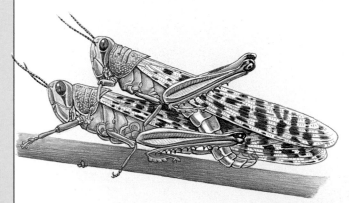

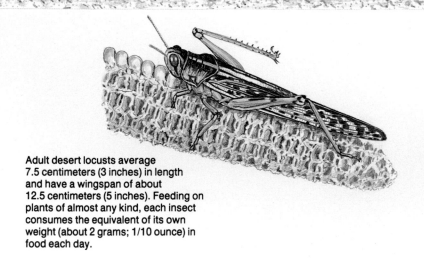

Aerial spraying with insecticides is used to regulate swarms but the most effective control involves poison-baiting hoppers on the ground, before they have a chance to swarm and fly.

The distribution of the desert locust, showing the maximum area liable to invasion during plagues and the areas where locusts are found during recessions.

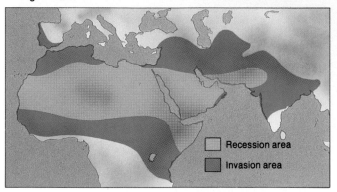

☐ Recession area

■ Invasion area

Adult desert locusts average 7.5 centimeters (3 inches) in length and have a wingspan of about 12.5 centimeters (5 inches). Feeding on plants of almost any kind, each insect consumes the equivalent of its own weight (about 2 grams; 1/10 ounce) in food each day.

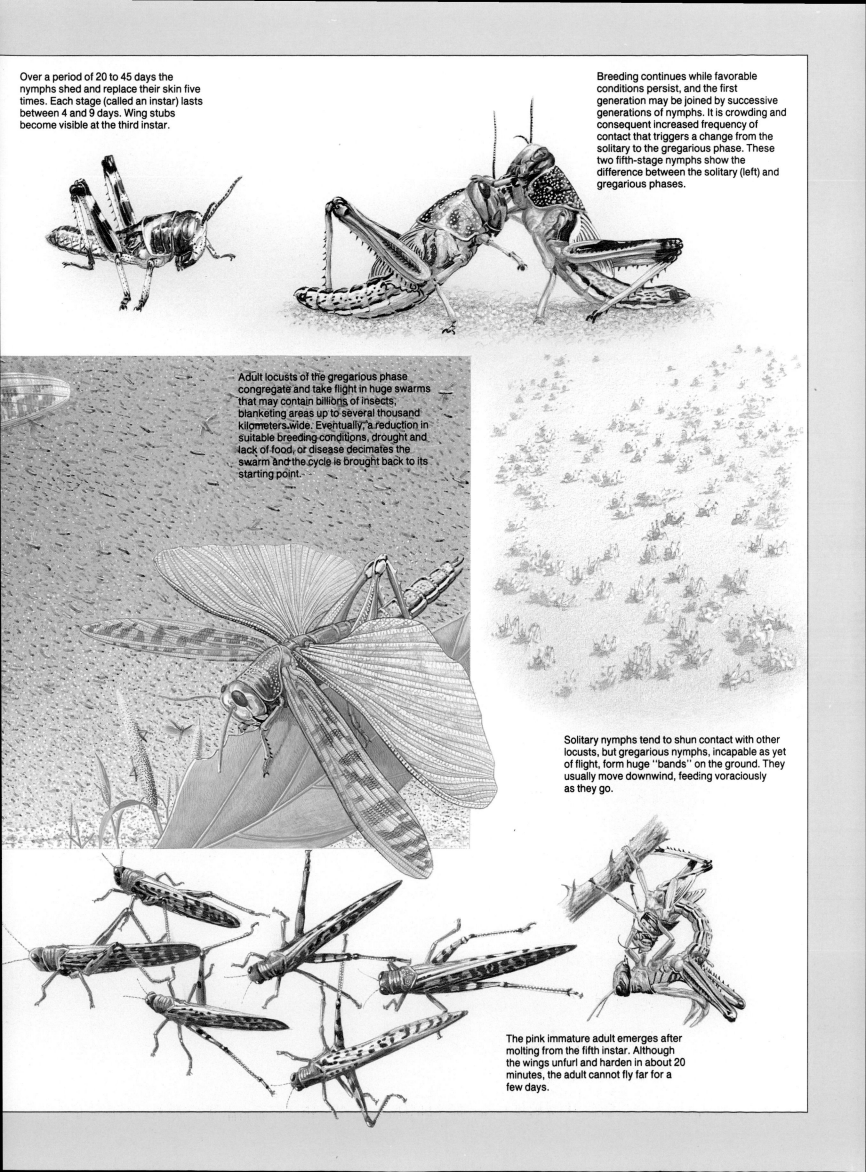

Over a period of 20 to 45 days the nymphs shed and replace their skin five times. Each stage (called an instar) lasts between 4 and 9 days. Wing stubs become visible at the third instar.

Breeding continues while favorable conditions persist, and the first generation may be joined by successive generations of nymphs. It is crowding and consequent increased frequency of contact that triggers a change from the solitary to the gregarious phase. These two fifth-stage nymphs show the difference between the solitary (left) and gregarious phases.

Adult locusts of the gregarious phase congregate and take flight in huge swarms that may contain billions of insects, blanketing areas up to several thousand kilometers wide. Eventually, a reduction in suitable breeding conditions, drought and lack of food, or disease decimates the swarm and the cycle is brought back to its starting point.

Solitary nymphs tend to shun contact with other locusts, but gregarious nymphs, incapable as yet of flight, form huge ''bands'' on the ground. They usually move downwind, feeding voraciously as they go.

The pink immature adult emerges after molting from the fifth instar. Although the wings unfurl and harden in about 20 minutes, the adult cannot fly far for a few days.

OTHER INSECTS

Terence Lindsey

Migrations, for many flying insects, are brief periods of activity between longer sedentary periods. Many non-flying insects also migrate, sometimes keeping on the move throughout their lives.

If we search carefully along the banks of any small pond shortly after sunset on a calm summer evening, we may well find a dragonfly nymph crawling slowly up the stem of a reed or some other aquatic plant. Dragonfly larvae, or nymphs, spend the early part of their lives entirely under water, hunting the larvae of other aquatic insects. They ultimately leave the water to carry out the transformation into a fully adult insect capable of flight. At dusk the harsh glare of the sun has gone but the air is still comfortably warm. Many larvae choose this time to begin their crawl to the surface.

This is a delicate and lengthy process, but if we were to patiently maintain our vigil, we would see the adult emerge from the split husk of its larval skin and its wings slowly unfold and harden. Little else happens until about an hour before dawn, when the insect rapidly vibrates its wings for half an hour or so. The dawn air is chill, and the flight muscles must reach a certain temperature before they can function effectively. Just before sunrise, the insect takes flight and heads away from the pond.

This dragonfly will probably remain in flight for some time, show little interest in food or sex, and even shun other ponds similar to the one in which it was born. It is

Jane Burton/Bruce Coleman Ltd.

as though its sole interest lies in making distance. Only after several days will it settle at a suitable pond, begin feeding, and take whatever action to attract a mate is appropriate to its particular sex and species.

The behavior of such a dragonfly is typical, in its major features, of the behavior of a vast number of flying insects. For example, almost all the species of aphids that fly are strongly attracted to ultraviolet light when they metamorphose into the fully adult (that is, flying) stage. They therefore seek blue sky and spend the first period of adulthood in flight. This period may last only a few hours, although if the plant on which they first land is unsuitable for any reason their journey may be extended in stages over several days. Either way, the first few hours of early adulthood constitute a clear-cut migratory phase. Within a few days the aphid's wing muscles atrophy and are reabsorbed, and flight thereafter is

impossible. Many species of mosquito, and a number of kinds of beetle, display behavior similar to the flying aphids.

The life cycle of many winged insects might be seen as comprising a relatively sedentary stage (the larva) in which food is almost the only concern, and an adult stage, also more or less sedentary, in which reproduction is of prime concern, with a brief but distinct period of travel in between.

In several respects these migratory flights are less casual than they might appear.

In the first place, they tend to be highly synchronized. Our dragonfly spent the night in transformation from larva to adult, but it then waited until dawn to actually take flight. Many other dragonflies probably emerged from the pond, and perhaps from other nearby ponds, that same night. And all of them would have waited until dawn to fly. In other words, individual insects may become ready for migration at various times,

▲ As nymphs, dragonflies live under water, breathing by means of gills lining a chamber in the rectum. For their size they are fearsome predators, feeding on almost anything they can catch and subdue, including frogs and small fish.

◀ (Opposite, top) Lupin aphids (*Macrosiphon albifrons*) on a flower stem. Aphids feed by sucking fluids from plants, and some species are serious pests in gardens and orchards. Many forms have wings and migrate by flight.

◀ (Opposite, bottom) Dragonflies have two pairs of wings which are very similar in size and shape, and which cannot be folded back along the body as in most other insects. Active by day, most species roost at night clinging to waterside vegetation—often, like this individual, accumulating the early morning dew.

63

Kim Taylor/Bruce Coleman Ltd.

▲ An aphid giving birth. Aphids are remarkable for the complexity of their life cycles. Many species have both winged and wingless forms, or forms that lay eggs and forms that give birth to living young, or forms that reproduce sexually and forms that reproduce by parthenogenesis (that is, in the absence of fertilization by the male). These forms often alternate seasonally or between generations within the same species.

but all then await a specific event, such as dawn, to actually take flight.

This tendency for a gradual accumulation followed by an abrupt flush of activity is a common feature of these migrations. For broadly similar reasons, aphids generally show two peaks in the daily pattern of their migration activity: one in the early morning, and the other in late afternoon.

Additionally, the insect migrants are usually all of the same age. We might contrast this with the migrations of many birds and mammals, in which it is common for migrating groups to consist of adults and immatures of all ages.

THE PATH OF MIGRATION
It might be thought that wind plays the dominant role in determining course and distance in the journeys of insects, such as aphids, that are weak flyers, but this does not tell the full story. Generally speaking, insects cannot glide: they remain aloft only while they flap their wings. It follows from this that the distance traveled is strongly influenced by the time the insect chooses to keep flying, so the insect has at least some degree of potential control over this factor. Experiments in a number of cases have ruled out mere fatigue as the reason for curtailing such flights.

Similarly, it is at least conceivable that a species might be able to evolve some behavioral mechanism prompting individuals to take flight at some event most likely to be followed by winds blowing in a preferred direction. At a given location, for example, a sudden drop in temperature might be most often followed by a southerly wind. Such climatic associations are not rare. We rely on them quite heavily in our weather-forecasting techniques, and some insects do indeed seem to behave as though they too were exploiting such relationships.

By no means do all insect migrations involve flight. Some species never fly, yet travel extensively. Among these are ants of the genera *Dorylus* (in Africa) and *Eciton* (in Central and South America). Widely known as driver ants and army ants, these insects spend their lives in pedestrian journeys.

Army ants are predatory, and live in colonies totaling several hundred thousand individuals. The colony constantly alternates between a nomadic phase lasting about 17 days and a sendentary stage of about 20 days. While on the march, the ants form temporary bivouacs at a different place almost every night; some remain through the day to guard the queen and larvae, while most others spread out to seek food. In midafternoon the raiders return and the entire colony moves off to a new camp.

G.I. Bernard/NHPA

The queen suspends egg-laying while on the move, but during the sendentary stage she rapidly becomes swollen with eggs, and within a week begins laying at the rate of well over 100 eggs per hour. While this crop of eggs hatches, the larvae of the previous crop spin their cocoons, emerging some days later as adults. The colony is then ready to resume its travels and the cycle begins anew.

▲ South American army ants camp periodically for a few days while the queen lays her eggs, but are otherwise constantly on the move through the rainforest.

▼ A colony of African driver ants on the march. Some workers carry the larvae while others forage along the column. Soldiers line the route facing outward, alert for trouble like riot police at a political rally.

BALLOONISTS AND HITCHHIKERS

Mark S. Harvey

Spiders and their kin—arachnids—are common inhabitants of virtually every terrestrial ecosystem on earth. From the slopes of Mt Everest to the ocean beaches, they play an important role as predators of insects, of each other, of other invertebrates, and occasionally, of vertebrates. Incredibly, some arachnids, the marine mites, have even invaded the sanctity of the oceans and may be found at the bottom of the deepest seas.

Arachnids can be recognized by the possession of four pairs of legs. Spiders are the most common example, but the group also includes scorpions, mites, ticks, pseudoscorpions, harvestmen, whip-scorpions, and several other minor groups. Together, they make up an ancient yet successful assemblage of beasts capable of producing horror and fear in humans.

exposed, prominent position, such as the end of a branch, rock or fence post, and faces into the wind. It then elevates its abdomen and produces a silken thread from the spinnerets located at the rear of the abdomen. This emerges as a sticky liquid which hardens on contact with the air. The thread is dragged from the spider by the wind, and may extend for several meters before the force exerted on it counters the weight of the spider and lifts the potential aeronaut into the air.

Once aloft, the spider is borne on the wind until it strikes another object such as a tree, or until it breaks the thread and descends gently to the ground. The small size and weight of ballooning spiders, usually less than 1 millimeter (1/25 inch) and 1 milligram (1/1,000 ounce), ensure a safe

Phil Devries/Oxford Scientific Films

How did spiders manage to get to Mt Everest long before Edmund Hillary and Sherpa Tenzing had ever contemplated their epic journey? How do arachnids colonize even the smallest oceanic islands, including newly emerged volcanic ones? Unlike insects, which usually possess wings and are able to fly vast distances to colonize distant shores, arachnids must rely on different migration techniques. The three groups that conduct long-range aerial dispersal are spiders, pseudoscorpions, and mites.

Spiders adopt a technique that is virtually unique within the animal kingdom—ballooning. The spider stands in an

landing. Ballooning spiders have been found in aerial surveys at altitudes of up to 5 kilometers (3 miles) and have been found alighting on ships far out to sea, thus highlighting the danger of falling to earth where there is none.

Adults of small species such as money spiders, or young members of larger species such as orb-weaving spiders, have been reported ballooning. Spiderlings of many other spider groups are also known to balloon.

A slightly different technique is used by some trapdoor spiderlings. Instead of allowing the wind to drag the silk from their body, they descend from an elevated position on a dragline. Silk pays out as the spider falls downward, and both spider and silk are caught by the wind and pushed horizontally until the thread breaks at the attachment point and the spider becomes airborne.

Pseudoscorpions, on the other hand, do not employ silken threads to move from place to place—they employ animals. These small animals, less than 5 millimeters (1/5 inch) in size, use pincer-like claws that resemble those of scorpions to attach themselves to the legs of insects and simply hold on for the ride. This behavior is termed "phoresy." For many years it was thought that the pseudoscorpions deliberately sought out flying insects as a means of reaching greener pastures. Modern views, however, hold that the migration is a result of the attachment behavior rather than a motivation for it. Some species are found in the fur of mammals or the feathers of birds. This association is probably a form of predation rather than a technique for travel, as the pseudoscorpions feed on ectoparasites such as mites and lice. However, they may be inadvertently transported if the host migrates. Pseudoscorpions have been found on remote islands, where they arrived either by hitching a ride with an insect or by rafting in clumps of vegetation and logs washed into the sea. Both methods are dangerous, as the host insect may not find suitable land, or the floating islet may break up before being cast ashore.

Like pseudoscorpions, many small mite species (less than 3 millimeters or 1/8 inch) are transported by other animals. Unlike pseudoscorpions, however, some mites possess remarkable structural modifications to aid them in attaching to the host. Nymphs of some species have sucker organs on the underside of their bodies while others secrete a stalk from modified anal glands that dries and hardens onto the host. Each technique assures solid adhesion and minimizes

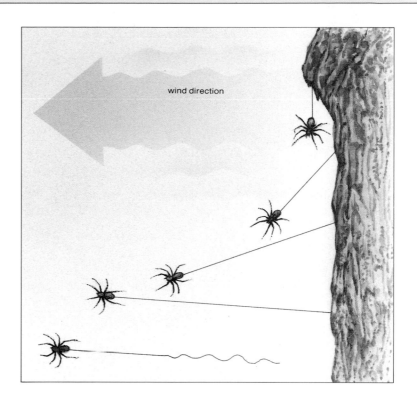

▲ To balloon, a *Ummidia* spiderling drops on a dragline of silk from the edge of a launching surface. The wind picks up the spider and as the dragline lengthens the spider is pushed away from the surface and lifted up and above the horizontal. Eventually the dragline breaks at the point of attachment and the spiderling drifts downward.

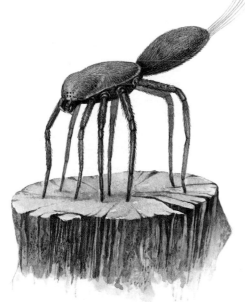

▲ One method of accomplishing ballooning. The spider stands on "tiptoes" facing the wind and squeezes out a drop of silk that is expanded further by the wind. When the pull on the threads is strong enough, the spider will float off into the air.

◀ (Opposite page) Mites infesting a dragonfly. Lacking wings, many mites and other arachnids solve their transport problems by hitchhiking and a successful parasite can go anywhere its host goes. Of course, it also stops when the host does.

the likelihood of mites inadvertently falling off or being cleaned or rubbed off by the host.

For mites that breed and feed in mammal dung, what better way to locate it than by means of a dung beetle? These mites, which are often adult females, cling to the underside of the beetles until they reach a suitably fresh patch of dung, then drop off and complete their duties before the dung dries and hardens. If no males are available at the new site, the females can lay unseminated eggs that hatch into males, thus allowing cross-fertilization to occur.

Water mite larvae attach themselves to aquatic insects and are thus transported to different water bodies if the insect migrates. They pierce the cuticle of the host with their specialized mouthparts and feed on its body fluids. Wide-ranging insects such as dragonflies and water beetles are often utilized, resulting in distributions that belie the small size of the mite—up to 2 to 3 millimeters (1/12 to 1/8 inch) in length.

A bizarre combination of pseudoscorpion and mite phoresy was reported in the early 1950s, when a number of mites were found attached to a pseudoscorpion which in turn was clasping a beetle. All that was needed was a spider ballooning past to complete the entire spectrum of long-range aerial migration by arachnids.

Spiders, pseudoscorpions, and mites are part of the aerial plankton that is continually present in our atmosphere—the spiders as balloonists, drifting on gossamer, and the pseudoscorpions and mites as hitchhikers, attached to an unwilling host. However, what goes up must come down, and these balloonists and hitchhikers can only hope that their landing is indeed on land.

AMERICAN BIRDS

Terence Lindsey

▲ The chestnut-sided warbler was apparently rare at the time of European settlement of North America but prospered with the destruction of the primeval eastern forests, and is now abundant and widespread in the east and northeast. It winters in Central America.

The urgent northward passage of wild geese is a familiar image of spring in North America, and for many people everywhere the passage of the seasons is most conspicuously marked by the appearance or disappearance of one kind of bird or another. In many ways, and for a combination of reasons, seasonal bird migration is more noticeable in North America than anywhere else in the world.

NORTH AMERICA

With an area well in excess of 20 million square kilometers (about 8 million square miles), the North American continent is essentially a gigantic wedge of land that extends from beyond the Arctic Circle almost to the equator. In the north it sprawls across nearly half the globe, from Alaska to Greenland, but it narrows in the south and is only a few dozen kilometers wide at the Isthmus of Panama. A number of its major geographic features have had far-reaching consequences for its native birds.

In Europe and northern Africa the major geographic features (the Alps, the Mediterranean Sea, and the Sahara Desert) run broadly east and west, thus acting as barriers to the north–south migration of birds. In North America, however, the major geographic features (the Rocky Mountains, Great Plains, the Mississippi River valley, and both coasts) run roughly north and south, and accordingly act to guide bird migration rather than hinder it.

The very breadth of the continent in the north means that large areas are remote from any oceans and their moderating influence on climate. Oceans act as huge heat sinks, storing solar radiation in summer and releasing it gradually in winter, and in their absence northern winters are particularly severe. The difference between summer and winter regimes in inland areas is much more exaggerated than in coastal regions at similar latitudes.

Cold, in itself, has little effect even on very small birds, so long as they can remain active. But increased activity means increased fuel (that is, food) consumption. Not only is food normally scarcer in winter, but reduced day length means that there are fewer hours available in which to search for it. This consideration affects insect-eaters in particular, and in cold climates small insectivorous birds face severe difficulties in gathering enough food by day to last them through the long, bitter night.

Even large birds are affected. For instance many waterbirds otherwise little troubled by climate are prevented from obtaining the limited food available in winter simply because the northern lakes and wetlands freeze over. For comparable reasons, many other birds (including hawks) find it advantageous to migrate to milder climates rather than face the rigors of the northern winter. There is, in fact, an approximate correlation between size, diet, and the propensity to migrate south for the winter. Fish-eaters and insect-eaters have little alternative, but seed-eaters can often achieve more favorable compromises because the availability of seeds is not always markedly reduced in winter. Some birds are capable of adjusting their diet seasonally while some others can make do, at least temporarily, on a diet very different from their normal one. Tree swallows (*Tachycineta bicolor*), for example, feed almost exclusively on flying insects but migrate northward in spring so eagerly that they occasionally misjudge the weather and become snowbound. In such circumstances they can sometimes survive for a day or two on small fruit and berries. Nevertheless, insect-eaters and small birds tend to be more active migrants than seed-eaters or large birds.

Since the region lying in the tropics is vastly smaller than that closer to the pole, the winter ranges of those birds wintering in the tropics are usually significantly smaller than their breeding ranges. The breeding distribution of the chestnut-sided warbler (*Dendroica pennsylvanica*), for example, is about ten times larger than its wintering distribution. Consequently, vast numbers of birds are crowded into a relatively small area each winter, and immigrants dominate the

local birdlife in Central America and northern South America to an extent unknown anywhere else in the world.

The arrangement of major geographic features has had a more subtle influence upon the evolution of North America's avifauna: it has permitted a greater

northward penetration of essentially tropical forms than might otherwise have been possible. Such tropical groups as the icterids (Icteridae), tyrants (Tyrannidae), wood warblers (Parulidae), and tanagers (Thraupidae) have evolved temperate forms that now commonly breed well to the north

▲ Snow geese (*Anser caerulescens*) breed on the Arctic tundra from western Greenland to northeastern Siberia. Large numbers migrate along a number of very narrow pathways to winter along the Gulf of Mexico. The birds congregate at well-defined rest stops along the way, though these points may change from year to year.

69

Among the most common and hardy of North American wildfowl, the mallard (*Anas platyrhynchos*) winters as far north as it can find food and open water.

The marbled godwit (*Linosa fedosa*) nests beside marshes and "sloughs" (shallow pounds) across the northern prairies, then retires to spend the winter along the Gulf of Mexico and on the Pacific coast from California southward.

of the Canadian border. However, the winter environment is particularly inhospitable to these essentially tropical forms, virtually all of which migrate back to the tropics. The wood warblers illustrate such factors, and can in many ways be viewed as typical of North American songbird migrants. These birds constitute a family with mainly tropical affinities and more than 50 of its total membership of about 126 species breed in North America, returning to the tropics in winter. They have penetrated North America with such success that, throughout the coniferous forests of Canada and the northern United States, wood warblers may be among the most common and conspicuous songbirds in summer.

They are also conspicuous in their seasonal migrations. Like other songbirds,

wood warblers tend to travel at night, moving northward in spring in relatively short stages of 300 kilometers (200 miles) or so. Large numbers may be held up temporarily by local bad weather, then move on all at once. Northward progress thus tends to be clumped in a series of waves possibly several days apart, and any observer fortunate enough to be in the woods just after dawn after such a wave has landed will be witness to one of the most extraordinary of all migratory phenomena. The trees literally swarm with activity and it is not at all unusual to find 10 or 20 birds of four or five species of wood warbler feeding in a single bush.

The wave motif is perhaps less marked in autumn, but the southward migration is no less impressive. On a mild, quiet, starry night in early autumn, any attentive observer can sense the scurrying traffic overhead, almost undetectable except for occasional quiet chirps and brief whistles as the birds stay in contact with each other. The whole whispered performance suggests nothing so much as a gentle rain of sound, drifting down from the night sky. Sometimes a winged form may be glimpsed for an instant outlined against the disk of the moon, but otherwise the hordes streaming southward remain invisible.

The routes and schedules used by migrating wood warblers are nearly as diverse as the species. A few, such as the yellow-rumped warbler (*Dendroica coronata*), are unusually hardy, migrate little, and sometimes winter as far north as southern Canada. Most others winter in Central America or the West Indies, some penetrating far into South America. A few, such as Kirtland's warbler (*D. kirtlandii*) have extremely restricted breeding and wintering quarters, and commute between them along very narrow pathways. Even some more widespread species use extraordinarily restricted routes. The blackpoll warbler (*D. striata*), for example, breeds as far northwest as Alaska, yet in autumn all birds move to the eastern United States to enter South America via Florida and the West Indies. The species is virtually unknown in Central America. Other wood warblers, such as the American redstart (*Setophaga ruticilla*), migrate directly southward across a very broad front to reach Mexico, the West Indies and northern and South America.

THE FLYWAYS

The total flux of seasonal avian migration in North America is enormous. Several hundred species, and thousands of millions of individual birds are involved in one way or another. Almost every species has its own schedule and itinerary. All this means that the seasonal pattern of avian migration across North America is an extremely complex one. Nevertheless, analysis reveals four major arteries of movement across the continent that have been distinguished and labeled as flyways.

Many birds of Quebec, Labrador, and the maritime provinces of Canada use the Atlantic Flyway, which flows along the east coast of the United States to Florida. Birds following this route often then island-hop through the West Indies to reach South America via Venezuela and Guyana.

The Mississippi Flyway has its origins in the Mackenzie River valley in northwestern Canada, but many users breed as far west as Alaska. These birds move south across central Canada, gradually funneling into the valley of the Mississippi River and the Gulf of Mexico. A wide range of species use this flyway, but the extensive wetlands that line the route make it ideal for waterbirds including vast numbers of ducks. Many of the songbirds that use the route continue their flight across the Gulf of Mexico and into Central and South America.

The Central Flyway also has its origins in the Mackenzie region, but its main southward trend is along the eastern-front ranges of the Rocky Mountain system, and it

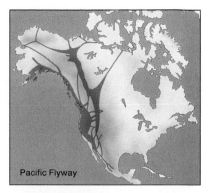
Pacific Flyway

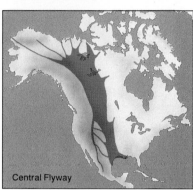
Central Flyway

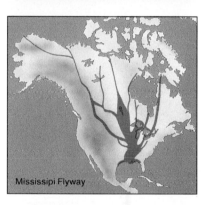
Mississipi Flyway

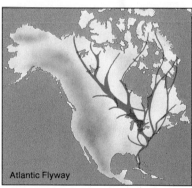
Atlantic Flyway

▲ The four major flyways used by migrating birds in North America.

has as its terminus the high central plateau of Mexico. Like the Mississippi Flyway, this route is also favored by many waterfowl.

Because the Pacific Flyway follows the more temperate climate along the American west coast, from Alaska to southern California, it is less important than the other three and is used by relatively few long-distance migrants. Rather, it tends to function more as a suburban branch line, with commuters continually getting on and getting off, as it were, along the way.

The oceans bordering the continent, the Atlantic in particular, also constitute flyways of some significance. Most users of these routes are shorebirds of the families Scolopacidae and Charadriidae that nest in the High Arctic and travel enormous distances to their winter quarters in southern South America.

SOUTH AMERICA

South America straddles the equator and has a gigantic latitudinal range stretching from 12°N to 55°S, or nearly 6,000 kilometers (3,700 miles). All climatic regimes from tropical to sub-Antarctic are represented, but two-thirds of its land area lies in the tropics while its southern extremity tapers away to a narrow point. This means that, for birds, the situation is the opposite of that found in North America—their potential breeding areas are small while wintering ranges may be vast.

Consequently, latitudinal migration of birds is a much less conspicuous phenomenon in South America than in North America. Nevertheless, many birds do migrate with the seasons, and several travel the entire length of the continent. Thus some swallows, such as the brown-chested martin

▼ These yellow-headed blackbirds (*Xanthocephalus xanthocephalus*) migrate to the southern United States and northern Mexico to spend the winter in large wandering flocks. They are often mixed with other species on scrubby open country and congregate in huge numbers in reedbeds to roost at night.

Robert A. Tyrrell/Oxford Scientific Films

◄ Even some tropical birds migrate seasonally. The violet-crowned hummingbird (*Amazilia violiceps*) crosses the United States border to breed in certain canyons in southern New Mexico and Arizona, but returns to Mexico in winter.

(*Phaeoprogne tapera*) and the Patagonian swallow (*Pygochelidon cyanoleuca*), migrate from the far south to winter in Central America and have been recorded as far north as Mexico.

Many areas serve simultaneously as a breeding range for some migrants and winter quarters for others. For example, temperate regions such as the central provinces of Argentina and Chile receive many migratory birds that come from tropical regions such as Amazonia to breed, returning in autumn. Such relatively short-range migrants include various tyrants (especially in the genus *Muscisaxicola*) and the giant hummingbird (*Patagona gigas*). The same regions also provide winter quarters for many birds that breed much further south. Waterfowl and shorebirds such as the Patagonian plover (*Charadrius falklandicus*) are prominent in

this group, but it also includes many smaller birds including at least one hummingbird, the green-backed firecrown (*Sephanoides sephanoides*), that breeds as far south as Tierra del Fuego.

Although latitudinal (or north–south) migration is less marked in South America than in North America, the reverse is true in the case of altitudinal migration. Soaring to many peaks exceeding 6,000 meters (20,000 feet), the Andes of South America are much higher than any mountain range in North America. These highlands contain substantial areas of potential breeding environment at very high altitudes, but are inhospitable in winter. Many birds, among them the Andean goose (*Chloephaga melanoptera*), breed in the highlands above 3,200 meters (10,500 feet) but descend to lower levels in search of snow-free conditions in winter.

EUROPEAN AND AFRICAN BIRDS

Chris Mead

▲ Sand martins are so-called because of their habit of excavating their nest-burrows in sandy banks and similar sites. They breed in colonies and are widespread across the northern hemisphere.

The intricately interleaved web of connections that European and African birds weave between distant places is only now being revealed in something like its full complexity. Many migrant birds travel much further than first thought, and not all migrations are north–south.

For centuries farmers throughout Europe have expectantly awaited the return of swallows (*Hirundo rustica*) each spring, but it is only within the past 60 years or so that bird ringing has begun to unravel the details of their journey and the winter quarters used by the birds. Earlier explanations of the swallows' disappearance and reappearance included the suggestion that they hibernated in the mud of ponds. In 1703 it was even suggested that they wintered on the moon since they were clearly much too delicate to survive a journey over the sea!

In the case of swallows that breed in England, their route out of the country, their strategy during their flight, and their ultimate destination are now well known. The birds gather together in flocks during August and September and undertake a fairly leisurely movement southward through Britain and across the Channel at its narrower, eastern end. They continue southward and slightly westward through France and Spain and cross the Mediterranean. This 2,000 kilometer (1,200 mile) journey is completed in about six weeks and made up of about 10 legs of 200 kilometers (120 miles), each of which is undertaken in just part of a day.

There is then the formidable barrier of the Sahara between the migrant swallow and tropical Africa—an enormous scorched area that offers little if any opportunity for feeding. However, a swallow in good condition, with enough fat to fuel its flight, can readily cross the 1,500 kilometers (930 miles) of desert in a couple of days to reach the rich feeding grounds of the Niger Inundation Zone, the wetland area along the inland course of the majestic River Niger. But even here the birds are only halfway through their journey and by mid-November they will be feeding in South Africa, right down on the Cape of Good Hope. As with

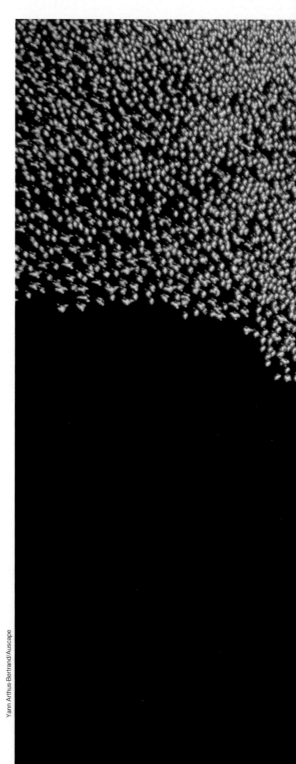

many Afro-European migrants the return journey is faster—it may take only five weeks—and rather more toward the east.

Such journeys are commonplace. Many millions of British swallows undertake them every year, and there are swallows throughout the rest of Europe. In fact, seasonally migrant birds were making their long-distance journeys millions of years before European explorers discovered the landmasses that are their destinations only a few hundred years ago. Other aerial feeders, like the sand martin (*Riparia riparia*) and house martin (*Delichon urbica*), make similar journeys but the swift (*Apus apus*) is

possibly the most amazing species.

In Europe almost all swifts now breed in the roofs of buildings, although in the surviving primeval forest on the Polish–Russian border some still nest in the hollow branches of the tallest trees. The parent birds return to their nesting sites at the beginning of May and will not have landed anywhere since they left the nesting site at the end of the previous July or early August. Their journey will have taken them southward through Europe and into west Africa. Here they spend the first part of their winter gradually filtering southward with the southern movement of the Inter-Tropical

▼ A flock of flamingos (*Phoeniconaias minor*) crosses Lake Nakuru in Kenya. The factors that influence the traffic of flamingos between the large salt lakes of East Africa are still not understood.

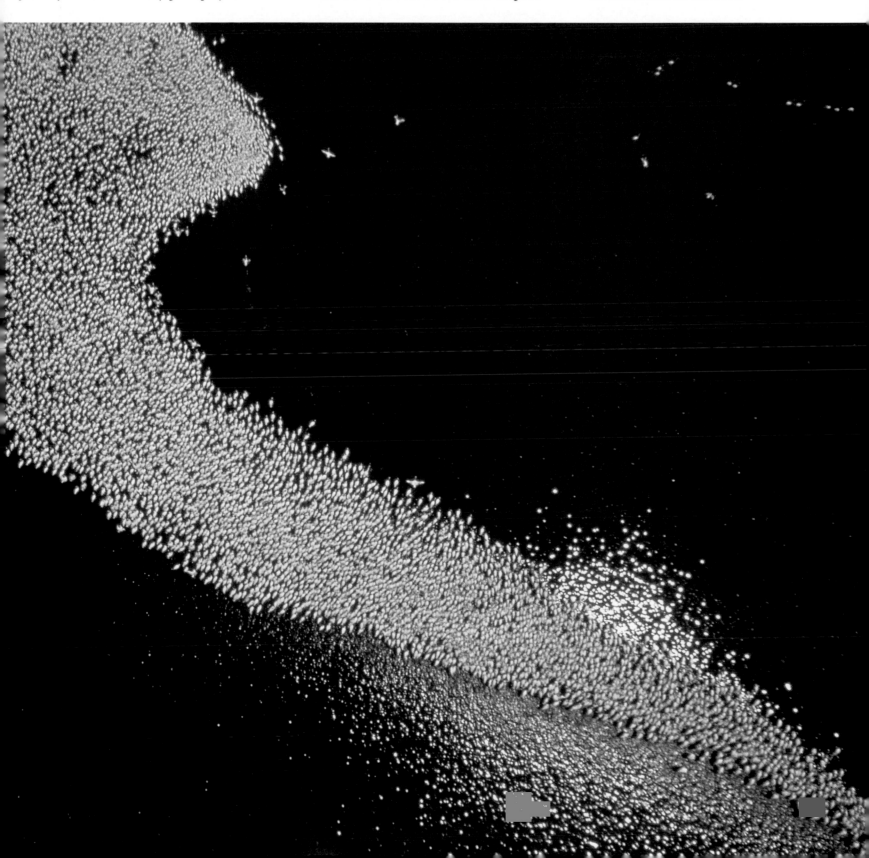

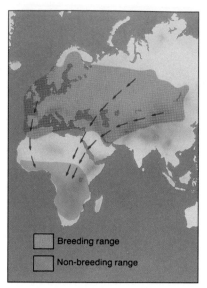

Breeding range

Non-breeding range

▲ The migration routes of the Eurasian swift (*Apus apus*).

▼ These lapwings huddling in an English snowstorm may be from Scandinavia. Many British lapwings move to Ireland or cross the English Channel in winter and are replaced by birds from Scandinavia.

Front—a climatic feature where the meeting of two airstreams sucks up insects from sub-Saharan Africa. However, the front disappears out into the Gulf of Guinea at the end of autumn, so the huge masses of European swifts then fly across mid-Africa to spend the rest of their winter and early spring in East Africa. Birds marked in Britain are most often found in Zaire on the way across, or wintering in Malawi. The 17,000 or 18,000 kilometer (10,500 or 11,100 mile) aggregate of their migration flight within a single year palls into insignificance compared with about a quarter of a million kilometers of their other feeding and sleeping flight during the year!

Such movements as these, from north to south in the autumn and reversed in the spring, are forced on the birds because of the seasonal changes to the weather in Europe. But these pressures do not simply give rise to north–south movements. The western seaboard of Europe is warmed by the Gulf Stream and many species—

particularly wildfowl and waders, finches, and thrushes from central and northern Europe—move west for the winter when snow cover and winter cold force them away. For some the movements seem simple, but their actual journeys are sometimes almost beyond belief.

For instance, it used to be thought that the flocks of redwing (*Turdus iliacus*) that fly westward across Europe and the North Sea came from the nearer breeding colonies in Scandinavia. These pretty little thrushes are now known also to come across from the eastern Soviet Union, and in subsequent winters they may travel southward to end up in the mountains between the Caspian and Black seas, in Turkey, or even—as one ringed bird has been recorded—in Iran. The birds are also able to respond to cold snaps during the winter by flying farther south or west, in the latter case aiming to reach the west of Ireland.

However, the redwings' navigation is not faultless. In January 1963 a redwing was

Chris Knights/Survival Anglia

ringed in a Warwickshire garden as a very severe spell of cold weather started to bite. Three days later it was found dead on a freighter crossing the Atlantic from America. It was 2,400 kilometers (1,500 miles) from its ringing site and had clearly missed Ireland. Thirty-five years earlier a lapwing (*Vanellus vanellus*), ringed as a nestling in the Lake District in England, had made the same mistake but, with favorable weather, it was found alive in Newfoundland.

Lapwings are conspicuous waders of temperate farm and moorland. Other waders of the High Arctic are much more regular and extensive globetrotters. Some species, common on European shores and on estuaries during the winter, breed so far to the north that their nests were not found until late last century, when Arctic explorers first penetrated far up Greenland's icy shores and into the bleak archipelago north of

Canada. Here birds such as the sanderling (*Calidris alba*) and knot (*C. canutus*) rub shoulders with the northernmost populations of such common species as the ringed plover (*Charadrius hiaticula*) and dunlin (*Calidris alpina*).

For these High Arctic birds the short window offered by the continuous daylight of their summer is packed with plenty, but so brief that delaying arrival will preclude any chance of completing their breeding cycle. Failed breeders reappear in Europe as early as the start of July and young birds, not yet able to breed, will not venture as far north as the breeding grounds.

The journeys of the knot are stupendous. Some populations of this medium-sized wader that arrive in or pass through Europe breed in the tundra of northern Greenland and Canada, or in Siberia. The vast flocks on European estuaries in the winter come

▲ An unusual feature of ruffs (*Philomachus pugnax*) is that no two birds are alike in the color or pattern of the decorative collar of feathers around their necks.

▲ Migrating waders characteristically congregate in mixed flocks of several species, yet they may have very different migration routes. Knots (*Calidris canutus*) (the larger birds in the picture) travel huge distances to winter in South America, southern Africa, and Australia, but the smaller dunlin (*Calidris alpina*) seldom crosses the equator on its migrations.

from the western population and reach Europe in a series of flights including, for many of them, a crossing of the Greenland icecap and of the North Atlantic. In the autumn, flocks from Siberia arrive for a short stay mainly on the massive estuaries of the southeastern parts of the North Sea.

They are on their way to winter off Mauritania in huge flocks on the Banc d'Arquin, the vast mudflats of the bulge of Africa. Some of them reach bays and beaches as far to the south as the Cape of Good Hope.

In some years the passage birds reach

(17 miles) per hour if the bird flew nonstop.

Enormous distances are traveled by the ruff (*Philomachus pugnax*), another wader. They breed across northern Europe and in Siberia, from there moving both east–west and north–south. Males have a very specialized mating display, which is designed to allow each female (known as a reeve) to select her mate. After fertilization, she breeds alone. Both sexes have the same seasonal migration, the eastern populations flying westward across much of Asia and the whole of Europe to appear in autumn on the marshes and bogs of Scandinavia, Germany, Holland, and Britain. They have already covered up to 7,000 or 8,000 kilometers (4,400 or 5,000 miles), but after a short stay they turn southward and form enormous flocks a further 5,000 kilometers (3,100 miles) away in the Niger Inundation Zone. The return journey in spring is more direct, with a stopover for fattening in areas such as the Po Valley in northern Italy.

The most spectacular and visible migration between Europe and Africa involves the soaring birds, particularly storks and raptors, that make their way along traditional routes in daylight, taking advantage of the rising hot air in thermals and the updraughts on hills and cliffs. Unable to provide their large wings with enough power to sustain flapping flight for more than a minute or two, these birds need to conserve their resources and are only able to make their long migrations by using their wings for soaring flight. In northern Europe there are fine viewing points in southern Scandinavia and Finland.

▼ The cattle egret (*Bubulcus ibis*) is a bird of very flexible migratory habits. In Europe it is seasonally migratory, but in north Africa populations move irregularly on only a local scale.

Britain in the autumn and several marked on the Wash, on the east coast of England, have been found within a short time in west Africa. The fastest was recovered more than 5,200 kilometers (3,200 miles) from its ringing site only eight days later. This represents an average speed of 27 kilometers

Michael Pitts/Survival Anglia

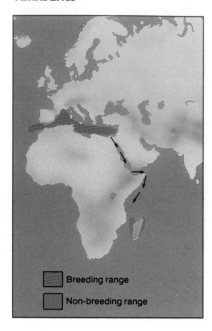

▲ The migration routes and breeding range of Eleanora's falcon.

▶ Most European ospreys (*Pandion haliaetus*) winter across Africa from Senegal to Ethiopia, mainly north of the equator.

Moreoever, the lack of thermals over even a narrow sea makes soaring impossible there, and so the most magnificent sites are at either end of the Mediterranean. In the west the Straits of Gibraltar and in the east the Bosporous and Eilat on the Red Sea are veritable meccas for birdwatchers.

The main activity is in the autumn, when the population is swelled by the young birds bred during the summer. White storks (*Ciconia ciconia*), honey buzzards (*Pernis apivoris*), eagles, and all sorts of other soaring birds pass overhead in a continuous stream lasting for three or four hours each day. In a good week, several hundred thousand birds may be logged at a single site. Once into Africa the streams disperse and the birds spread out, with some of the white storks flying through the Rift Valley in Ethiopia and Kenya to reach the southern-most parts of the continent.

Many bird species have specialist migrations and some even rely on other migrating birds for their own livelihoods. The timing of the breeding season of Eleanora's falcons (*Falco eleonarae*) around the shores of the Mediterranean allows them to feed their young on the immature passerines that stream across Europe in August and September. Later the falcons themselves migrate to a distant winter home, a journey first hinted at by the distribution of specimens taken for museums and later confirmed by a handful of ringing recoveries.

The birds from colonies all along the Mediterranean fly eastward and then south to the island of Madagascar, off East Africa.

Many of the small birds on which the Eleanora's prey are migrating warblers. There are many species, most of which have special areas at which they congregate to stopover and fatten up. These areas (and their destination) offer feeding opportunities similar to those in the birds' summer quarters to the north.

The recent lack of rain and increasing desertification in sub-Saharan areas have had an immediate effect on several species. Birds such as the whitethroat (*Sylvia communis*), redstart (*Phoenicurus phoenicurus*), sedge warbler (*Acrocephalus schoenobaenus*), and sand martin that winter inland in west Africa, have been badly affected and breeding populations in Britain have declined. The whitethroat populations are now stabilized at a level roughly 30 percent of the number recorded in the 1960s. Very similar species, wintering in areas unaffected by these changes in climate, seem to have maintained their populations. For example, lesser whitethroats (*Sylvia curruca*), which winter inland in central East Africa, are still present in good numbers.

Some of the most extravagant migrations are undertaken by species that spread far across Europe and into Asia following the latest glaciations. As the ice pushed slowly southward, birds that were already migrating

Francois Gohier/Auscape

north and south had to adapt their routes to the new conditions. For many species, their ranges were split by the advancing icesheets and, over the thousands of years of glacial isolation, many of these birds evolved into separate but related species or, in some other cases into related but distinct subspecies.

As the ice retreated the range of many seasonal migrants spread northward into the newly warmed areas—but the birds retained their ancestral wintering areas. Africa, for instance, holds the wintering population of both the willow warbler (*Phylloscopus trochilus*), one of the smallest migrants weighing only 7 or 8 grams (2/10 to 3/10 ounce) in the breeding season, and the wheatear (*Oenanthe oenanthe*), the northernmost representative of the chat family of small thrushes. Indeed, some wheatears regularly cross the Bering Sea to breed in Alaska at the eastern end of their range, and western birds are to be found on

Ellesmere and Baffin islands to the west of Greenland. All stream down into Africa for the winter, with the most distant birds facing journeys of well over 15,000 kilometers (9,300 miles) each way.

▲ ▼ The swallow (*Hirundo rustica*) breeds commonly across North America (where it is known as the barn swallow), Europe, and Asia and winters in South America, Africa, and Southeast Asia.

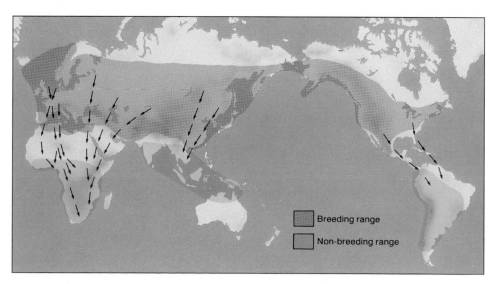

Breeding range

Non-breeding range

ASIAN AND AUSTRALIAN BIRDS

Duncan Parish

Half the world's shorebird species use the Asia–Pacific Flyway, a 10,000 kilometer (6,200 mile) migration route extending from the Arctic tundra to Australia. Remarkably, some birds fly up to half this distance nonstop.

Brian Chudleigh/Australian Nature Transparencies

▲ Most numerous on tidal mudflats, the bar-tailed godwit (*Limosa lapponica*) is typical of a wide range of migratory waders that nest in Siberia and winter mostly in Australia.

Shorebirds are characterized by relatively long legs and bills that are adapted to feed in shallow water or soft mud. There are 200 species of shorebird around the world, of which about 100 use the Asia–Pacific Flyway. Those using this flyway range in size from the eastern curlew (*Numenius madagascariensis*) with a wingspan of about a meter (40 inches) and weighing about 750 grams (26 ounces), to the sparrow-sized red-necked stint (*Calidris ruficollis*) with a weight of about 30 grams (1 ounce).

Most shorebirds begin their lives in the Arctic tundra or high latitude forests of

Siberia. Here, in May and June, during the brief northern summer, there is a superabundance of food as all living things work fast to reproduce. Swarms of insects and freshwater life make easy pickings for shorebirds, enabling each pair to hatch three to eight young. But summer is short-lived and the snows of winter sometimes come early, so the adult birds start to depart the nesting areas in July, leaving their young to fend for themselves.

The parents head south, flying cross-country over the open tundra to the pine forests of the taiga and then on over the

Frans Lanting/Minden Pictures

open steppes of Mongolia and northern China. Their destination is the coastal marshes and mudflats of northeastern Asia, where they will stay for between one and three weeks. These coastal wetlands are rich in food, such as shellfish and worms, that provide them with the energy reserves needed for the long flight that is the next stage of their journey. On departure, they will first head southeast, following the coast. The larger species, such as curlews and knots will then head south directly across the Pacific toward Australia.

The birds climb to a height of 3,000 to 4,500 meters (10,000 to 15,000 feet) and head off toward their destination, cruising at a speed of 40 to 80 kilometers (25 to 50 miles) per hour. The smaller birds must stop to rest and refuel on Pacific islands or in Southeast Asia, but the larger ones can reach New Guinea or northern Australia directly from eastern China, a three-day nonstop journey of over 5,000 kilometers (3,100 miles). They arrive exhausted on the coast of northern Australia in late August—about six weeks after leaving their breeding quarters 10,000 kilometers (6,200 miles) to the north.

One of the main arrival points for the shorebirds into northwestern Australia is the 300 kilometer (185 mile) stretch of coast between Broome and Eighty Mile Beach. The tidal range here is so high that at low tide the mudflat stretches 6 kilometers (4 miles) out to sea and supports nearly one million shorebirds during a migration season. When the tide races back in, the birds aggregate at particular roosts with populations of up to 100,000 birds.

For some shorebirds, this is their journey's end and here they remain for the next six months. For others, it is merely a transit point. After recovering from their flight across Asia, approximately 500,000 shorebirds make a further journey of some 3,000 kilometers (1,850 miles) across the center of Australia to coastal wetlands in the far southeast. To do this they cross deserts almost as hostile, from the birds' perspective, as the open ocean itself. They remain in the south until March, when they will start their northward migration back across Australia and Asia to their Arctic nesting grounds.

These gigantic journeys between the High Arctic and the wetlands of the southern hemisphere can be achieved only by a series of enormous leaps, each of which is possible

▼ The sanderling (*Calidris alba*) breeds as far north as there is land and differs from almost all waders in its preference for ocean sand beaches rather than estuarine mudflats. Here it feeds in a very distinctive manner: it dashes up the beach, barely ahead of the wash of each breaking wave, only to turn and follow it back as it retreats, rapidly snatching at minute animals momentarily exposed in the film of water.

AUSTRALIAN BIRD MIGRATION

Terence Lindsey

Winters in Australia are nowhere especially rigorous, and regular seasonal migration among birds, of the kind so evident in the northern hemisphere, is a relatively inconspicuous phenomenon in Australia. Nevertheless, many birds do so migrate.

Winters are most severe in Tasmania, in the far south. A few birds, such as the orange-bellied parrot (*Neophema chrysogaster*), swift parrot (*Lathamus discolor*), silvereye (*Zosterops lateralis*), and flame robin (*Petroica phoenicea*) migrate to and from Tasmania. Some of these, such as the orange-bellied parrot, do little more than cross Bass Strait to the mainland while others, including the silvereye, continue up the east coast as far as Brisbane in Queensland. Several of these breed only in Tasmania.

On the Australian mainland, several species of honeyeaters—notably the yellow-faced honeyeater (*Lichenostomus chrysops*) and white-naped honeyeater (*Melithreptus lunatus*)—migrate from their breeding grounds in the mountain forests of the southeast to winter quarters in the coastal heaths and woodlands of northeastern New South Wales and southeastern Queensland. These birds migrate by day, moving in small parties through the treetops, and at certain favored spots in the Blue Mountains west of Sydney it is possible to watch this migration in progress, the birds streaming northward across the ridges at a rate of several thousand per hour. Their precise destination remains unknown. In fact, though tens of thousands of migrating honeyeaters have been banded over the past few decades, few have ever been recovered, and it is suspected that the birds adopt a nomadic (and hence virtually untraceable) mode of life through the winter.

In the rainforests of eastern New South Wales there are a number of birds that are not resident. These include the dollarbird (*Eurystomus orientalis*), common koel (*Eudynamis scolopacea*), and black-faced monarch (*Monarcha melanopsis*). These birds migrate northward after breeding, but little is known of their routes and destinations. Some are known to winter in New Guinea, but this destination remains merely conjectural for several others, based on little more than failure to find the bird wintering in Australia.

Even in the tropical rainforests of northeastern Queensland there are several species, such as the red-bellied pitta (*Pitta erythrogaster*) and the white-tailed kingfisher (*Tanysiptera sylvia*), that cross Torres Strait to winter in New Guinea. Why these birds should find it necessary or desirable to risk this sea crossing twice a year remains a mystery, since both origin and destination are tropical. The puzzle is made especially intriguing by the fact that virtually all are birds of coastal lowland forest: in contrast, similar birds in the cool highland rainforests nearby are resident.

It is notable that most of these movements are associated with one of Australia's major geographical features, the Great Dividing Range, a chain of mountain ranges that parallels the east coast from the far south to the tip of Cape York Peninsula. In Australia, the annual migration of breeding birds is an essentially eastern affair, and most of those that migrate are birds of forest or woodland.

▼ Budgerigars (*Melopsittacus undulatus*) can be found almost anywhere in interior Australia, often in huge flocks. Their distribution is constantly adjusting to the changing pattern of local drought and erratic rainfall across the continent. Superimposed upon this pattern of apparently random dispersal is a marked overall tendency to move north in winter and south in summer. Such complex webs of interacting migratory, dispersive, irruptive, and nomadic tendencies are characteristic of the movements of many birds in the arid interior of Australia.

Graeme Chapman/Auscape

Richard Kirby/Oxford Scientific Films

only if the birds can refuel in a hurry. They must be able to gather food at a rate several times faster than that needed to fuel the search for it in the first place. In general, this is possible only in wetlands and, in particular, those extensive mudflats that occur most often where large slow rivers meet the sea.

In fact, the sheer weight of fuel the birds carry presents its own set of difficulties. For example, at takeoff a red-necked stint may well be carrying a burden of fat exceeding 90 percent of its normal body weight. The bird will gradually burn up this excess fat in the course of its ensuing nonstop flight of well over 24 hours.

The work involved in hoisting this burden to an effective cruising altitude itself uses up a significant amount of the fuel carried.

Once this altitude is reached, a bird's best option is to continue until all its available fuel is exhausted. Paradoxically, the bird confronts serious risks in any attempt to land before its supply of fuel is used up. It is quite likely, for example, that if it does this it will come down where it cannot refuel quickly enough to continue. Such a risk is a subtle one, but no less great than that of running out of fuel and drowning.

It is the sophistication of the means by which these extraordinary birds manage such difficulties, quite apart from the huge distances traveled, that makes shorebirds among the most fascinating of all migrants.

Meanwhile, what happened to those young birds left behind in July by the departing parents? They stayed in Siberia until they were six to eight weeks old and then flew south in August and September to follow their parents. These birds know instinctively where to migrate and how to navigate and will visit many of the sites their parents used, reaching southern Australia in November and December.

Shorebirds in Asia do not migrate in a direct north–south route. Instead, they follow a path that maximizes their chance of reaching their destination safely. Some follow a great circle route, while others follow the coastline, from their breeding grounds in the far northeast of Siberia to Indochina, before turning southeast to make a landfall in northwestern Australia.

The larger shorebirds such as the great knot (*Calidris tenuirostris*) have a flight range of 5,000 kilometers (3,100 miles) and are able to take advantage of southeasterly winds blowing to the southeast off the coast of China each August and September to help them on their way out across the Pacific or

▲ The rare Asian dowitcher (*Limnodromus semipalmatus*) nests in loose colonies in flooded meadows at a few known sites scattered across Siberia and Mongolia. Very little is known of its migrations, but it apparently spends the non-breeding season mainly in Southeast Asia.

South China Sea. Given a good tail wind these birds can easily reach the northern shores of Australia without stopping.

What sort of hazards do these birds face? Apart from natural ones such as storms or strong winds, and the very nature of their migration tactics, shorebirds also run the gauntlet of human-related threats. Many of the key sites shorebirds use for resting and feeding are under threat from large-scale development projects. The government of South Korea plans to reclaim 155 tidal embayments along its west coast, removing the feeding grounds of many seabird migrants. The Chinese government plans to reclaim up to six million hectares of coastal land in the next 20 years. The Nagoya Council in Japan plans to turn one of the country's most important shorebird staging sites into a rubbish dump. Seventy percent of the coastal mangroves and adjacent mudflats in the Philippines have been cleared or affected by agricultural projects.

As well, the birds fly over some of the most densely populated countries in the globe, where they have been hunted for food or sport for thousands of years. Modern firearms have made hunting very destructive and it is estimated that between half and one and a half million shorebirds are hunted each year. This represents a massive 10 to 30 percent of the entire populations of birds.

A number of initiatives have been taken in recent years to identify and protect critical shorebird sites in Asia and Australia by the Parties to the Ramsar Convention of 1971, and by organizations such as the Asian Wetland Bureau and the Royal Australasian Ornithologists' Union. In addition, the Australian government has recently supported an initiative to assess the levels of shorebird hunting in the region and identify alternative means of livelihood for the hunters. It is hoped that this combination of efforts will ensure the continued survival of these birds and their fascinating migrations.

▼ The sharp-tailed sandpiper (*Calidris acuminata*) prefers non-tidal wetlands and often occurs at such places as sewage farms and on the shallow margins of interior lakes. It breeds in Siberia, and recent census work suggests that most of the birds spend the non-breeding season in southeastern Australia.

Klaus Uhlenhut/ Australian Nature Transparencies

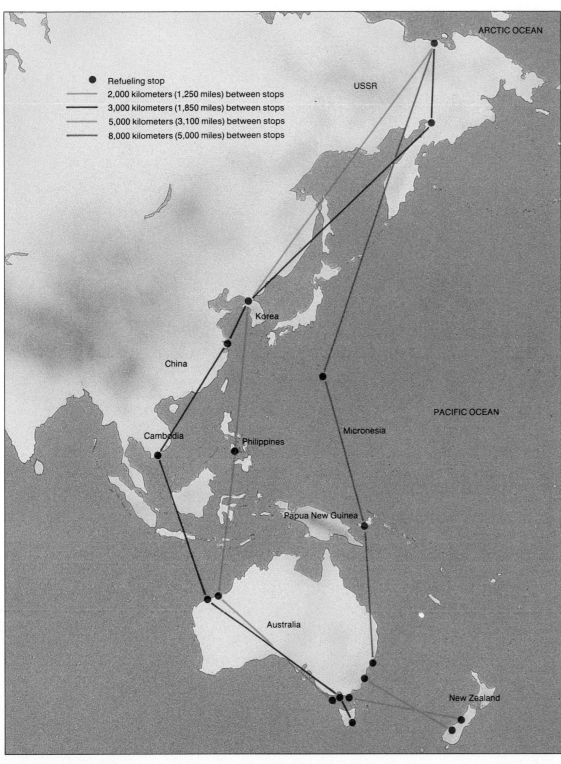

◆ Refueling stop
—— 2,000 kilometers (1,250 miles) between stops
—— 3,000 kilometers (1,850 miles) between stops
—— 5,000 kilometers (3,100 miles) between stops
—— 8,000 kilometers (5,000 miles) between stops

ARCTIC OCEAN

USSR

Korea

China

Cambodia

Philippines

Micronesia

PACIFIC OCEAN

Papua New Guinea

Australia

New Zealand

◀ Most migrating waders cannot make the distance between their breeding and wintering areas in one flight. In general, the need to stop for refueling is greater for small waders, which can carry less fuel, than it is for larger species.

Smaller waders such as the red-necked stint can carry sufficient fuel for about 2,000 kilometers (1,250 miles), and the scarcity of suitable island feeding stops forces them into a zigzag northward path along the eastern coasts of Asia. On the other hand, larger waders such as the great knot can carry enough fuel for 5,000 kilometers (3,100 miles), and can therefore take a more direct route.

▼ By March, waders on their wintering grounds have begun to molt into their breeding plumage and fatten up. They are now ready to leave on their annual migration to their Arctic breeding grounds.

SEABIRDS

Peter Fullagar

Seabirds range from the polar icecaps to the tropics, and sometimes migrate or forage over huge distances. But there is much variation in their migratory behavior and the evidence for its regularity is not always clear-cut.

▲ Atlantic puffins (*Fratercula arctica*) from Britain are known to visit the coasts of Greenland and Newfoundland.

Oceanic birds are known to range far and wide, but little is known about most species' movements, and few are known to follow a regular pattern. Their migrations are often dictated by prevailing winds and many are best described as nomadic. Many seabirds breed at remote localities on coastal islands along the shores of the continents or on islands and atolls scattered throughout the oceans. Some are known to breed at very few sites, often a particular island or even very small areas on it. Nevertheless, the adult birds may range widely over the surrounding seas in their quest for food. A wandering albatross (*Diomedea exulans*) is known to have made a round trip of more than 15,000 kilometers (9,300 miles) in a single foraging trip during its partner's incubation shift. Amongst larger seabirds, such distances must be commonplace.

The young of many seabirds have a long adolescent, or pre-breeding, life—two or three years, and sometimes as many as ten—and during this time they may also

D. Parer & E. Parer-Cook/Auscape

range far from their birthplace. They remain mostly at sea but as maturity approaches they spend increasingly lengthy periods in reconnaissance at breeding sites. Even those seabirds with wide distributions commonly return to the same general area and colony in which they were hatched and reared.

Seabirds can be divided broadly into those inhabiting tropical seas, those of temperate oceans, and those of the polar regions. Many are characteristic of certain oceanic or coastal regions within these broad climatic zones. Tropical seas are separated by major continental landmasses, but polar regions are continuous. Southern oceans run almost circumpolar across a broad span of latitudes.

Tropical seabirds like the frigate birds, boobies, tropic birds, and many species of terns have wide distributions and have often, but not always, evolved regional species within the separate sea areas. Because of the relatively constant food supply, some tropical seabirds show almost continuous breeding activity and a few have breeding seasons that are spaced at other than annual intervals. Most can best be described as dispersive in their movements, with no clear pattern of migration.

In temperate and subpolar seas, annual periods of higher productivity necessitate

seabirds having regular annual breeding seasons to ensure that available foods are efficiently exploited. Many seabirds in these regions are also regular migrants, often between hemispheres. Nevertheless, a large number of gulls, terns, auks, and penguins undertake no more than local movements from their breeding colonies. Occasionally food abundance is so great that large populations of seabirds can be supported indefinitely. The most famous of these regions are the rich feeding areas in the Humboldt Current that flows north along the

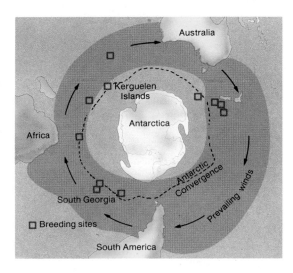

▲ Gannets and boobies, like this blue-footed booby (*Sula nebouxii*), dive for their food, often in spectacular plunges from a height of 30 meters (100 feet) or more.

◀ Wandering albatrosses in courtship display. (Opposite page) Pair-bonds are often permanent in seabirds, but dissolve in the vast distances between breeding seasons, to be renewed on return to the nest each season.

◀ Little is known of the wandering albatrosses' movements between breeding seasons. Some populations seem less migratory than others but the birds occur, at least as vagrants, throughout the oceans of the southern hemisphere.

western coastline of South America and has, in the past, supported enormous numbers of seabirds, especially boobies and shags.

Perhaps the most notable examples of restricted ranges are to be found among the Southern Ocean shags. Heavy-bodied and short-winged, these birds are incapable of regular long-distance flight and have become local foragers. These seabirds occur on most subantarctic islands and most populations show distinctive characteristics suggesting isolation at each island or island grouping. The power of flight has been lost altogether in the flightless shag (*Nanopterum harrisi*) of the Galapagos Islands. The only long-distance migrants amongst shags and cormorants are the larger winged and essentially inland populations of northern hemisphere species such as the double-crested cormorant (*Phalacrocorax auritus*)

▲ A blue-eyed shag (*Phalocrocorax atriceps*) flies in with material for its nest on the South Orkney Islands.

90

and the great cormorant (*P. carbo*). These migrate in winter because the waters they use in summer become frozen.

Seabirds adapted to the polar regions have either become specialized in seeking food continuously within these extreme conditions or migrate to and from them to capitalize on the plenty of summer. Some species move from one polar sea area to the other, remaining in constant summer polar conditions. Migrating birds often need to be able to switch to entirely different food resources when at their non-breeding haunts.

Patchiness of feeding locations in many areas has led to the ability of many seabirds to cover large areas of sea in search of localized concentrations. Upwellings of nutrient-rich waters, mixing of cooler and hotter currents, continental slopes, and sheltered waters can all provide important regions at which seabirds concentrate. Different species specialize in different foods and in the manner in which they obtain them. There are scavengers and there are predators on other birds and mammals. Some scoop up food at the surface, while others feed by diving after faster-moving prey below the surface. Penguins pursue all their prey from below water, using their flippers to propel themselves, and auks, though they have retained their powers of flight, do much the same. In many ways auks and penguins represent mutually

Frans Lanting/Minden Pictures

exclusive groups of birds that are very similar in their habits, biology, and ecology. Auks occur in the northern hemisphere and penguins in the southern hemisphere.

Some birds need daylight to find their prey, but detailed studies of seabird diets show that many of them include high concentrations of food species that surface only at night and descend to the depths (in a vertical migration) during the day.

▲ A wandering albatross (*Diomedea exulans*) incubates its single egg on South Georgia. Both adults incubate the egg in alternate shifts lasting about a week until the egg hatches after about 80 days.

▼ Many of the larger seabirds breed in packed colonies in which all activities are closely synchronized, as in this colony of king shags (*Phalacrocorax albiventer*) in the Falkland Islands.

Frans Lanting/Minden Pictures

THE ANNUAL CYCLE OF THE SHORT-TAILED SHEARWATER

JUNE/JULY/AUGUST
Arriving in late June, short-tailed shearwaters (*Puffinus tenuirostris*) spend their nonbreeding season in the North Pacific. Many birds pass through the Bering Strait into the Arctic Ocean, while others disperse east toward the North American coast.

SEPTEMBER
Adults spend several weeks on the return flight to their nesting colonies in southern Australia. Colonies may contain tens of thousands of birds, and are usually situated on grassy offshore islands. Many young birds remain in the northern Pacific all year.

APRIL/MAY
The chick reaches its peak weight and puts on feathers. Parents and chick leave independently for their wintering grounds in the North Pacific.

→ Migration direction
Wintering range
Breeding range

OCTOBER/NOVEMBER
After repairing their nesting burrows, courting, and establishing a pair bond, the birds leave for the open sea to feed and regain condition for a period of about three weeks.

FEBRUARY/MARCH
The chick is fed in alternate visits by both parents, once every three days or so.

DECEMBER/JANUARY
The egg is laid during the last few days of November and incubated by both parents in alternate shifts lasting about two weeks each. The egg hatches in mid January.

TRANS-EQUATORIAL MIGRATIONS

Long-distance vagrancy is particularly well known in petrels and, from time to time, black-browed albatrosses (*Diomedea melanophrys*) have been found in the North Atlantic, far from their normal range in the southern oceans. It is likely that a quirk of weather conditions or some other chance occurrence directs them off course. In any event, the individuals involved are then "locked" into the North Atlantic, presumably because they are unwilling or unable to retrace their paths.

A manx shearwater (*Puffinus puffinus*) banded as a chick on an island off the west coast of Britain was found beachcast in South Australia at the end of the following year. These birds breed on many islands in the eastern North Atlantic, foraging over waters of the continental shelf off western Europe and northern Africa. There is good evidence from other band recoveries that at the end of the summer breeding season they migrate to the South Atlantic coasts of Brazil, Argentina, and South Africa. It seems most likely that the vagrant that reached Australia had moved far eastward to cross the southern Indian Ocean.

Regular trans-equatorial migrations are known for several seabirds, but few species' migration routes are known in detail. Without doubt one of the most famous seabird migrations is that of short-tailed shearwaters (*Puffinus tenuirostris*), popularly known as "mutton birds." This species performs an annual journey from its numerous breeding islands scattered along the coasts of South Australia, Tasmania, Victoria, and southern New South Wales to reach the cool waters, but rich feeding areas, of the Bering Sea near the Alaskan coast. The story of this migration was first pieced together by noting the location of beachcast specimens. These showed a distribution around the perimeter of the Pacific Ocean which, combined with date of discovery and information on prevailing winds, led to the idea of the migratory pathway being a giant figure-of-eight. However, more recent studies suggest that, although the birds certainly fly north to Arctic waters, their return is probably direct. There is no clear evidence of southward migration off the west coast of North America and the few specimens collected there are probably vagrants. Similarly, a few birds move westward from Australia and are found in the north of the Indian Ocean.

There are possibly 10 million breeding pairs of the short-tailed shearwater and

Jonathan Chester/Extreme Images

probably an equal number of pre-breeding and non-breeding birds. Most years they return to Australia in late September or early October and on some occasions masses of birds can be seen streaming down the southeast coast of New South Wales, wave after wave heading south with as many as a quarter of a million birds passing per hour at the height of the passage.

The sooty shearwater (*Puffinus griseus*) is closely related to the short-tailed shearwater but has a wider breeding range. A few nest along the southeastern coast of Australia, but many millions occur on the islands around New Zealand and off the southern tip of South America. Sooty shearwaters also migrate to the northern Pacific, but do so by both eastern and western routes. Others move into the North Atlantic from the breeding colonies on the western side of South America. In the southern summer both species go well south and some are known to reach the edge of the pack-ice off the coast of Antarctica.

The flesh-footed shearwater (*P. carneipes*) is another trans-equatorial migrant, but on a lesser scale, making an annual round trip from the island group of Lord Howe in the north Tasman Sea to the continental shelf surrounding Japan and off Korea. The pattern of recovery of banded individuals clearly shows the timing of the passage north and south. The closely related great shearwater (*P. gravis*) breeds on the South Atlantic islands, forages widely each summer in the cooler waters of the South Atlantic, and migrates to the North Atlantic at the end of the breeding season.

▲ Black-browed albatrosses at sea. Cormorants and gannets are birds of shallow coastal waters and are relatively sedentary, but albatrosses and petrels are truly oceanic and avoid land. They routinely travel vast distances between breeding seasons.

POLAR SEABIRDS

Many of the seabirds that breed in polar regions remain as close to their breeding colonies as they can but solid sea ice and winter darkness force them to move to the edge of the iceshelf or find open water within the pack. In both the Arctic and Antarctic permanent open areas of water become crucial for some of the most hardy species that are truly polar birds. These include the Ross's gull (*Rhodostethia rosea*) and ivory gull (*Pagophila eburnea*) of the Arctic regions that very rarely venture south. However, another gull of truly High Arctic breeding range, Sabine's gull (*Larus sabini*), is migratory and flies as far south as South Africa and the west coast of Peru.

The Arctic tern (*Sterna paradisaea*), with a widespread breeding distribution in high latitudes of the northern hemisphere, also migrates south to the pack-ice edge along the Antarctic coastline. In doing so it passes from a northern summer to a southern one, annually accumulating some of the longest daylengths experienced by any bird. Young birds and some non-breeding adults may stay south or dally along the way at places where feeding is good. However, breeding adults in the northern parts of their range must move back to the polar seas at the first signs of spring thaw. Otherwise they will not complete the breeding cycle and have their young on the wing before winter returns.

Only nine species of birds are truly Antarctic. Of these Wilson's storm-petrel (*Oceanites oceanicus*), weighing only 35 to 40 grams (1 1/5 to 1 3/5 ounces), is the smallest. Nesting in cracks or crevices in exposed rock, it has a brief period each summer in which to complete its breeding cycle. It then migrates north and can be found in the northern Indian Ocean and the North Atlantic.

Several species of fulmarine petrels breed in Antarctica, using any suitable sites around the coastline. The snow petrel (*Pagodroma nivea*) and the Antarctic petrel (*Thalassoica antarctica*) almost never leave the region of the southern pack-ice. These and the two species of penguin that are true inhabitants of Antarctica—the emperor (*Aptenodytes fosteri*) and the Adelie penguin (*Pygoscelis adeliae*)—generally remain within the pack-ice zone or nearby southern oceans. The southern fulmar (*Fulmarus glacialoides*)

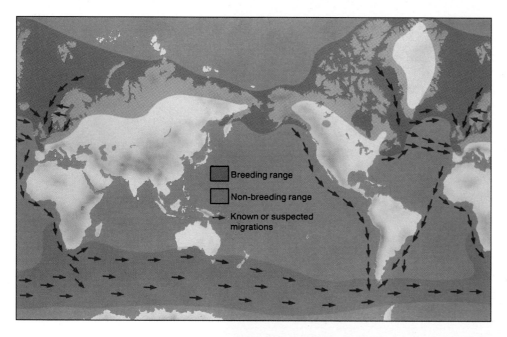

Breeding range

Non-breeding range

Known or suspected migrations

▶ ▲ An Arctic tern feeds its well-grown young. This tern is notable for the extent of its seasonal migrations: its breeding range extends northward to the shores of the Arctic Ocean, and many birds winter at sea in the packice fringing Antarctica. The young migrate independently of their parents, and typically spend up to four years in the Southern Ocean before returning north to breed for the first time.

Hans Schouten

also breeds in Antarctica and has a non-breeding range that extends little farther than the coldest waters of the southern oceans.

Nevertheless, one species of fulmar—the northern fulmar (*Fulmarus glacialis*)—has colonized Arctic seas. It seems reasonable to suppose that these populations are derived from Antarctic birds that reached Arctic regions and established breeding colonies, eventually evolving distinctive features differentiating them from their southern fulmar relatives.

Many other polar seabirds migrate great distances. The South Polar skua (*Catharacta maccormicki*) is known to have reached northern Pacific waters in the non-breeding season and has been found in the northern summer mixing off the coasts of Greenland with its North Atlantic counterpart, the great skua (*C. skua*). Again, it is tempting to conclude that this northern species evolved from an Antarctic colonist.

Three species of predatory jaegers—the pomarine (*Stercorarius pomarinus*), Arctic (*S. parasiticus*), and long-tailed jaeger (*S. longicaudus*)—breed on the Arctic tundra, exploiting the abundant summer wildlife.

Long-tailed jaegers prey on lemmings. These small rodents have cyclical periods of abundance spanning several years and the birds can only breed successfully in years of high lemming numbers. Each autumn the jaegers head south, reaching coastal areas off southern America, Africa, Australia, and New Zealand. On migration and in their non-breeding range they must change their feeding habits to those of a marine predator. All jaegers are cleptoparasitic; they feed by aggressive pursuit of other seabirds to steal food after making them disgorge their last meal. They can often be seen harrying feeding parties of other seabirds. In common with several other species of long-distance migrant seabirds, it seems that younger birds travel the farthest and often remain in these distant areas for a year or more.

As with jaegers, we know most about seabird movements when, paradoxically, they are near or over land. The technical difficulty of studying migrations over the open sea remains enormous. Yet, what little we have discovered suggests that seabirds may yet prove to have the most fantastic journeys of all birds.

▲ The giant petrels belong to a group of seabirds known as fulmars, and play the role of scavengers in subantarctic animal communities. They feed opportunistically, and congregate like vultures at seal or whale carcasses washed ashore or floating in the sea.

BATS

M. Brock Fenton

Several lines of evidence suggest that bats achieve long-distance orientation through vision and spatial memory. Although echolocation represents a remarkable pattern of behavior analogous to radar, there is no evidence that it plays an important role in bat migrations.

Along the Kathleen River in the Yukon Territory in Canada, little brown bats (*Myotis lucifugus*) often form maternity colonies in caches or in buildings such as cabins. Since these colonies can house over 100 adult female bats it is relatively easy for an astute observer to monitor their seasonal comings and goings. At 60°N bats are not a large component of the mammal fauna, which perhaps reflects the challenges of being nocturnal at a latitude where the summer nights are short. In early May, a visitor to a known bat colony would probably find none. By mid-June the visitor could count over 100 pregnant females, while by the end of the month the colony size would have doubled, as each female would have borne her single young. By the middle of August the colony would be virtually deserted once more.

Just north of the equator in West Africa, bats are a more prominent component of the mammal fauna in terms of biomass (the total weight of living organisms within an area),

numbers of individuals, and numbers of species. Straw-colored fruit bats (*Eidolon helvum*) are abundant in many parts of Africa, where their relatively large size (250 to 300 grams; 9 to 11 ounces) and tendency to roost in large numbers in the crowns of trees make them conspicuous. In parts of Abidjan on the Ivory Coast, from October until January, tens of thousands of these bats can be seen roosting in trees around the city. Just after the young are born, the colonies dwindle in size—and tens of thousands of straw-colored fruit bats appear in savanna locations to the north.

Wherever bats are found—be it in Australia, Africa, Europe, or North America—their seasonal appearance and disappearance at known colony sites is a recurring theme. In some cases there is evidence of repeated seasonal movements to and from specific sites by known individuals, usually bats carrying numbered bands. Flight gives bats mobility, making it easy for them to cover relatively long distances at relatively low cost, and band returns occasionally

provide details of the distance and timing of bat migrations. Furthermore, banding studies have revealed that bats are long-lived animals and that individuals in some species return to the same roosts year after year.

However, studies of bat movements are still few. Bats are small nocturnal animals, with most of the 900 or so species having adult body masses of less than 20 grams (3/4 ounce) and many less than half that. This makes them inconspicuous, which partly explains why the day roosts of most species remain unknown, why little work has addressed the details of bat orientation, and why most of the evidence about bat migration comes from species that form conspicuous colonies.

As well, not many bats can be fitted with radio transmitters, or "active" tags. Bands ("passive" tags) produce only limited or sometimes misleading information, but transmitters exceeding 5 percent of a bat's body mass significantly interfere with maneuverability and agility. Recent studies using larger bats with very small radio

◄ (Opposite page) Tent-building bats (*Bilobatum* species) of Central America, like these in Costa Rica, bite along the stems of large leaves, causing them to curl and form a protective "tent."

▼ Mexican free-tailed bats (*Tadarida brasiliensis*) emerging from a maternity cave in the American southwest at dusk.

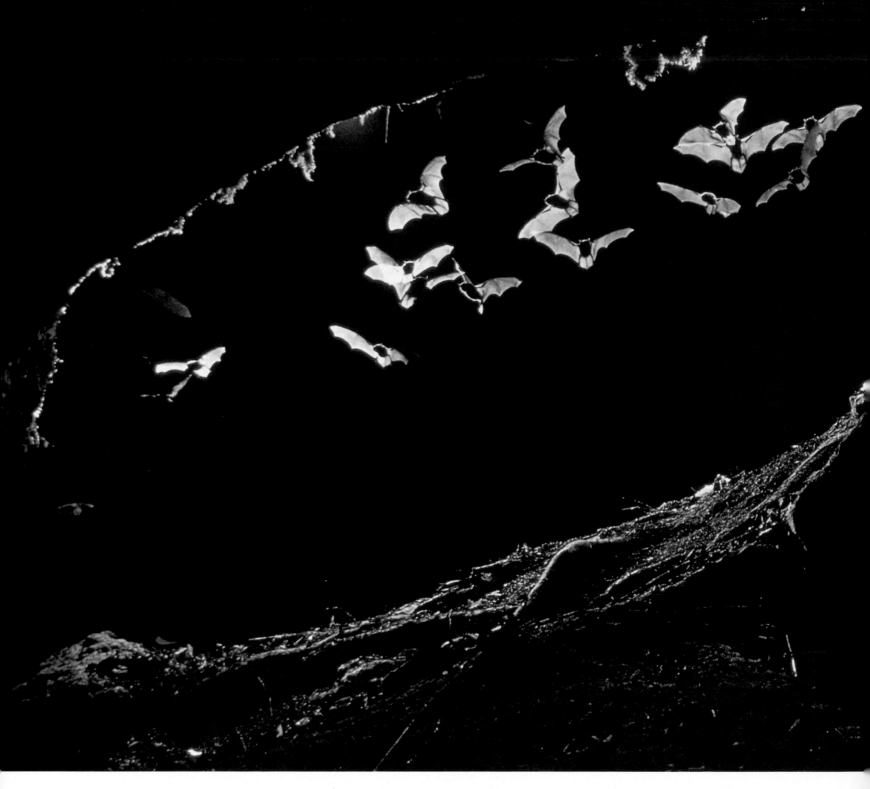

▲ The Mississippi myotis (*Myotis austroriparius*), a colonial bat that inhabits the southeastern United States, lives in caves and (except in Florida) hibernates through the winter. Captured and tagged individuals have been known to return to their roosting caves from release points up to 70 kilometers (44 miles) away.

transmitters weighing less than a gram (1/30 ounce), have begun to throw new light on bat orientation and on their occasionally unpredictable choice of roost sites.

ORIENTATION

Like most species of mammals, bats gather information about their surroundings by looking, listening, and sniffing. It seems reasonable to assume that a bat trying to find its way from one place to another, or trying to locate its preferred roost mates would use all these senses. However, the bats' most famous mode of orientation is echolocation, an active mode of orientation

involving the use of sound.

Echolocating bats use the echoes of sounds they produce to locate objects in their path. They produce their echolocation calls by clicking their tongues (for megachiropteran bats) or in their larynxes. Returning echoes are detected by the bats' ears. The bats use the difference between the time and frequency of the original sound and its echo to collect information about their surroundings. Not all bats can echolocate and there is considerable variation among bats in the use made of this remarkable system of orientation.

Biologists presume that the 750 or so

on a cloudy night. In the air, however, echolocation is effective only over short distances. Although a big brown bat (*Eptesicus fuscus*) can detect a 20 millimeter (4/5 inch) diameter sphere at 5 meters (16 1/2 feet) or a large rock face at perhaps 50 meters (165 feet), it probably cannot use echolocation for long-distance orientation.

In the 1960s, a landmark study was conducted on orientation behavior in the greater spear-nosed bat (*Phyllostomus hastatus*). Since these bats were large enough (60 to 100 grams; 2 to 3 1/2 ounces) to carry radio transmitters, detailed information about their in-flight orientation could be

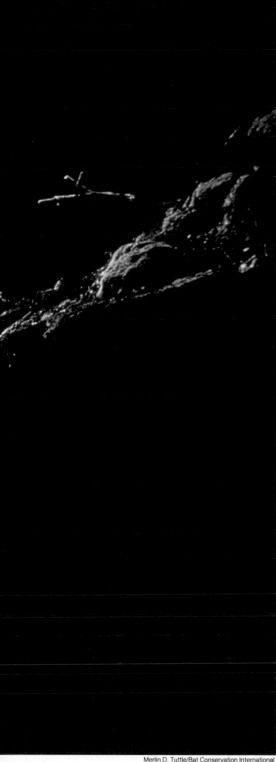

species of bats in the suborder Microchiroptera can echolocate, but to date this mode of orientation has been demonstrated in just one of the 150 or so species of bats in the suborder Megachiroptera. Furthermore, there is considerable diversity in the details of echolocation among the Microchiroptera, from call design to the distances over which bats can use echolocation.

Echolocation permits animals to operate effectively in the dark or where there is little light. This means that an echolocating bat can orient itself in the pitch black of a deep cave or locate flying insect prey in a forest

▼ A little brown bat (*Myotis lucifugus*) disturbed in its hibernation site. This widespread North American bat migrates from parts of its range in autumn to congregate in caves where the animals become torpid. One banded little brown bat moved more than 800 kilometers (500 miles) between hibernation sites in Ontario.

Wayne Lankinen/Aquila

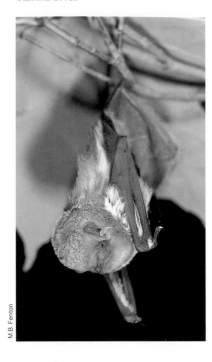

▲ The red bat (*Lasiurus borealis*) is among the most widespread of North American bats. Though the evidence to date is circumstantial, it seems to be strongly migratory and has been recorded on ships far out at sea. It is a solitary species that roosts in trees.

collected. In the study the bats were divided into an experimental group whose eyes were covered with goggle-like blindfolds, a treated control group whose eyes were covered by transparent goggles, and an untreated control group not wearing goggles. Bats in each group were released at different distances from their cave roost and their flight paths were monitored.

The bats in both the control groups flew directly back to their cave roosts from distances of up to 16 kilometers (10 miles). At 24 to 32 kilometers (15 to 20 miles) these bats took more scattered routes to their home caves. However, the experimental bats with the goggle-like blindfolds took circuitous and meandering routes, even at distances of 9.5 kilometers (6 miles), although they finally arrived back at their home cave. At distances of 56 kilometers (35 miles), the treated and untreated control bats showed the same kinds of circuitous and meandering routes exhibited by the blindfolded bats at 9.5 kilometers. These results highlight the importance of vision in the long-distance orientation of bats and also suggest that they rely on a spatial memory

of specific settings or areas to find their roosts, their young, or perhaps, preferred feeding areas, when they are operating in familiar areas.

Studies using passive tags could not have collected such information. However, studies of homing by bats deprived of their vision suffer from a separate limitation. Day-flying bats are particularly vulnerable to attacks by raptors and other birds. Since a blind bat would be unable to distinguish dependably between night and day, it is possible that lower rates of return by blinded animals reflect mortality rather than an inability to find their home roost.

Further studies have shown the importance of cues other than echolocation in short-range orientation by bats. Hungry big brown bats have been used to study the role of local cues in the location of potential feeding areas. When the bats were released at an abandoned airfield, they tended to fly toward the sound of a frog chorus, a reliable indicator of a wet area where insect abundance might well be high. These bats appeared to be using sound as a cue for short-distance orientation.

HOME RANGES

The data from the greater spear-nosed bats introduces the question of spatial memory and emphasizes the importance of knowing the home range of study animals. We still know little about the home ranges of bats and the available data demonstrate considerable variability both within and between species. Big brown bats typically fly for less than two hours a night and in this time may make round trips of up to 5 or 10 kilometers (3 to 6 miles), depending upon local weather conditions and prey availability. Spotted bats (*Euderma maculatum*), however, typically cover 10 to 20 kilometers (6 to 12 miles) a night, spending over five hours in flight, and in this behavior resemble large mouse-eared bats (*Myotis myotis*). Hoary bats (*Lasiurus cinereus*), on the other hand, may cover more than 40 kilometers (25 miles) in their foraging flights which can also last over five hours. In the tropics, larger bats such as Indian false vampires (*Megaderma lyra*) or large slit-faced bats (*Nycteris grandis*) have much smaller home ranges, usually less than 2 kilometers (1 1/5 miles) in diameter. None

Jean-Paul Ferrero/Auscape

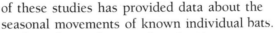

◀ This tube-nosed bat (*Nyctimene* species) is an Australian member of the suborder Megachiroptera, or Old World fruit bats. These bats feed on nectar and fruit, wandering large distances in synchrony with the flowering and fruiting seasons of the trees and shrubs on which they feed. Tube-nosed bats utter distinctive whistling calls and are characterized by their tubular nostrils and the bold yellow spots splashed across their wings and ears.

of these studies has provided data about the seasonal movements of known individual bats.

The radio-tracking studies that have provided information about home ranges have also demonstrated that while some species of bats typically return to the same roost day after day, others change roost sites quite unpredictably. Furthermore, this pattern can differ within a species. In one study in Canada, big brown bats roosting in buildings in eastern Ontario returned to the same site day after day and season after season, while those roosting in trees in British Colombia changed their roost unpredictably from night to night. Such data reveals a basic flaw in homing studies that have not used active tags and have relied on presumed roost fidelity to provide a clear indication of successful homing.

BAT MIGRATIONS

In the New World, bats in the genus *Lasiurus* are widespread and some species have often been suggested to be long-distance migrants. For example, in summer red bats (*Lasiurus borealis*) and hoary bats range over much of North America, probably occurring almost as far north as the tree line. These species, which roost in the foliage of trees and shrubs, have never been found in Canada or most of the United States in winter. Furthermore, there are

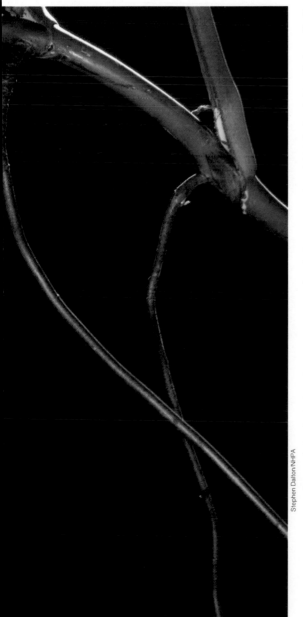

Stephen Dalton/NHPA

◀ Some bat species may range 40 kilometers (25 miles) or more from their daytime roosts, spending as many as five or six hours on the wing every night. Others, such as this Indian false vampire (*Megaderma lyra*), seldom wander more than a kilometer or two from their roosts. False vampires feed on small reptiles and mammals, as well as large insects.

▶ The straw-colored flying fox (*Eidolon heluum*) is abundant and widespread across much of Africa. Feeding largely on fruit, it migrates seasonally and like many other flying foxes, it roosts (or "camps") conspicuously in trees in densely packed assemblies that may number tens of thousands of bats.

Merlin D. Tuttle/Bat Conservation International

records, usually from people sampling migrating birds, of red and hoary bats passing through known migration way stations such as Point Pelee on Lake Erie. In southern Manitoba and in southwestern Ontario, hoary bats generally appear around the end of May, but most have left these areas by the middle of August. Red bats often appear earlier in May, but in Manitoba the southward migration begins in mid-July.

After mid-August red bats are uncommon in either Manitoba or Ontario. The occurrence of red bats in Bermuda and in the Galapagos, and their frequent observation on ships off the east coast of North America, shows that they are capable of long-range flight. Hoary bats can also fly huge distances. They occur in Hawaii, in the Galapagos, and have been recorded from Iceland and the Shetland Islands.

Although there are no band recoveries documenting point-to-point movements by red or hoary bats, there is strong circumstantial evidence that they are seasonal migrants. Furthermore, at a study site in southwestern Ontario, some individually marked hoary bats returned to the same foraging areas three summers in a row. There is also comparable data for some noctule bats (*Nyctalus noctula*) in Europe.

In other species, the picture is more complicated. In the American southwest a number of caves house huge populations of Mexican free-tailed bats (*Tadarida brasiliensis*). Many of the caves are nursery colonies, seasonally occupied by up to five million bats. Banding studies have revealed that many of the bats that summer in the southwestern United States pass the winter in central Mexico, 1,000 to 1,500 kilometers (600 to 900 miles) away. Some populations of these free-tailed bats show little evidence of seasonal migration, however, and some biologists use this distinction to justify treating the two populations as being taxonomically distinct. Since studies of these bats have not produced genetic evidence supporting this distinction, the exact mixture of seasonal migrants and year-round residents remains unknown.

Banding studies have revealed that many species of European and North American bats show regular patterns of movement between summer and winter roosts, some of them involving journeys of over 100 kilometers (60 miles). These bats range in body mass from species weighing 5 to about 30 grams (1/6 to 1 ounce). The winter roosts are usually caves or mines—sites characterized by cool, above-freezing temperatures and high humidity—where the bats enter a state of torpor, passing the winter in hibernation. Other species hibernate in hollow trees or buildings, where winter temperatures sometimes fall below freezing. Since there is no clear evidence that bats can supercool (that is, lower their body temperatures below freezing point without themselves freezing), hibernation in such sites is presumably restricted to areas where the periods of subfreezing conditions are relatively brief. In response to subfreezing temperatures, some hibernating bats arouse from torpor and move to alternative sites. Other species increase their metabolic rates to maintain their body temperatures above freezing.

Other species of bats, for example big brown bats, appear to be more sedentary. Recoveries of banded big brown bats, largely from the northeastern United States, rarely show them moving more than 50 kilometers (30 miles) from the banding site.

For the time being, we lack information about most of the issues central to the questions surrounding bat migration.

▼ Bats of the family Molossidae have a tail that extends substantially beyond the margins of the tail membrane, and are known as free-tailed bats. Some species, including these Mexican free-tailed bats, breed and roost in large caves that may shelter many millions of bats. Mexican free-tailed bats are strong, fast flyers.

Part 3

OCEAN ODYSSEYS

As phenomenal as the migrations of many birds, but less visible, are those undertaken by fishes, crustaceans, and marine mammals. Many appear to have their origins in the era when dinosaurs still roamed the earth.

LOBSTERS

In self-protective lines up to 60 individuals long, lobsters may walk for days across the ocean floor

OCEANIC FISHES

Hidden from researchers' eyes until recently, fishes display a pattern and range of migration as various as those of terrestrial animals. Plankton, too, migrate up and down through the water column.

EELS

European and North American eels breed in their hundreds of millions in the Sargasso Sea but, amazing to recount, no adult has ever been seen there.

SALMON

Every year salmon swim upstream, sometimes traveling huge distances, jumping rapids and waterfalls when necessary, to spawn where they were spawned years earlier.

MARINE TURTLES

Traveling huge distances from their feeding grounds to breed, marine turtles display navigational skills that have yet to be explained.

SEALS, SEA LIONS, AND WALRUSES

Born out of the water, these amphibious mammals are not famed migrators, but they too sometimes travel extensively.

WHALES

While some whales only migrate over short distances, others undertake vast annual round trips, living off reserves of blubber for half the long journey.

LOBSTERS

William F. Hernnkind

In mid-autumn, western Atlantic spiny lobsters migrate from the shallows to deeper, calmer water. They arrange themselves in queues of up to 60 individuals, each lobster touching the one in front, and walk for several days and nights across the ocean floor.

Some 50 species of spiny lobsters (family Palinuridae) are found in shallow to moderately deep waters (about 200 meters; 650 feet) around the world, mainly in the tropics, but also in temperate latitudes. Some lobsters migrate very little, while others migrate almost continuously, the extent of their movements dictated by how each species exploits the ecological, physical, and topographical conditions within its range.

Tropical reef dwellers, like the beautiful spotted lobster of the Caribbean (*Panulirus guttatus*), and a suite of Pacific species, each of which is found in a particular zone of the Great Barrier Reef, probably spend their entire bottom-dwelling existence within a kilometer (5/8 mile) radius of the reef patch where they landed as post-larvae. At the other extreme is the ornate lobster (*P. ornatus*) of northeast Australia, which treks continuously for months, covering several hundred kilometers between its nursery area and distant spawning grounds across the Gulf of Papua.

The western Atlantic spiny lobster (*P. argus*), is also a great traveler, its geographic range extending from Brazil northward to Bermuda, and including the Caribbean and the Bahamas. Within this vast region its remarkable walking ability enables it to exploit the resources of just about every saline shallow coastal shelf, island, and bay. These lobsters exhibit nearly the full range of movement patterns seen in all lobster species, but also make spectacular formation movements during explosive mass migrations, which appear to be unique among crustaceans.

Western Atlantic spiny lobsters of the Bahamas range nomadically over a mosaic of marine habitats, including seagrasses, algal plains, and patches of sponge, sea whip, and coral. They feed and wander about the thousands of square kilometers of shallows from 2 to 10 meters (6 1/2 to 33 feet) deep on the Great and Little Bahama Banks. In early autumn juveniles and adults are typically found scattered across the banks, denning up in any available crevice, underneath uprooted seagrass mats, and even resting in tail-to-tail rosettes (a side-by-side radial arrangement with tails touching in the center) around the base of bushy sea whips. At this time of year the sea is clear and calm (bar the occasional hurricane), with temperatures just below 30°C (86°F). Eating seems to be the main activity, since the sexually mature individuals will have spawned on the oceanic reef margins in spring and early summer. The adults now plough their caloric resources into molting and body growth, before regenerating their copious gonads in the winter. The juveniles are at their highest growth rate, and those less than two years since settlement do little else but forage, feed, and molt.

▲ Spiny lobsters begin life as transparent larvae called phyllosomae ("leaf-like"). They live among the oceans' plankton, drifting with the currents until they reach their adult forms.

▶ Portrait of a spiny lobster. Members of this group (family Palinuridae) are most conspicuously characterized by their lack of the formidable claws usually typical of lobsters. Many species are strongly patterned and brightly colored.

▶ As autumn storms disturb the shallow waters of the Great Bahama Bank in the West Indies, spiny lobsters begin to move en masse, migrating southward along the eastern edge of the Florida Straits.

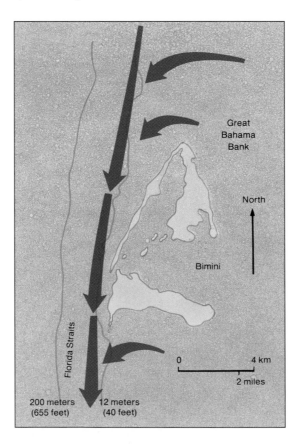

Great Bahama Bank

North

Bimini

Florida Straits

0   4 km

2 miles

200 meters (655 feet)   12 meters (40 feet)

▶ Spiny lobsters on autumn migration wind about the tightly circling leader as a queue transforms into a defensive rosette. Once formed, with all the lobsters facing outward or upward, a predator is confronted by spine-laden antennae at all angles of attack.

▶ (Opposite) With the gregariousness typical of their family, New Zealand rock lobsters (*Jasus edwardsii*) cluster in a rock crevice. In Australasia, where "true" lobsters do not occur, spiny lobsters are called "lobsters," "rock lobsters," or "crayfish" and are an important part of the commercial fishing industry.

▼ Spiny lobsters on autumn migration form queues, each animal maintaining contact with the one in front as the group marches steadily across the ocean floor.

MIGRATION FROM THE SHALLOWS

In mid-autumn the weather abruptly changes, as high pressure fronts sweep down from North America. Winds intensify to 20 to 30 knots, the skies darken, rain falls, and temperatures plummet. As the storms move across the open ocean, they generate swells that sweep over the shallows, churning the sediments and clouding the water. Wind-driven currents increase, while waves create surging oscillations in the shallow water. Turbulence accelerates the heat transfer from warm seas to cold air, so that water temperatures decline in concert with air temperatures. At the end of several stormy days, the banks' waters are white-capped, murky, cold, and tumultuous.

Off the west shores of the Bimini Islands on the edge of the Great Bahama Bank, just across the Gulf Stream from Florida, storm-churned bank water can be clearly seen flowing around the islands and forming a sharp demarcation line where it meets the crystalline water of the Gulf Stream. Scuba divers along this margin can see single-file, head-to-tail lines, or queues, of lobsters, ranging from 2 to over 60 individuals, continuously appearing from the cloudy waters and traveling southwestward into the clear, slightly deeper waters (10 to 30 meters; 30 to 100 feet) along the edge of the bank. The migration may continue for up to several days, queuing lobsters moving both day and night. Lobsters finding scattered rock ledges or patch reefs fill up all available cover and even pile up on themselves when resting briefly. Large tail-to-tail rosettes of lobsters also form on the open sandy bottom where no cover exists. Individuals in these rosettes continuously change as queues arrive and join up, while others trail off to form new queues behind restless "leaders."

Now and then a queue leader will stop to probe the sand for prey. As the queue waits, the followers may also probe about or, more typically, dance about from side to side while always retaining physical contact with the animal ahead. Those acquiring prey keep their place in line when the queue moves on, using their two front pairs of legs to manipulate the food while their hindmost three pairs do the walking.

The migratory pathways pass through areas rarely inhabited by lobsters at other times of year—probably because shelter is scarce. Occasionally, queues in the open are attacked during the day by predators, especially queen triggerfish. The lobsters respond by quickly forming a rosette, the lead lobster turning on its own body length, causing its followers to wind around it like a coiled chain. When the last queue member is wound in, the group members turn outward to present a hemispherical array of long, horny antennae. The occasional loss of an antenna is not necessarily a major problem because it will regrow at the next molt. Less than 1 percent of migrants are ever seen alone, and solitary lobsters quickly join passing queues.

After several days, the stream of lobsters subsides and there are comparatively few lobsters remaining in the pathway crevices near Bimini. The rest appear to gradually drop off their queues farther down the pathway. Eventually, the thousands of migrants disperse over 30 to 50 kilometers (20 to 30 miles) of habitat scattered along the edge of the bank. Some lobsters descend the precipitous drop into deeper water. Near Grand Bahama Island on the Little Bahama Bank, queuing migrants have been observed from a research submarine at a depth of over 200 meters (660 feet).

Legends maintain that the migrant lobsters actually cross the ocean floor, and eventually resurface in the shallows of either the Little Bahama Bank or the Florida Keys. However, this species of lobster cannot acclimatize to the cold seawater temperatures (below 10°C; 50°F) found at the bottom of deep ocean straits. Lobsters fitted with ultrasonic transmitters and released in deep water off Key West in Florida, where the temperature was 7°C (45°F), became moribund within minutes, and within 24 hours their flesh had been entirely devoured by hordes of scavenging crustaceans.

Tag-and-recapture studies of lobsters in Cuba, Florida, and the Bahamas suggest that there is no particular geographic terminus to the lobsters autumn mass migration. Migrants scatter widely after the initial period of mass queuing, and some lobsters have been recaptured the following summer back on the shallows. Sexually mature lobsters remain along the edge of the bank among scattered reefs. There has been no confirmed recapture of a tagged lobster across a deep strait, despite the tagging of tens of thousands of lobsters in the region over a period of nearly 30 years.

Kim Westerskov/Oxford Scientific Films

Doug Perrine/Innerspace Visions

▲ A western Atlantic spiny lobster in its typical habitat in shallow waters among coral reefs. Spiny lobsters forage over a variety of habitats on the sea-floor, retiring to crevices among boulders or coral to rest or when alarmed. It is still not clear why these animals migrate en masse each autumn, and when they do they appear to have no fixed destination.

WHY MIGRATE IN AUTUMN?

Because so many environmental factors change during the storms that characteristically trigger these autumn migrations, the immediate stimuli that induce mass queuing have not been fully investigated, but a number of hypotheses have been advanced. Among the contenders are sharp temperature drops, shelter deprivation, hunger, and intensified water motion.

A number of experiments have been carried out on lobsters in large laboratory pools. Thus far, the only stimulus to consistently induce continuous queuing is increased water motion. Both stepped-up current flow around the pool and turbulent (nondirectional) water pulses caused lobsters resting in a pool's central den to emerge and start queuing within a few hours, then continue to migrate throughout most of the two-day experimental period. The lobsters may travel several kilometers despite the confinement and obstacles, those queuing in currents mostly walking with the current, those in turbulence walking equally clockwise and counterclockwise.

It would be of particular interest to test whether experimental cues act only upon lobsters already primed to an internal migratory state—expressed either as migratory restlessness or heightened responsiveness to key stimuli. Occasional mass queuing under calm water conditions in both the field and in laboratory pools indicates some variation in the level of sensitivity among lobsters. Other studies show that the most active lobsters usually

lead queues, so perhaps their behavior encourages others to become migratory. It is also thought that declining day length and hormonal changes associated with growth might be linked with autumn migration.

HOW LOBSTERS FIND THEIR WAY

The compass direction of autumn migration differs among localities, but is consistent from year to year at each site. Off Bimini, autumn migrants head southward, while migrants along Florida's east coast travel northward. Lobsters change direction to circumnavigate islands or to follow channels through shallow water, which suggests that local cues serve as guideposts.

Field experiments and ultrasonic tracking studies of lobsters settled in a home area have displaced them from their home dens then released them in both nearby familiar and distant unfamiliar areas. Within the normal foraging range, a displaced lobster usually walks home to the den area from which it was captured, even when it has opaque eye-caps fitted, and cannot see. Likewise, eye-capped lobsters released in unfamiliar areas walk in a straight course, but in directions related to local water movement. In the presence of wave surge, lobsters move upwave, which is generally offshore. In the absence of surge but in flowing water currents, lobsters generally move with the current, but if chemical attractants are present, hungry lobsters will walk upstream, continuously sampling the water with their primary odor receptors on the paired forward antennules, y-shaped appendages next to the longer, unbranched spiny antennae. If there is no water movement, lobsters become disoriented.

Water movements, chemical features, and topography vary widely during migration, which argues against such movements being guided by a single stimulus. Many autumn migrations appear to involve movement from disturbed areas to more protected locations near the lee side of islands or along the ocean margin, and strong downcurrent and upwave responses may serve as initiating and course-correcting guideposts. Traveling either upwave, in the direction of ocean swells, or downcurrent, when storm water driven onto shallows flows seaward, as winds calm and/or shift direction, would lead Bimini migrants in autumn from the bank shallows to the Bimini pathway area. Once in the pathway, however, other directional responses must come into play, as water movements in that region are variable. Perhaps lobsters sustain direction in such conditions by geomagnetic cues.

THE ADVANTAGES OF QUEUING

Queues are the most striking and characteristic feature of mass migrations. Queue members maintain their positions by having the tips of their antennules and the tips of their foremost legs almost constantly touching the abdomen of the lobster in front. This contact is not disrupted even by the removal of a lobster's antennae. When, in experiments, antennules are removed, the lobster increases the frequency with which it touches the lobster in front with its foremost legtips. If these are removed, the lobster then uses the tips of the second, now foremost, legs. This ensures that the queue is sustained even if the lobsters cannot see. Water motion caused by the lobster ahead is possibly used by a follower to regain lost contact while chemical stimuli allow it to recognize that it is following a fellow lobster.

Queues are a most efficient surveillance formation for a moving group. The eyes, antennae, and other receptors of all members can be used to detect approaching predators, while the vulnerable abdomen of each (except the hindmost animal) is defended by the weaponry of its follower. When a queue is threatened, defensive pods or rosettes form to repulse predators that could easily kill a solitary lobster. Several other lobster species also form rosettes when threatened.

Queuing also makes mass migration a good deal easier, as it greatly reduces drag. A lobster walking in the wake of another lobster encounters only about half the drag

force that it would if walking alone. Reduced drag may provide substantial metabolic savings, given the rapid migratory walking speed, sometimes exceeding 1 kilometer (5/8 mile) per hour, which the lobsters sustain for several days. The lead position in the queue is frequently exchanged.

Yet another possible, but unproven, benefit of queuing is improved orientation. As the most active lobsters usually lead queues, and as it is only well-oriented lobsters that move about continuously over long distances, it may be true that lead lobsters always have strong directional ability.

Perhaps the most challenging questions about mass queuing migrations relate to their evolutionary origin and adaptive function. They are not related directly to movements to mating or spawning areas: such movements are made gradually by individual adults in the early spring. Food resources are not noticeably in decline in the areas from which migrants flow, and the migrations are not made to especially food-rich areas. Experimentally, starvation does not cause lobsters to migrate in autumn.

Although not fully tested, the most widely held theory about these lobster migrations is

▲ A juvenile with an adult spiny lobster. Adults of some species grow to as much as 15 kilograms (about 35 pounds) in weight.

that the lobsters move to avoid deteriorating conditions, such as rough and cold seas. While the autumn storms that trigger the localized mass movements do not create life-threatening conditions, repeated severe cold fronts, which occur around once every 10 years, can reduce water temperatures to such a degree that molting lobsters die and others become too moribund to feed or effectively move about. Efficient behavior adapted to prompt mass exodus when conditions deteriorate may have evolved as an important component of the lobster's unique lifestyle.

OCEANIC FISHES

Ronald Thresher and Ann M. Gronell

The blank face of the ocean hides movements of animals on a scale we are only just beginning to comprehend. Journeys may extend just a few meters or across entire oceans; the travelers range from tiny reef fishes to the gigantic tunas of the high seas.

Compared with the ever-changing nature of life on land, the steady roll of ocean waves and the regular movements of the tides are reassuringly constant. But within the depths, movement and change are as pervasive and dramatic as on land, merely being harder to see and comprehend.

Marine fishes migrate in order to exploit a moving food source, to spawn in the habitat most favorable to the survival of offspring, or to find a benign environment during difficult times (such as overwintering grounds). Journeys can occur daily and involve movements of only a few meters, or

take years to complete and cover thousands of kilometers and several oceans. Vertical migrations also occur up and down the water column, perhaps without change in geographic position.

THE MOVEMENTS OF REEF FISHES

Among marine fishes, migrations of a few meters to several hundred are common, taking place over either hours or a few days. A variety of coastal fishes move toward the shore and back with the tides, foraging over submerged tidal flats for a few hours each day. Regular foraging migrations also occur on a day-night cycle. On Caribbean coral reefs, for example, colorful schooling fishes known as "grunts" (the noise they make when they are caught by an angler), from the family Haemulidae, mill in large numbers around the reef during the day. At dusk they gather into separate schools that

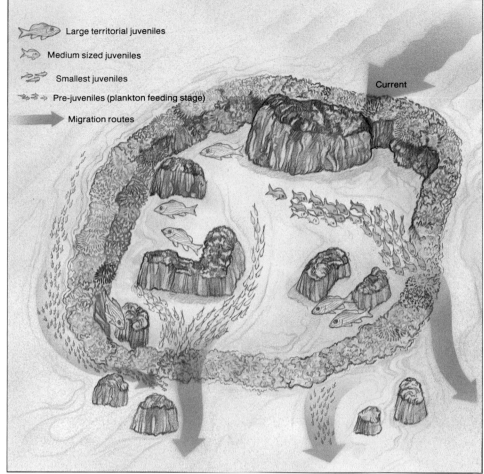

Large territorial juveniles

Medium sized juveniles

Smallest juveniles

Pre-juveniles (plankton feeding stage)

Migration routes

Current

follow regular paths away from the reef and into the surrounding seagrass meadows. There they scatter and spend the night feeding on invertebrates. The schools re-form shortly before dawn and retrace their paths back to the reef, each returning to the spot where its members traditionally spend the day. This daily migration allows the grunts the best of two worlds: shelter from predators in the nooks and crevices of the reef during the day, and access to abundant food in the seagrass meadows at night, when the risk of being preyed upon is low. Each school uses its particular path day in, day out, for many years, and the routes are learned by each generation of juveniles when they join the school.

These migrations greatly benefit the reef ecosystem. Coral colonies, like plants, require sunlight and nutrients in order to grow, most corals relying on currents to carry food to them. Those colonies occupied during the day by schools of grunts grow faster and are healthier than colonies without grunts, because of the rich nutrients provided by the grunts' excrement.

Many fishes make daily and tidal migrations over small distances to particular places in their territory in order to spawn.

▲ Researchers studying the small-scale daily migrations of young grunts on one small coral reef (or microatoll) found that routes and staging areas were constant. Different age groups stay together during the day. Toward evening the fish congregate in certain (staging) areas, then at dark move out on regular paths to nearby seagrass meadows to feed.

◄ (Opposite page, top) The lizard fish (family Synodontidae), or grinner, is carnivorous. It hides in the sand alongside the migration paths used by grunts with only its head exposed, waiting to attack as the grunts move away from the shelter of the reef flats to feed.

◄ A school of bluestripe grunts (*Haemulon sciurus*) at Key Largo, Florida. So-called because of the sound they make when caught, grunts gather in schools to shelter in coral reefs by day, and disperse over nearby seagrass meadows to feed at night.

Kevin Deacon/Dive 2000

▲ Angelfishes inhabit coral reefs, and are notable for their tameness. They can often be approached by a swimmer or diver, and may turn gracefully as if inviting inspection. This is a blue angelfish (*Pomacanthus semicirculatus*), which occurs along Australia's Great Barrier Reef.

Some species spawn once a month, rather than daily. Fishes may travel 10 to 20 kilometers (6 to 12 miles) and begin to assemble several days before spawning, which typically occurs at a site near the edge of the reef, on or close to the night of the full moon. The place and time ensure that tidal currents are at their strongest to carry the eggs away from the reef. Some species use the same spawning sites over many generations. For hundreds of years fishermen in these waters have used their detailed knowledge of fishes' movements to make good catches at these sites and on the migration routes leading to them.

HERRINGS—SHOALING FISHES OF THE NORTH ATLANTIC

The shoaling fishes common at temperate latitudes migrate in greater numbers and over longer distances than tropical reef fishes, but the patterns are much the same. The North Atlantic herring (*Clupea harengus*) is a good example, having been studied extensively because of its economic importance. Over the centuries, fortunes have been made from the huge catches of herrings made at spawning sites.

Herrings migrate simultaneously on two planes. Firstly, each day the schools migrate up and down the water column, following the daily vertical movements of the plankton on which they feed. Secondly, they migrate seasonally in large circles, following oceanic currents, between spawning, feeding, and overwintering grounds.

Spawning gatherings of herrings occur at a large number of places, in different seasons, and only last a few months, after which the fish disperse. In the nineteenth century it was thought that the herrings swam north to the Arctic Circle for the summer, moving south in great waves from under the Arctic icefields as the water cooled. One branch of this wave was thought to flow into the fjords and estuaries of northern Europe to overwinter and spawn, the other moving to the North American coast.

Scientific work earlier this century was directed at answering two questions about herrings. Did fishes that spawned in the spring also spawn in the autumn, and vice versa, and did herrings return to their birthplace to reproduce? If herrings returned to their natal spawning grounds to spawn, then particular regional stocks were not part of some great herring wave, and could be managed more or less separately. And if spring and autumn spawners were not one and the same, then they too could be

These places tend to be pieces of coral or rock that are higher than the surrounding terrain, from which the spawning fishes then ascend, shedding their eggs and sperm as they rise. By beginning the ascent from a prominent place the fish remain close to shelter until the last possible moment. In most small species, spawning ascents are so fast that predators have little time to attack before the pair is back in the shelter of the reef. Larger fishes, who are less at risk of attack, rise to spawn more slowly. The spawning ascent increases the chances of the fertilized eggs being carried away by currents from hungry mouths on the bottom.

As territory sizes grow, or social units become more scattered, the distances fishes swim to assemble also increase. Large male angelfishes, such as the emperor angelfish (*Pomacanthus imperator*), routinely swim hundreds of meters each evening to meet and spawn with the widely scattered females in their harems. As the distances traveled increase, larger numbers of fishes tend to be involved. Spawning shifts from a paired to a group activity, and the preferred sites are no longer scattered rocks and coral heads, but large promontories or passages across the reef. The number of fishes that come together to spawn varies widely, depending on the species, from five to ten for some angelfish and wrass, to thousands in some species of parrotfish, goatfish, and sea bass.

managed as independent stocks.

The behavior of inshore fishes can be observed by divers, which is one of the reasons why so much is known about them. Observations of shoaling fishes in particular locations are of limited use, however, and other techniques to study migratory behavior are needed. The most common of these is the tag-and-recapture method. Fishes are caught, tagged, then released. When a fish is recaught, the place and time of recapture are noted. By comparing the tagging and recapture details from thousands of fishes tagged at different times of the year, migration routes can be plotted. Such studies, however, have many limitations. Tags are difficult to apply to small fishes, and cannot be used at all with minute larvae. Recovery rates are extremely poor (only a few percent) and may well be biased. Carrying a tag may also distort the very behavior that is being studied, as a tagged fish probably does not swim as well as one without a tag.

Scientists are now working on alternative tracking methods, such as the use of archival tags that record data continuously. These tags will record water temperature and depth, from which "guesstimates" can be made of the water mass in which the fish is

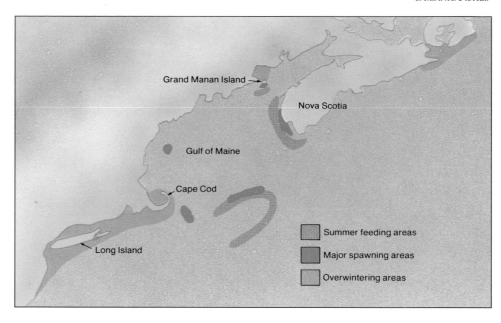

swimming. Light levels will also be registered, enabling day length to be calculated, and hence latitude. The intention is to have tags that will record data for six months, then detach automatically, float to the surface, and broadcast the data to a passing satellite.

Tagging studies of herrings have shown that most adults "home" to the same spawning ground each year, and that they

▲ Distribution of Atlantic herring in the Gulf of Maine and Scotian Shelf area during the summer feeding, spawning, and overwintering phases of the adults' annual migration cycle.

▼ Herrings characteristically travel in vast schools. This makes them relatively easy to harvest commercially, and a great deal of research has gone into determining the movements and spawning schedules of the various species.

Peter David/Planet Earth Pictures

▲ Many deep ocean fishes confine their migrations to vertical movements within the water column. Lanternfishes like this one (*Myctophus asperum*) spend the day at depths of 300 to 400 meters (980 to 1,300 feet) but ascend to the surface to feed at night.

also spawn only in one season of the year, some in spring, others in autumn, and a few in winter. Generally, the farther north a population is found the more likely it is to spawn in spring or summer. In many parts of the species' range, however, populations that spawn in the spring coexist with stocks that do so in the autumn.

Further proof of homing arose when scientists found that water temperature affects the development of bones in herring larvae. They discovered that the number of vertebrae in the backbone of a herring larva increases as temperature decreases, as a result of slower growth. Along the coast of Norway, where the waters in the north are much colder than in the south, there are marked differences between herring populations with regard to numbers of vertebrae. When research was carried out in the region, it was found that in a given spawning ground adults generally had the same number of vertebrae as the larvae from that area.

Research has also been done on the innermost structure of a herring otolith (a small bone in the fish's ear that detects movement, orientation, and acceleration). It has been found that otoliths differ in appearance depending on the time of year the larva hatches. Otoliths of adults that spawn in the winter almost invariably resemble the newly formed otoliths of winter-spawned larvae.

It is now clear that rather than consisting of one huge mixed population, there are at least 15 herring populations in the northern Atlantic. These populations are defined according to their general location (for example, the Atlanto-Scandian group), their spawning area (for example, the Dogger Bank stock), and the season in which they spawn. Some stocks are separated by wide stretches of ocean, while others intermingle, separating only during spawning periods.

After hatching, herring larvae largely drift passively, and it is thought that separate stocks develop wherever ocean currents keep larvae in a particular area throughout their development. Stocks tend to be associated with banks or headlands where large eddies form through the steady sweep of ocean currents. In areas where currents are more variable, or where there are no prominent topographic features to create eddies, larvae from different spawning beds mix freely and stocks are more scattered.

The extent to which juveniles and adults migrate depends largely on the availability of food. If an area is well supplied with nutrients, which is often the case where there are eddies and banks, it is likely to be both a larval nursery and an adult feeding ground, and the net movement of fishes during their life cycle will not be great. Migrations are short and to specific spawning areas within the general range. But in some regions food supplies alter from season to season, causing large-scale migration. Adult herrings from southern Norway follow the food supply north in summer, feeding in the central Norwegian Sea. They then swim west and south to feed and overwinter off Iceland before returning to the southern Norwegian coast to spawn in the spring.

TUNA—FISHES OF THE HIGH SEAS
Tuna are true oceanic fishes swimming constantly and rarely approaching land. The fastest of all marine creatures, they have evolved remarkably streamlined body shapes, to the point of having extra fins along the rear edges of their bodies to reduce drag. They can reach burst swimming speeds in excess of 100 kilometers (62 miles) per hour.

Tuna can be divided into two groups on the basis of their migratory patterns. Most of the smaller tuna, such as the bonito (*Sarda orientalis*) and skipjack (*Katsuwonus pelamis*), migrate in a random fashion throughout large areas, with some individuals moving one way and others the opposite. In its undirected movements, the skipjack covers the entire tropical South Pacific. Specimens tagged near the west coast of North America have been found off Hawaii; others tagged in the South Pacific have been caught near the Asian coast. Reflecting this mobility, skipjack are genetically very similar over the entire Pacific. This suggests that there are no regular migrations to specific spawning areas for particular parts of the overall population. Studies using ultrasonic tags, which allow the movements of a fish to be followed for a few days (if a fast boat is used), suggest that skipjack regularly migrate in and offshore around Pacific islands. They spend the day cruising about a particular reef or bank, and then move offshore at night to feed on the fishes that migrate vertically to the surface. So far as scientists know, spawning also occurs offshore.

In contrast, migrations by the larger tuna tend to be more directed. Bluefin tuna, or tunny, are among the largest of all fishes. They live for about 20 years and do not reproduce until they are 5 or 6 years old. A fish that cruises at 5 to 10 kilometers (3 to 6 miles) per hour can cover large areas of ocean in 5 years, and a lot more in 20. Exactly how far they travel has been the focus of much study.

As is the case with herrings and many reef fishes, migrations are made by bluefin tuna to specific spawning grounds. Atlantic bluefin tuna (*Thunnus thynnus*) collect to spawn in the Gulf of Mexico and in the Mediterranean Sea. Mixing between the two populations appears to be slight. In the Pacific, one species of bluefin tuna (*T. orientalis*) spawns only in a small area southeast of Japan, while another, the southern bluefin tuna (*T. maccoyi*), spawns only off the south coast of Indonesia.

An outline of the movements and biology of southern bluefin tuna has now been established, although considerable research remains to be done. Spawning occurs between October and January in the Java Sea, a region of warm water just south of Indonesia and northwest of Australia. Following spawning, eggs and larvae drift for a few days. The larvae then become mobile and begin to school. Even at this stage, when they are only a few millimeters long, they are voracious predators. Most, if not all of the rapidly growing larvae and juveniles head south, migrating down the west coast of Australia. At the age of about 1 year, it is thought, they reach the southwest corner of Australia and turn east. Over the next four to five years the juveniles, which are up to about 60 centimeters (23 inches) long and

weighing up to around 20 kilograms (44 pounds), are found in schools along the southern coast of Australia. As they mature, they slowly filter east and south, eventually moving into the Southern Ocean—the band of very cold water around Antarctica, which is rich in food. The adults remain in these cold latitudes for most of their lives, ranging west to the South Atlantic and east to the southern tip of South America. Once a year a proportion of these fish head north in large schools to the tropics to spawn.

Such extensive movements pose formidable problems for those wishing to study these fish. Techniques used to study migrations in less mobile species are totally inadequate. How, for example, do you track a bluefin tuna fitted with an acoustic tag when the fish can swim three times faster than the maximum speed of a fisheries research vessel? Scientists have so far

▼ The various species of tuna (family Scombridae) tend to congregate in dense schools as young fish, but disperse to lead more solitary lives when fully mature.

CONFLICT OVER FISHERIES: THE SOUTHERN BLUEFIN TUNA

Like most other tuna, the southern bluefin tuna (*Thunnus maccoyi*) supports valuable commercial fisheries. One such fishery is close to the south coast of Australia, where shore-based boats catch juveniles (2- to 5-year-olds) for canning. The species also supports a high seas fishery, Japanese, Taiwanese, and Korean long-line trawlers catching adult fish mainly for the Japanese sashimi market. Adult southern bluefins are extremely valuable: one fish can be worth US$20,000 on the sashimi market.

The Japanese object to the Australians catching immature fish because it is wasteful and reduces the number of adult fish. As fishing pressure has increased and catch rates have declined over the last decade, the Japanese have requested that the Australian government restrict the shore-based fishery for juveniles. Australian fishermen, however, are unconcerned about the number of adults left, providing enough remain to reproduce. They resent having their catches and profits reduced to support a foreign fishery which, they believe, should catch fewer adults in order to ensure a viable population.

Neither the Japanese nor the Australian fishermen are prepared to stop fishing, and each group accuses the other of catching too many fish. As matters stand, the southern bluefin tuna is threatened with extinction. Negotiation and cooperation between the two countries depends to a large extent on knowing exactly what proportion of the juvenile stock is subject to the shore-based fishery.

▲ A small fortune in bluefin tuna on deck. Tuna inhabit the open ocean, and are the fastest of all fishes. They are so streamlined that many have shallow grooves in the body. The fins fit into these when not extended.

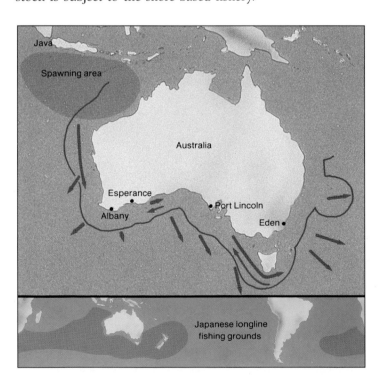

▲ Southern bluefin tuna spawn in the Java Sea. Once hatched, the baby fish move south. They gradually accumulate in coastal waters off southern Australia, where they remain until they reach maturity after several years. Then they disperse into the deep waters of the Southern Ocean.

Scientists suspect that juveniles trickle into the Southern Ocean all along the southern Australian coast. While the bulk of them may well stay in Australian waters until near sexual maturity, the tag-and-recapture data from which the basic migration pattern has been determined are not good enough to show what proportion of them use this route, and whether this proportion varies annually. If many juveniles bypass Australian waters altogether, then controlling the shore-based fishery is relatively unimportant and the Japanese could have the freedom to control their catches as they see fit. If all juveniles are subject to Australian fishing, however, controls over the Australian fishery are essential.

captured few bluefin tuna that are less than 1 year old, despite considerable efforts to find them off the west coast of Australia. They must be present by the tens of thousands, but exactly where is unclear. Researchers also do not know what age the juveniles are when they leave Australian waters and enter the Southern Ocean, or what proportion of the adult stock migrates north every year to spawn. Given these limitations, estimating the size of the population is impossible.

ORIENTATION ACROSS THE OCEANS

How does a fish navigate thousands of kilometers, across several oceans, to the one small region in which it spawns? Experimental work on coral reef fishes that make daily feeding and spawning migrations, suggests that fishes orient to conspicuous features, such as a coral outcrop. When scientists moved a particularly prominent piece of coral or rock on a regular grunt migration path, the fish altered course to travel via this repositioned feature. Those species that migrate along the shoreline probably orient themselves this way. American shad (*Alosa sapidissimus*) migrate north every year from the coasts of Florida and Georgia to southern Canada in summer, and then travel south again for the winter. En route, they enter rivers, where they spawn. These fish appear to follow preferred water temperatures north, as the ocean warms in summer, and then south, as temperatures decline in the autumn. The precise migration route, however, is dictated by coastal topography, the fish swimming parallel to the coastline.

More complex orientation methods are required to account for other forms of migration. Many fishes travel directly in and offshore each day, from the places where they shelter at night to inshore feeding grounds. At least some of these fishes use the sun to orient themselves. Parrotfishes that are taken offshore and then released, swim directly inshore on sunny days, but swim about aimlessly when it is overcast. It has been suggested that large oceanic fishes, such as tunas, use sun-compass orientation, but this fails to account for migration that takes place at night and on overcast days. It also seems inconceivable that tuna, whose eyes are designed for seeing underwater, can see the night sky sufficiently clearly through the choppy surface of the sea to plot their course by the stars.

Two other techniques have been proposed to explain the phenomenal orientation and homing abilities of oceanic fishes. The first is direct magnetic orientation. Some studies, particularly in sharks, suggest certain fishes are capable of detecting the earth's magnetic field. Essentially, they have a built-in compass. For some forms of migration, such as movements on and off banks to forage at night, a shark could simply reverse its bearing at dawn to return to its daytime shelter. The second technique involves electro-reception. Again, most of the work has been done on sharks. Recently it has been found that they have numerous pits—lateralis pits—on the head and snout that are sensitive to electrical fields. Studies with small species indicate that they use this sense to locate prey buried in sand, detecting the weak electrical field generated by the nervous activity of a hidden fish or crab. Perhaps this sense also helps sharks find their way in the open sea. When currents in the ocean cross the earth's magnetic field they create electrical fields that would certainly be strong enough for sharks to detect. To a shark, the ocean might well be a complex world of interweaving magnetic and electric fields, through which the currents pass like well-marked highways.

Do tuna use similar mechanisms to find the Java Sea? There is no evidence that they have sense organs like the lateralis pits on sharks. Researchers remain baffled. Perhaps fishes, in their exquisite adaptation to an oceanic existence, have senses of which we are unaware and read signs in their environment that we cannot see.

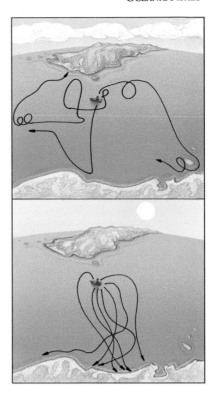

▲ Paths of adult parrot fish (*Scarus guacamaia* and *S. coelestinus*) released during the afternoon in Balley's Bay in Bermuda. Individuals released under complete cloud cover (top) could not orient themselves home. Individuals released during bright sunshine (bottom) oriented home immediately.

Marty Snyderman

▲ The blue shark (*Prionace glauca*) roams the tropical and subtropical oceans of the world. The recent discovery that sharks can detect minute electrical fields leads to speculation that perhaps they navigate by following the web of interactions between the earth's magnetic and electrical fields

PLANKTON

Michael J. Kingsford

lankton is the collective name for animal and plant organisms that drift in oceans and lakes. The word plankton is Greek for "wandering" or "drifting," but for many forms of plankton, directed movements are extensive and critical to their survival. Most planktonic organisms are less than 2 millimeters (1/12 inch) long, but some can be up to 3 meters (nearly 10 feet) in length, as in the case of large jellyfish. In general, the larger the size of plankton, the greater control they have of their movements. Plankton are made up of phytoplankton ("plant-plankton" in Greek) and zooplankton ("animal-plankton"). Most marine animals have a planktonic larval stage after they hatch from eggs. Larvae are, therefore, members of the plankton. Animals that only spend part of their life in the plankton are called meroplankton. Holoplankton are animals that spend their entire lives as part of the plankton.

▼ Clustered around a central mouth, the oral arms of a jellyfish gather food. The animal moves by rhythmic, muscular contractions along the rim of the flotation "umbrella."

VERTICAL MIGRATION

Both phytoplankton and zooplankton migrate vertically, that is they move up and down the water column. The best known migrations occur on a daily basis (diel migrations). The vertical movements of phytoplankton are generally achieved by controlling the quantity of gas, oil, or salt within the organism. Production of gas or oil, or the removal of salt will cause the organism to rise, while reversing the process will cause it to sink. Some migrate with the assistance of mobile whip-like hairs called flagellae. Zooplankton move by swimming with legs, stiff hairs, fins, and/or by moving their bodies.

In nocturnal migrations plankton move toward the surface at night and descend to deeper waters during the day. Reversed migration is when they move toward the surface during the day, descending to deeper water at night. Nocturnal migrations are the most common. The distances that phytoplankton migrate are poorly described while the distances that zooplankton travel are known to vary considerably. Some species only migrate through the upper

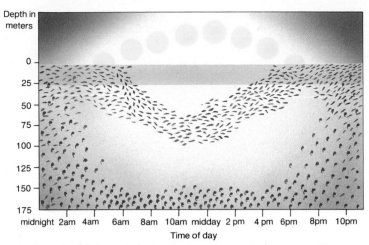

Depth in meters

midnight 2am 4am 6am 8am 10am midday 2 pm 4 pm 6pm 8pm 10pm
Time of day

▲ The cycle of daily vertical migration is continuous in deep oceans. Near dawn zooplankton migrate to deep water and away from the photic zone where phytoplankton abound (green band). At dusk, planktonic animals such as copepods (red) and mysids (blue) swim to the surface to feed on the phytoplankton and remain inconspicuous to predators.

100 meters (330 feet) of the water column, whilst others travel over 1,000 meters (3,300 feet) each night. The migratory behavior of zooplankton is plastic, as they may alter the range of depths over which they migrate according to the time of year, depth of the water column, and the timing of reproduction.

While a variety of mechanisms control the timing of zooplankton migrations, light is probably the most influential factor. As light levels drop at dusk, certain types of plankton rise toward the surface. Then, when light levels increase toward dawn, they return to the depths. The timing and scale of zooplankton migration is also influenced by the presence of food or predators, which the plankton detect visually, by taste, or touch. The distance zooplankton migrate can be influenced by changes in water temperature, while others only migrate during periods of reproduction.

The benefits of migration are varied. Many zooplankton feed on the phytoplankton that grow only near the surface of the water, where the sunlight can reach them. The concentration of predators that hunt by sight is much greater in these surface waters, so the zooplankton stay in deeper water during the day, migrating upward at night. In this way they reduce the chances of being seen by predators.

Small animals that live on the bottom during the day often become temporary members of the plankton at night. Many of these animals are adults rather than larvae, and are thought to migrate in order to disperse or reproduce. In some species the members of only one sex migrate, and their bodies are structurally modified to enable them to live both on the bottom and in the plankton. For example, male amphipods (genus *Parawaldeckia*), sandhopper-type animals, have larger eyes and swimming legs than the females.

HORIZONTAL MIGRATION

Plankton rarely make active horizontal migrations, although there are a few examples of such movements. In the Palau islands of the Pacific, large jellyfishes (genus *Mastigias*) make daily migrations of up to 1 kilometer (5/8 mile) across small lakes. These jellyfishes have a symbiotic relationship with the algae living in their bodies, and it is thought that the migrations maximize the exposure of these algae to sunlight.

Copepods (small animals related to prawns and rock lobsters) in lakes have also been found to migrate daily between the shore and open water.

Some zooplankton use tidal currents to carry them to suitable habitats. Such passive horizontal movements are mostly made by larvae of estuarine animals such as crabs, barnacles, and flatfish. By migrating vertically in the tidal currents they control their horizontal movements, and thus avoid being swept out to sea. For example, larvae may migrate toward the surface on the incoming tide, to travel as far upstream as possible, and then move toward the bottom on the outgoing tide, to minimize downstream movement.

Larvae from a variety of adults that live in coastal regions, spend time developing in the ocean before returning to the coast. For example, larvae of rock lobsters are carried offshore by winds that influence surface waters, then, when they migrate to deeper waters (often as a negative response to light), ocean currents carry them toward shore. Sometimes, as has been found for crabs, larvae may remain in deep currents early in life so they are transported offshore. Later in their development they migrate to surface waters and are then carried onshore by the winds and waves.

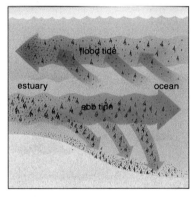

◀ Vertical migration of larvae in an estuary. Larvae migrate to the surface on the incoming (flood) tide so that they are transported into the estuary. On the outgoing (ebb) tide they migrate toward the bottom so that they are not flushed from the estuary.

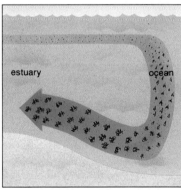

◀ Transport of larvae away from coastal environments into ocean waters during their early development, and back to nursery areas late in development. Depending on local conditions of oceanography, larvae may drift offshore in surface waters (top) or bottom waters (bottom). Midway through development they migrate toward the surface or bottom waters so that currents facilitate their transport to coastal nursery areas.

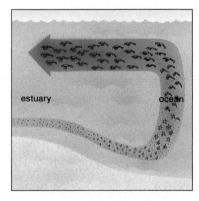

▶ (Following pages) Copepods and amphipods are often especially abundant in plankton associations. Other planktonic organisms include the young of various molluscs, corals, crabs, and other crustaceans.
Peter David/Planet Earth Pictures

EELS

Ann M. Gronell and Ronald E. Thresher

▲ Adult European or common eels frequently burrow in bottom mud or loose gravel looking for food, or lie in wait, half-hidden, waiting for prey.

We know that the spawning grounds of European and North American freshwater eels are in the Sargasso Sea. But no adult eel has ever been caught there and the eels' long journeys are among the most mysterious of all animal migrations.

The Sargasso Sea. In popular fiction the name conjures up images of ghostly ships on a vast, still sea of weed and wandering seabirds. In fact the Sargasso Sea, which is located south of Bermuda in the western North Atlantic Ocean, is a focus of the great clockwise North Atlantic current and a region of clear tropical water, slight winds, and low biological productivity. It is also the start and end of one of the longest oceanic migrations undertaken by any fish—the so-called "freshwater eels."

Eels are widespread and abundant in the ocean. Their elongate, snake-like shapes grace such diverse ecosystems as tropical coral reefs and the oceans' depths. There are about 720 species in the order of true eels, Anguilliformes, distributed in 21 different families. Our knowledge of the biology of most of these species and families is sparse and generally limited to taxonomy (mainly of adults). We also have information on their geographic distributions and, to a lesser extent, diets and reproductive ecology. The last is of interest here.

Little is known about the reproduction of most species. This is partly because eels tend to be secretive and usually are active only at night. However, the order has a characteristic and distinctive larval stage, known as the leptocephalus. These bizarre-looking creatures, sometimes known as leaf fishes, are only a few centimeters long and occur only in the ocean. They cannot control the chemical composition of their blood and other body fluids, and consequently cannot survive the relatively dilute water of freshwater streams, rivers, and lakes.

Which brings us back to the Sargasso Sea and one of nature's most dramatic and poorly known migrations. Despite the fact that an eel's early life must be spent in the oceans, there are 15 species that live most of their lives in fresh water. All are in the family Anguillidae and genus *Anguilla*. Two of these—the European eel (*Anguilla*

anguilla) and the American eel (*A. rostrata*) are found in the Atlantic Ocean. Virtually identical in ecology, behavior, and appearance, these eels have been separated into different species because of their ranges and another rather subtle difference— American eels have, on average, eight fewer vertebrae than their European counterparts. Females of each species grow much larger than males, live much longer, and are common in a variety of freshwater habitats, from small, muddy ponds to fast-flowing rocky rivers. Most males, however, appear to remain in estuaries.

That the females inhabit freshwater habitats, but the larvae require salt water to survive dictates the first and most conspicuous element of the migration of the eels—their downstream movement. In autumn, millions of females make their way to the estuaries, where they join with the males. These downstream migrations form the basis of trap fisheries wherever *Anguilla* is found, though the European fishery is by far the largest. As many as 17,000 tonnes (37,500 pounds) of *Anguilla* are caught annually in the rivers of Europe and one small lake on the French coast of the Mediterranean has been estimated to produce between 500,000 and 600,000 eels annually. From the entire coast of Europe literally hundreds of millions of eels migrate down rivers every autumn, pouring into the ocean and onward until they leave the continental shelf. And there, they disappear. Completely and utterly. It is little wonder that such a massive and dramatic movement of animals, supporting a very valuable fishery, inspired immense curiosity as to what drives it, where the fish go, and as importantly, where the fish reproduce.

Early this century, these questions were more than just rhetorical ones. The eel fishery is of vital economic importance to many countries and to ensure that over-fishing did not affect future catches, it was necessary to know where the parents of the returning juveniles originated. Once it had been generally concluded that spawning occurred at sea, the question remained as to whether it occurred near shore, perhaps close to the river mouths, or farther away. If the former, then it was likely that each river system supported its own local population of eels and that catching too many migrating adults could eliminate the population and bring about the collapse of the local fishery. However, if the eels consisted of a single population with a common spawning area somewhere far out at sea, then rivers could be overfished locally with little or no effect on the numbers of returning juveniles. Catch limits could be ignored and fishermen could

▼ It takes young eels about two to three years to cover the distance from their hatching area in the Sargasso Sea to the mouths of freshwater rivers and streams in North America and Europe. Here they change from the larval leptocephalus stage to a transparent form more closely resembling the adults. At this stage they are known as elvers.

EELS—MYSTERY AND MYTHS

Fredrick Ehrenstrom/Oxford Scientific Films

The way in which eels reproduce has always been a mystery. This mystery was fueled by two strange but inescapable truths about the fish—the prodigious downstream movements of the females and the fact that no one ever caught a female full of eggs. To the naturalists and fishermen of pre-twentieth century Europe, however, why the eels migrated and where the young eels came from was far from obvious. The eggs and small juveniles of other fishes, far less common, were easily found and well known but eels were a great riddle.

Where data are sparse, imagination fills the gap, and all sorts of myths developed about eel reproduction. Aristotle suggested that eels arose spontaneously in mud. A much later observer, noting immense numbers of small eels in a gravel bank being excavated, suggested something similar— that eels reproduce more or less underground, or in riverbeds at least. A popular myth, current until the beginning of the twentieth century, held that eels arose from horse hairs that had fallen in the water. Parasitic worms that look a little like tiny eels grow on horse hair and it was thought that they grew into adult eels once they fell into a pond or river.

Others suggested that eels were either live-bearing (due to the frequent presence of eel-like parasites in their tissues) or the offspring of the marine, live-bearing fish, *Zoarces viviparous* (which explained why eggs and small larvae were never found). Even today, in Germany and Italy, the common name of *Zoarces* is "eel-mother."

It is also common to find leptocephali longer than the juveniles that develop from them. Like a caterpillar turning into a butterfly, the transformation can be dramatic. At the end of their larval stages, the fish actually shrink in length. This unusual feature, not widely recognized, led to one of the most spectacular, but wrong, discoveries in recent popular marine biology. During the cruises of the Danish research vessel *Dana,* a leptocephalus was caught that

▲ One of the most persistent of early myths "explaining" the origin of eels was that they were the young of this fish, the eelpout *Zoarces viviparous*, which gives birth to live young.

measured 1.8 meters (6 feet) long. We now know it to be the larva of a species of deep-water notacanthiform. At the time, however, people reasoned that if a 15 centimeter (6 inch) *Anguilla* larva develops into a 2 meter (6 1/2 feet) adult, then a 1.8 meter larva would yield an adult eel 23 meters (76 feet) long. The larva of the sea serpent had been found!

The Bettmann Archive

▲ Eel migrations became entangled with older myths involving sea serpents.

exploit the local downstream migrations of females to their hearts' content.

To answer this economically important question, in 1905 the Danish government commissioned Johannes Schmidt to lead a fisheries research team to find the spawning grounds of the Danish eel populations. Previous attempts had consisted of trying to catch ripe females at sea. This worked well with many other fishes, but had failed miserably for eels. Despite the migration of literally millions of eels into the ocean each year, only a few had ever been caught there and none had been caught away from the continental shelf. (This is still true.) Further, none of the females carried particularly well-developed eggs. For this reason, Schmidt approached the problem from the other direction. If you can't find or track the adults, find and track the larvae. When you find the youngest, then you have found the spawning grounds. In what is now considered a classic piece of research, Schmidt arranged for the collection of larvae from ships all across the Atlantic.

The results were stunning. Small larval *Anguilla* were caught all right, but nowhere near Europe. Rather, the youngest larvae were caught more than 3,000 kilometers (1,860 miles) away—in the Sargasso Sea. Larvae increased in size as they were caught closer to their native coasts.

Although we still do not know the details of what happens at sea, the general outline is clear. Each year the males and females of both Atlantic species move offshore, descending to depths of 150 to 800 meters (490 to 2,600 feet). They converge on the Sargasso Sea, tens of thousands of tonnes of eels probably in huge shoals, swimming through the ocean depths. The trip from Europe takes at least five to six months of continuous swimming aided by the currents; that from the American coast takes somewhat less (or it is possible that the European adults spend an extra year in transit and rely more heavily on transport by the currents).

As determined by the location of the smallest identified larvae (sometimes only hours old), spawning by the European species occurs south and southeast of Bermuda, whereas the American species spawns farther to the west. Both species apparently spawn at depths of between 200 and 700 meters (650 and 2,300 feet). Spawning has never been observed, but in other types of eels it often involves one or more males seizing a female with their jaws just behind her head and then, while

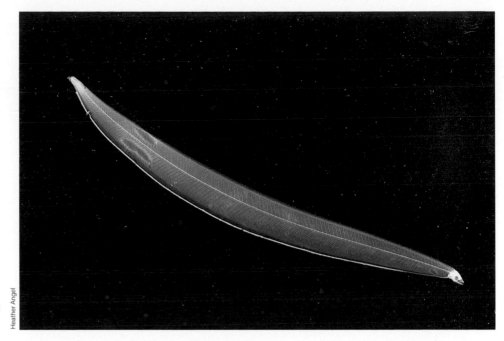

Heather Angel

wrapped in a spawning embrace, shedding eggs and milt. The fertilized eggs drift surfaceward, hatch into the leptocephalus, and begin the long journey back to the coast. The adults then die, so far as we know, their millions of decaying, spent bodies presumably littering the sea bottom south of Bermuda.

And the return journey begins.

The paths of the American and European larvae are much the same at the onset of the return journey. Drifting westward as they grow, the leaf-like larvae are caught in the Gulf Stream—the warm poleward-flowing current that originates in the American tropics and sweeps along the eastern coast of the United States before turning east toward northern Europe. Larvae of the

▲ Eel eggs are laid and fertilized at great depths in the Sargasso Sea near Bermuda, and drift slowly to the surface. They then hatch into tiny leaf-shaped transparent larvae, known as leptocephali.

◄ So persistent is the eels' trek upriver that some individuals may leave the water altogether, and wriggle through wet grass toward isolated swamps and ponds.

John Lythgoe/Planet Earth Pictures

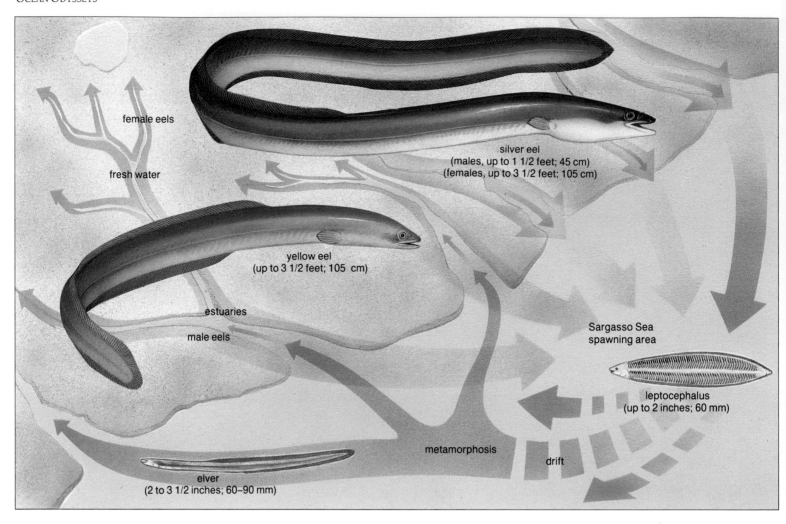

female eels

fresh water

silver eel
(males, up to 1 1/2 feet; 45 cm)
(females, up to 3 1/2 feet; 105 cm)

yellow eel
(up to 3 1/2 feet; 105 cm)

estuaries

male eels

Sargasso Sea
spawning area

leptocephalus
(up to 2 inches; 60 mm)

metamorphosis

drift

elver
(2 to 3 1/2 inches; 60–90 mm)

▲ The life cycle of the American eel (*Anguilla rostrata*). Adults spawn in the Sargasso Sea. After hatching, the larvae drift to the North American coast where they metamorphize into glass eels or "elvers." As they move up the estuaries of freshwater rivers, they grow larger, becoming yellow (or juvenile) eels. Finally, as they mature, they start back down the rivers, transforming into the sea-going silver eel. Their eyes enlarge and their gonads develop.

American *Anguilla* ride the Gulf Stream for about six to eight months, turning westward from it and migrating into coastal estuaries where they transform into juvenile eels. Larvae of the European species stay in the warm oceanic current for a period of two and a half to three years. Comparisons of Gulf Stream current speeds with length of larval duration suggest that the movement of larvae destined for America is essentially passive. European eels probably take some active part in their transport to make it back to the coast of Europe and the Mediterranean Sea within three years. At the end of this larval period, the developing eels shrink in total length, take on a rounded appearance, and move inshore and toward the bottom. They appear to be attracted to fresh water by chemical cues (in at least some cases, the "smell" of bacteria on decaying leaves), though details of the process have not been fully determined. It is unlikely that larvae "home" to the river systems from which their parents emerged three years earlier.

The juvenile eels, largely transparent and about 6 to 7 centimeters (2 1/2 inches) long, form thick columns of individuals, swimming close along river and estuary banks as they move upstream. The return of the "glass eels," as they are called, takes place from autumn through to late spring, occurring at different seasons in different places. These juveniles work their way upriver with remarkable persistence, crawling up and over small waterfalls and, it has been suggested, even traveling overland on damp nights to reach the isolated ponds and lakes where they will grow.

So, the cycle begins again.

Despite the large amount of research done on Atlantic eels, much remains a riddle about their migration. What separates the larvae of the American species from those larvae destined for Europe? We know there are slight differences between the species in morphology, and they separate readily using biochemical genetic techniques. But why don't we get the occasional European eel attracted to American shores, and vice versa?

To account for this phenomenon, in 1959 it was suggested that the two species are, in fact, identical. According to this theory, European eels do not migrate to the Sargasso Sea to spawn but die off the European coast, before reproducing. The only eels to reach the Sargasso Sea and spawn are American eels. The larvae produced by these adults are swept northward in the Gulf Stream and those that are swept past the American coast and grow to maturity in Europe are "surplus" fish, an evolutionary dead end. After they make their downriver trip in autumn they simply swim a short distance off the coast, and die.

Superficially, the structural and genetic differences between the American and European species of *Anguilla* falsify this hypothesis. However, because these differences in morphology and genetics can also result from strong selection on very young larvae, the only way to prove conclusively that *Anguilla anguilla* migrates to and spawns in the Sargasso Sea is to catch one there. And so far, no adult *Anguilla*, of either species, has been caught anywhere near the Sargasso Sea.

Assuming that conventional wisdom is correct, and that both the American and European eels migrate to and spawn in the Sargasso Sea, we are still left with what is perhaps the biggest riddle—why? What is so special about the Sargasso Sea that an animal with a relatively feeble swimming ability would undertake a migration of thousands of kilometers, in the depths of the ocean, in order to reproduce and die there? Nothing about the Sargasso Sea suggests it to be a particularly good spot in which to spawn planktonic larvae. If anything, because of a typically low level of nutrients in the waters of the region, it would seem a less suitable spawning ground than a lot of other spots much closer to home.

We cannot know why an animal does something. We can only guess at the adaptive significance of a behavioral pattern. Our first clue comes from examining the behavior of other species of *Anguilla*. The migratory behavior of the North Atlantic *Anguilla* seems not to be unique to these species. Although details are lacking, it appears that *Anguilla* species in the Pacific also migrate offshore and into deep water to spawn. The distances traveled are much less, but the pattern is similar. So the question becomes not "Why does the European eel migrate?" but "Why does it migrate so far?"

The answer to this question may lie not in the biology of the species, but in its history. Eels are an old fish lineage, and the group to which they belong can be recognized in the fossil record to at least the early Cretaceous period, some 130 million years ago. In the Cretaceous, the world was a very different place. Warm and wet, dinosaurs still stalked

the land and swam in the seas while primitive birds clambered among the flowering plants which had just burst onto the evolutionary scene. More importantly from our perspective, the distribution of landmasses and oceans was quite different from that of today. According to the theory of continental drift, the rift zone that ultimately formed the Atlantic Ocean had at this time only just split apart the European and American continental landmasses. We can never know for certain, but it is likely that the ancestors of the modern Atlantic species of *Anguilla* spawned in the relatively small body of deep water between the spreading continents. In the 100 million years since then, as the Atlantic Ocean grew and the distance between America and Europe increased minutely each year, perhaps the eels have remained faithful to this original spawning ground. Each year, they swam just a little farther to reach it, with the result that the European species now undertakes one of the most prodigious migrations in the entire vertebrate world.

▲ Eels fall prey to a wide variety of fish-eating birds and other animals. Here, a gray heron attempts to subdue an eel.

▼ The drift of leptocephali from eel spawning areas in the Sargasso Sea. The position of the eels is shown at yearly intervals. The leptocephali drift with the ocean currents, reaching the coast of North America within two years and the European coast one to two years later.

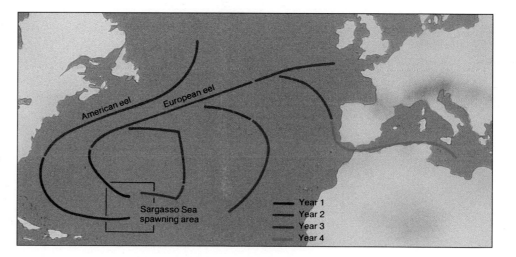

SALMON

Thomas Quinn

Every year many millions of salmon travel from far out in the oceans to the rivers where they were spawned years earlier. They swim sometimes huge distances upstream, jumping rapids and waterfalls, to spawn and then die.

For years anglers and scientists suspected that adult salmon migrating upriver were returning to where they were spawned, noting that salmon differed in appearance, and in times of migration, from one river to another. Tagging studies have recently confirmed this.

The term salmon usually refers to Atlantic salmon (*Salmo salar*), native to Europe and North America, and the species of Pacific salmon (genus *Oncorhynchus*), found in North America and Asia. The family Salmonidae however, also includes trout and chars. The life cycles of all these fishes are variations on themes of migration.

UP FROM THE GRAVEL

The eggs of salmon, trout, and chars are fertilized by the male and buried by the female in a gravel depression which she constructs, usually in a cool stream. She lays about 2,000 to 4,000 eggs, depending on her species and size. They develop in the darkness and require only a supply of clean, well-oxygenated water. After a few months the eggs hatch. Each hatchling, or alevin, has a large, bright orange yolk sac attached to its middle. The alevin will remain in the gravel for several weeks or more until this yolk sac with its stored food has been exhausted.

▲ Humpback salmon (*Oncorhynchus gorbuscha*) congregate in readiness for spawning. The salmon and trout constitute a family of fishes characterized by their heavy demand for oxygen and are most common in cool northern rivers and streams. Salmon (and some trout) species spend much of their lives in the sea, returning to their natal streams to breed and die.

▼ Migratory patterns of Atlantic salmon in the Northern Atlantic.

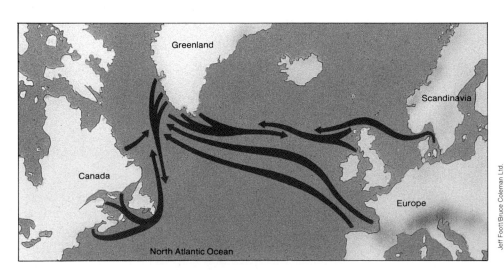

In the spring, when there is no yolk left, the tiny salmon, known as fry, wriggle up through the gravel and out into the stream to begin foraging on their own. While cool, clean streams are safe places for eggs to incubate, they provide little food for hungry young fry. Some species, such as chum salmon (*Oncorhynchus keta*) and pink salmon (*O. gorbuscha*), leave the stream soon after emerging from the gravel and migrate to the ocean. Sockeye salmon (*O. nerka*) also leave the stream, spending a year or more in a lake before migrating to sea.

Most other species, such as Atlantic salmon, brown trout (*Salmo trutta*), rainbow trout (*Oncorhynchus mykiss*), coho salmon (*O. kisutch*), and chinook salmon (*O. tshawytscha*), stay in the stream for up to one or two years before migrating to sea. They set up territories which they defend aggressively, feeding on insects and food particles that drift downstream. When there is sufficient food, territories are small, but if it is scarce each fish must defend a larger

▼ Sockeye salmon leaping a waterfall in a Canadian river on the way to their spawning grounds.

area in order to find enough to eat. Fishes that are unable to establish territories are forced downstream into less favorable areas.

DOWN TO THE OCEAN

In spring, the young salmon, known as smolts, leave the safety of their freshwater rearing areas, and swim rapidly toward the sea. Collectively, the rivers flowing into the North Pacific and Atlantic Oceans are filled with billions of these young salmon, running the gauntlet of predators, chiefly birds and larger fish. These migrations usually take place at night and are often precisely timed. For example, in 1981 about 193 million sockeye salmon left just one lake, Babine Lake in British Columbia, Canada. Half the fishes left on four consecutive nights, converging on the outlet from distant points of the lake, which is 160 kilometers (100 miles) long.

▲ Salmon eggs are laid in the gravel bed of rivers and streams, and hatch in about two months. The young remain in the gravel another month until the yolk sac is completely absorbed, then wriggle free to begin life in the open stream.

The seaward journey is considerably more hazardous for the fishes when there are dams. The Columbia River in the western United States once flowed freely from its headwaters in British Columbia, and its major tributary, the Snake River, ran unimpeded from Idaho, Montana, and Nevada. Now the upper reaches of both these rivers are blocked by huge dams, and the lower reaches consist largely of a series of lakes, created by further dams. The seaward progress of young salmon is slowed by the slack water in the reservoirs and when they reach the dams they are often swept into the turbines and killed. The surviving fishes emerge downstream in a dazed condition, to be confronted by predatory fishes and birds. It has been estimated that 15 percent of the smolts are lost at each dam, which has a devastating cumulative effect.

WHY DO SALMON GO TO SEA?

If the journey to sea is so perilous, why do salmon migrate there at all? In fact, some do not. The benefits and costs of such migrations vary from species to species.

Salmon eat fish, squid, krill, and other small organisms. The oceanic waters of the northern latitudes, where salmon and trout are plentiful, provide the fishes with more food than do the rivers and lakes, so they grow more quickly. Seagoing (anadramous) trout and salmon are much larger at a given age than those that remain in freshwater environments, which is beneficial when the time comes to reproduce. Large females can lay more eggs than small ones, and large males can battle successfully for access to females.

Nevertheless, the disadvantages of going to sea are considerable. Ordinary freshwater fishes die in salt water, and even salmon will die if they are forced into salt water before their kidneys, excretory systems, and gills have had time to adapt. In addition to the physiological stress of this bodily transformation for life at sea, salmon face a formidable range of predators both in their passage down and upriver and while they are in the ocean. At sea they are eaten by large fishes, birds, and mammals such as seals and killer whales.

For some salmon, such as the pink salmon, the benefits of oceanic migration outweigh the costs, and all members of the species go to sea. For others, such as the rainbow trout, the benefits of migration are roughly equalled by the costs, and only some populations go to sea. Still others, such as the lake trout native to North America (*Salvelinus namaycush*), and the huchen of Europe (*Hucho hucho*), spend their entire lives in freshwater environments.

LIFE ON THE HIGH SEAS

Atlantic and Pacific salmon often travel tremendous distances to reach their ocean habitats. Many Atlantic salmon from both Europe and North America converge on food-rich waters off the west coast of

Greenland. From England this is a one-way journey of about 4,000 kilometers (2,500 miles).

In the Pacific Ocean most young salmon swim north, forming a great, diffuse river of fish about 8 to 30 kilometers (5 to 20 miles) offshore. They enter the ocean in late spring and by autumn they are present in vast numbers in the Gulf of Alaska, near Kodiak Island. They then seem to move south into open waters. Little is known about salmon migrations during winter, but in spring they travel north and west. Dispersed, rather than in schools, they swim near the surface, following the warming water and the rich supplies of food.

The salmon spend from one to four or more years at sea. In the spring and summer of their last year at sea their movements become more directed, and they begin their long journey home to spawn.

FINDING THEIR WAY HOME

What guides the salmon in this remarkable homeward migration? It seems they use both the earth's magnetic field and the sun's position as navigational aids. Not only do they find their way home, but they return at a specific time, year after year. For example, about 80 percent of the millions of sockeye salmon homing to Bristol Bay, Alaska, arrive within a two-week period. Just a few months earlier, these fish would have been spread out over a great expanse of ocean. It appears that they can detect changes in day length, which indicates the time of year, and thus have an internal calendar. This probably tells them when it is time to begin their homeward journey.

The salmon swim homeward on a constant course for weeks, at rates of up to 60 kilometers (40 miles) per day. Once they reach coastal waters they often have to make

▲ Sockeye salmon spawning. On returning to the breeding stream from their ocean feeding grounds, these salmon stop feeding and the males turn bright red, with dull green heads. After spawning they are exhausted through lack of food, the journey from the sea, and the stresses of breeding. All die within a few days.

133

Randy Time/DRK Photo

▲ Recently classified as a salmon, the rainbow trout (*Oncorhynchus mykiss*) is well-known to sport fishermen everywhere, and has been introduced to many parts of the world. Some populations migrate to the sea for some part of their life cycle; others do not.

their way around countless islands, and as they do not always retrace their outward paths, this can be problematic. Generally they reverse course and swim out to sea again for a few hours before turning and resuming their homeward orientation. Where there are many islands the fishes spend much time backtracking, their journey resembling the path of a pinball on the downward slope of a table.

THE FINAL LEG OF THE JOURNEY
In spite of the ravages of predators and fishermen, many salmon reach the mouths of the rivers from which they originated. They either spend several days or weeks in the estuary, or immediately swim upriver. In order to return home, the physiological processes that enabled them to go to sea must be reversed. At this stage they also lose the silvery appearance of marine fishes and start to take on their dramatic spawning colors. Sockeye salmon, for example, are bright red with green heads.

For some salmon the trip to their spawning ground is short. Others, such as those from the upper reaches of the Yukon River, have to swim as much as 3,000 kilometers (1,900 miles) upriver. This is an exhausting undertaking, made even more

remarkable by the fact that salmon do not eat during this final phase of the trip. Those fishes that had to negotiate dams on the way downriver, have to cope with them once more on the way back up. Some early dams were built without provision for salmon passage, but many now have ladders. Salmon ascend ladders by jumping from one pool to the next, working their way upstream. Without a ladder, the salmon's efforts to migrate upstream would be frustrated and they would be forced to jump in vain or spawn below the dam.

On their journey upriver to the stream they left years earlier, salmon may pass dozens of rivers suitable for spawning, many with their own salmon species. It is their sense of smell that enables them to identify their own spawning grounds. Juvenile salmon learn the particular smells of their home river before they leave for the ocean, and they home to these on their return journey.

By the time the salmon reach their spawning grounds their appearance has changed greatly. Males have developed long, hooked jaws and sharp teeth—weapons they will use to battle for females. They may also grow a large hump on their backs, most notably in the case of the pink (humpback) salmon. The snouts and teeth of females also develop but not to the extent of males. Their colors resemble those of males but tend to be less dramatic.

The female chooses a place for the nest where there is good water circulation, and makes a depression in the gravel by turning on her side and sweeping her tail rapidly upward. When prime sites are in short supply females fight fiercely for the best spots. Males will court a female until she has spawned all her eggs, fertilize them, then leave her for another female. The female will guard her nest, to prevent other females from digging up the eggs.

After spawning, a small proportion of the fishes of some species, such as steelhead trout (*Oncorhynchus mykiss*), Atlantic salmon, and brown trout, survive and return to the sea, later to repeat the migration. The most numerous species of the Pacific salmon, however, make the cycle only once, dying after they spawn.

OVERFISHING AND HABITAT DEGRADATION

The return of salmon to coastal waters and rivers has always provided fishermen with rich catches, and in Europe there have been traditions and laws for centuries to regulate salmon fishing. Despite these, many runs have been badly depleted. Commercial fishing is now so efficient that complex regulations need to be enforced to ensure that stocks remain viable.

In common with many long-distance migrants, salmon range over a variety of habitats. During their lives they are found in small streams, beaver ponds, lakes, large rivers, estuaries, coastal waters, and the open ocean. Degradation of any one of these habitats will put the fishes at risk. When salmon fail to thrive it is a sure sign that the waters in which they are living have been spoiled.

While there are still a large number of runs of Pacific salmon, particularly in British Columbia and Alaska, many populations have been reduced or destroyed. Populations of Atlantic salmon in North America and Europe are much smaller than they once were. There are many reasons for these losses. Overfishing, logging, roadbuilding, dam construction, and pollution have all had an effect. Rivers have become silted and clogged with logging debris, water temperatures have increased through the removal of trees. Atlantic salmon must also contend with dangerously low pH levels associated with acid rain.

A common response to the loss of so many spawning and rearing areas has been to build hatcheries, but these are a poor substitute for natural production. By boosting salmon numbers they also encourage heavy fishing, resulting in the overfishing of nearby wild runs. As a result, hatchery fishes are increasingly taking the place of wild stock.

If salmon numbers are to be maintained and safeguarded, much more care must be taken of their natural habitats, and fishing must be effectively regulated.

▲ Many populations of salmon have been decimated by overfishing, the construction of dams, and water pollution. The Atlantic salmon is a commercially important species, and attempts are being made to produce them in hatcheries and fish farms like this one in the Loftolen Islands, Norway.

◀ Salmon returning to their breeding streams to spawn provide food for many predators, like this bald eagle in Alaska.

THE LIFE CYCLE OF THE SOCKEYE SALMON

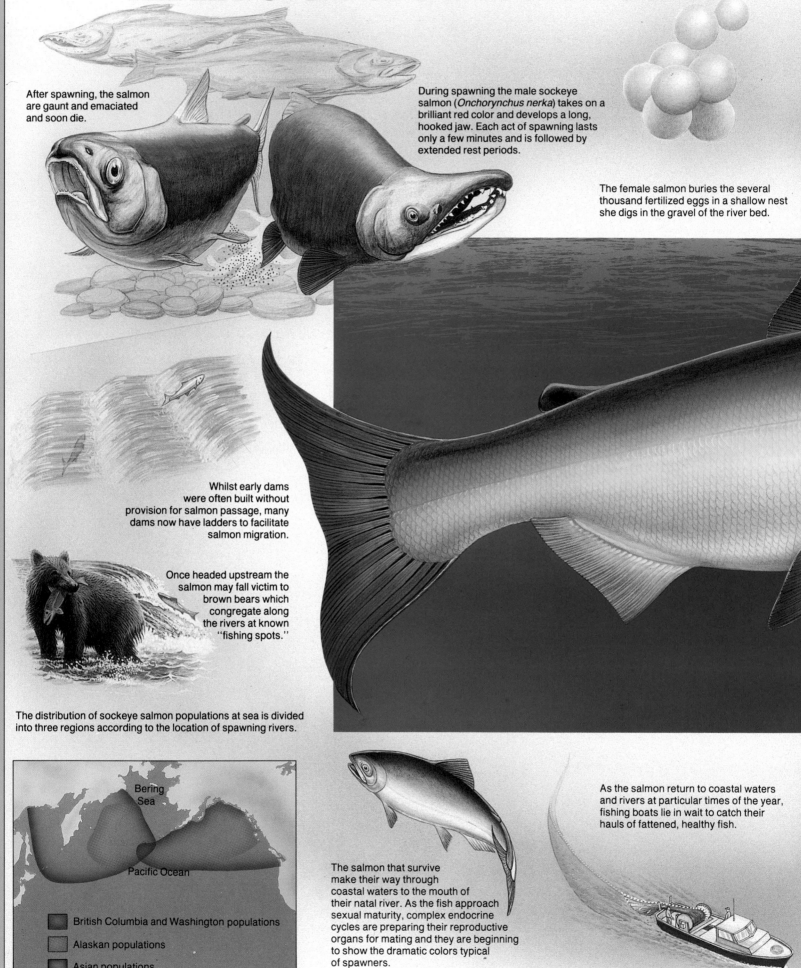

After spawning, the salmon are gaunt and emaciated and soon die.

During spawning the male sockeye salmon (*Onchorynchus nerka*) takes on a brilliant red color and develops a long, hooked jaw. Each act of spawning lasts only a few minutes and is followed by extended rest periods.

The female salmon buries the several thousand fertilized eggs in a shallow nest she digs in the gravel of the river bed.

Whilst early dams were often built without provision for salmon passage, many dams now have ladders to facilitate salmon migration.

Once headed upstream the salmon may fall victim to brown bears which congregate along the rivers at known "fishing spots."

The distribution of sockeye salmon populations at sea is divided into three regions according to the location of spawning rivers.

Bering Sea

Pacific Ocean

British Columbia and Washington populations

Alaskan populations

Asian populations

The salmon that survive make their way through coastal waters to the mouth of their natal river. As the fish approach sexual maturity, complex endocrine cycles are preparing their reproductive organs for mating and they are beginning to show the dramatic colors typical of spawners.

As the salmon return to coastal waters and rivers at particular times of the year, fishing boats lie in wait to catch their hauls of fattened, healthy fish.

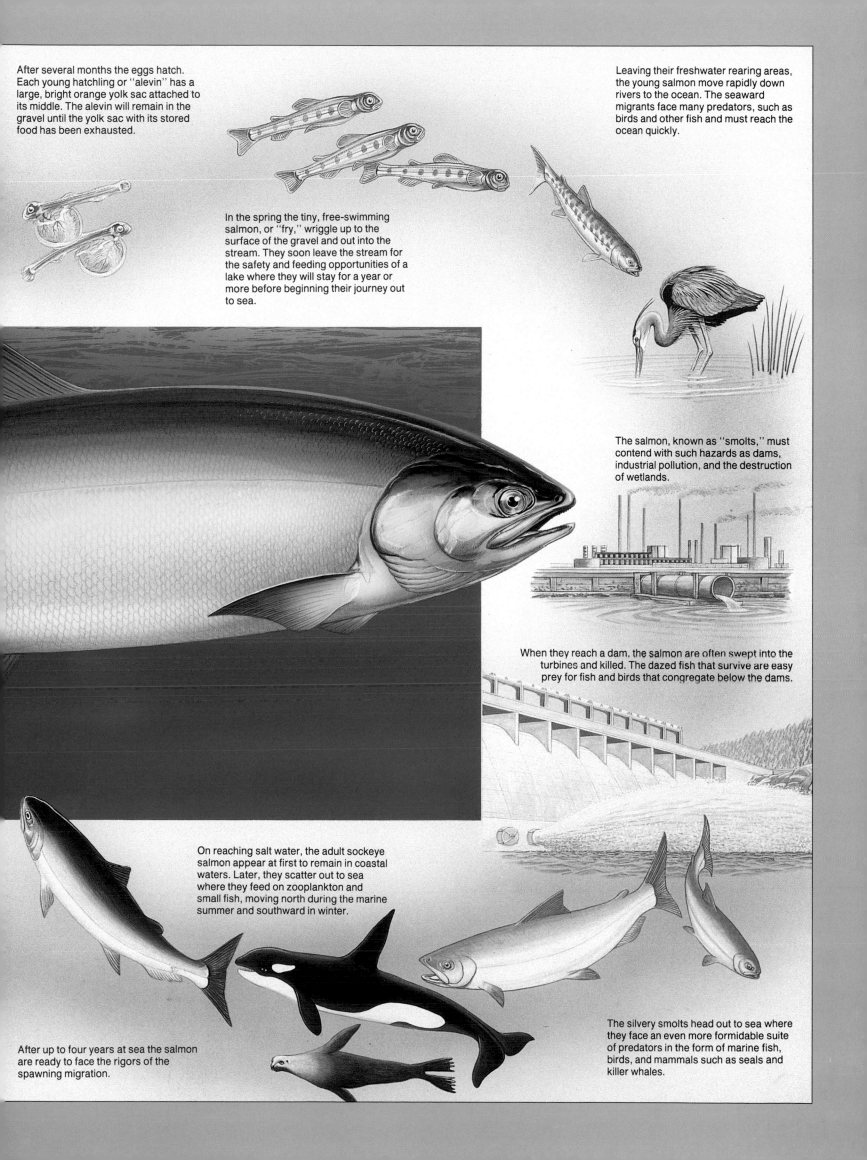

After several months the eggs hatch. Each young hatchling or "alevin" has a large, bright orange yolk sac attached to its middle. The alevin will remain in the gravel until the yolk sac with its stored food has been exhausted.

In the spring the tiny, free-swimming salmon, or "fry," wriggle up to the surface of the gravel and out into the stream. They soon leave the stream for the safety and feeding opportunities of a lake where they will stay for a year or more before beginning their journey out to sea.

Leaving their freshwater rearing areas, the young salmon move rapidly down rivers to the ocean. The seaward migrants face many predators, such as birds and other fish and must reach the ocean quickly.

The salmon, known as "smolts," must contend with such hazards as dams, industrial pollution, and the destruction of wetlands.

When they reach a dam, the salmon are often swept into the turbines and killed. The dazed fish that survive are easy prey for fish and birds that congregate below the dams.

On reaching salt water, the adult sockeye salmon appear at first to remain in coastal waters. Later, they scatter out to sea where they feed on zooplankton and small fish, moving north during the marine summer and southward in winter.

After up to four years at sea the salmon are ready to face the rigors of the spawning migration.

The silvery smolts head out to sea where they face an even more formidable suite of predators in the form of marine fish, birds, and mammals such as seals and killer whales.

MARINE TURTLES

Colin J. Limpus

Long-lived relics from the age of the dinosaurs, giant marine turtles are a common feature of the tropical seas. These animals migrate huge distances from their feeding grounds to particular regions where they mate and lay their eggs, but scientists cannot yet explain how they navigate over open ocean with such accuracy.

▲ A newly hatched green turtle makes a dash for the comparative safety of the open sea. Hatchlings are extremely vulnerable to predation on land and in inshore waters.

▼ Mating loggerhead turtles (*Caretta caretta*). Both males and females mate with a series of partners over a breeding season. The female stores the males' sperm and, after the courtship period is over, uses it to fertilize about four clutches of eggs, each clutch containing around 125 eggs.

Many fascinating discoveries have been made recently concerning marine turtles, and with them has come an appreciation of the complexities of their migrations. The precision with which marine turtles can cross large expanses of open ocean to make a landfall on a specific locality is best illustrated by the green turtles (*Chelonia mydas*) that feed along the Brazilian coast of South America. Each year thousands of these turtles migrate 2,300 kilometers (1,500 miles) eastward from the Brazilian coast out into the middle of the Atlantic Ocean to their nesting beaches on Ascension Island. As this island is only 11 kilometers (7 miles) wide, the trip is an amazing feat of navigation.

BREEDING PATTERNS

The life history of most marine turtle species can be summarized as follows. Adult males and females migrate up to thousands of kilometers from their home feeding areas to their traditional nesting beaches, which are known as rookeries. Mating occurs in the neighborhood of the rookeries, with the mating period varying between the sexes. The female is sexually attractive to males for about a week, and during this time she is inseminated by a series of different males. She does not use the sperm received at this time, but stores it. The male is sexually active for about a month, during which time he usually mates with a series of different females. At the end of the courtship period,

Jean-Paul Ferrero/Auscape

he returns home. When the female has completed her mating she moves up to 100 kilometers (60 miles) to the immediate vicinity of her nesting beach. Here she commences egg production, using some of the stored sperm to fertilize the eggs. It takes approximately two weeks for her to prepare a clutch of eggs. When they are ready, she hauls out onto her nesting beach and lays a clutch of about 120 eggs. Her first clutch for the season is normally laid about four weeks after mating. Having laid the eggs, she returns to the sea and waits near the nesting beach while she prepares her next clutch of eggs, again fertilizing them from her sperm store. When this is completed she returns to her nesting beach and lays a second clutch, again of about 120 eggs, some two weeks after the first. This is repeated throughout the nesting season, with some turtles laying up to 11 clutches of eggs at two-weekly intervals. All the eggs from any one female are usually laid within a few hundred meters of each other.

During the nesting season the female remains in a relatively small area of sea adjacent to the rookery, known as her internesting habitat. At the end of the season, she returns to her home feeding area. For the months that she has been absent she will have spent very little time feeding, living instead off fat reserves stored up before the breeding migration began.

▲ Egg laying complete, a loggerhead turtle fills in her nest cavity with sand before returning to the sea.

▼ Green turtles living off the coast of Brazil migrate to Ascension Island to mate and lay their eggs, a navigational feat that remains one of the great mysteries of animal migration.

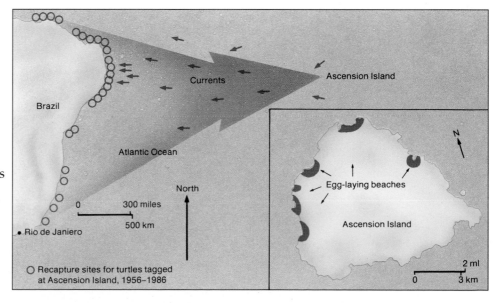

Currents

Ascension Island

Brazil

Atlantic Ocean

North

0   300 miles

500 km

Rio de Janiero

○ Recapture sites for turtles tagged at Ascension Island, 1956–1986

Egg-laying beaches

Ascension Island

N

2 ml

0   3 km

139

The same female does not usually breed in successive years. For most species, it will be two to eight years before she makes another breeding migration. When she does, she will usually return to the rookery where she previously nested. The males make their breeding migrations more frequently than the females, returning to mate in the same areas in successive breeding seasons. In the absence of human interference, the adult marine turtle can be expected to have a long breeding life, repeating these migrations many times over several decades.

WHEN THE EGGS HATCH

Once the female has buried her eggs deep in the sand above the reach of the tides, she provides her offspring with no further parental care. The eggs incubate in the moist sand, warmed by the sun, the temperature of the sand surrounding the eggs determining how long they take to hatch. They can take 13 weeks in cool sand, whereas they hatch within 7 weeks in warm sand. The temperature of the nest during mid-term incubation also determines the sex of the resulting hatchlings: warm nests can produce all female hatchlings, while cool nests can produce all males. Marine turtles do not have sex chromosomes as humans do. After emerging from their eggs, the hatchlings

have to dig their way up for several days to reach the surface. They wait until after dark to move away from the nest, thus avoiding the potentially lethal hot surface sands of daylight hours. Throughout the entire process of departure from the nest and dispersal from the rookery, the hatchling turtles have no large turtles present to follow or to mimic; they are entirely driven by instinctive behavior. Once they leave the nest, the hatchlings immediately scurry seaward, seemingly attracted to the dim glow of light reflected off the ocean surface, which makes the seaward direction brighter than the landward direction. Even on a moonless night there is enough light to guide them out to sea.

On most beaches, relatively few hatchlings are taken by crabs and birds. It is once they are in the water that they are at greatest risk. When they reach the sea the hatchlings immediately swim for the open ocean, and as they cross the shallow inshore areas many are eaten by fish or sharks. Only after several days of frenzied swimming do the little turtles rest and start feeding on the planktonic animals they encounter on the surface. In some places the young turtles hide among floating seaweed mats.

It appears that the young turtles then drift with the ocean currents for several years,

▼ After hatching in their underground nest chamber, the young turtles scramble to the surface. It may take them several days to reach the open air, but when they finally emerge it is usually at night.

perhaps making one or more circuits of the full ocean current system (ocean gyre) before changing to a bottom-dwelling lifestyle in continental shelf waters. Little is known of this post-hatchling period, but once the turtles take up life on the ocean floor the picture is clearer. They colonize many different habitats, from coral reefs to muddy estuaries, and feed on a wide range of foods, depending on the species. For example, green turtles are herbivores and feed mostly on seagrasses, algae, and mangroves; loggerhead turtles (*Caretta caretta*) are omnivores, and feed on a mixture of sponges and algae. Leatherback turtles (*Dermochelys coriacea*) feed on large planktonic animals like jellyfish throughout their lives.

THE BREEDING MIGRATION

When a young turtle settles in a feeding area on the ocean floor, it remains in that general vicinity for the decades that it takes to grow from a hatchling into an adult. When they finally reach adulthood, turtles preparing for a breeding migration take more than a year to lay down the fat reserves that they will need for the journey. In the months before the breeding migration, the female produces the many hundreds of mature follicles in the ovaries that she will use as yolks in egg production. At the same time, the male is preparing for migration by producing and storing vast amounts of sperm. Only those adults that have laid down extra fat reserves and prepared their gonads for breeding will leave the feeding areas. Immature turtles and adults that are not breeding that year remain in the home feeding areas.

Tagging studies have shown that female turtles living in the one feeding area neither all nest at the same rookery, nor commence migration together. Indeed, they depart individually over a period of weeks and subsequently arrive at the mating area alone. Except when mating, the marine turtle has an essentially solitary existence throughout the breeding migration, even though vast

▲ A green turtle at sea. Immature turtles spend several years drifting with the currents of the open ocean. As they near maturity individuals of most species seek out feeding areas, usually in warm, shallow, offshore waters, to settle down in.

141

numbers of them may come together to nest at traditional rookeries.

No one has ever followed a turtle in the wild through its life from hatchling to breeding adult. However, because marine turtles breed at traditional rookeries and because adults display a strong preference for a particular nesting beach, both within a single breeding season and between successive seasons, it is assumed that most

▲ A hawkesbill turtle (*Eretmochelys imbricata*) rests on the bottom of the sea. Marine turtles are among the most solitary of animals and, except when mating, seldom make contact with other members of their own species.

must return to breed at the beach at which they were born.

After more than 30 years of research, however, the paths followed by marine turtles during their migrations are not clear and the mechanisms by which they find their way remain a mystery. Even the much discussed imprinting process through which the hatchling is bonded to its natal area remains unexplained.

THE TURTLE'S SENSES

The turtle has to be self-sufficient from birth, given that it receives no parental care or guidance and may live a significant part of its life without contact with other turtles. Even when they do meet, marine turtles have little capacity for communication with each other. They are mute, and appear to be limited to chemical cues in the form of secretions transmitted through the water and visual cues contained in some postures at courtship and when feeding.

In contrast, marine turtles are very well equipped to detect environmental cues. They have an acute sense of smell and well developed eyesight, with color vision, especially in the blue-green end of the spectrum. Although they have no external ears, they can hear low frequency vibrations that are beyond the range of human hearing, but include the noises generated by waves breaking on a beach. Via their internal ears they can also detect "up and down"ness using the balance organ that responds to forces resulting from the earth's gravitational field. In common with many other migratory species, marine turtles can also detect changes in the earth's magnetic field. Recent research suggests that the turtle's in-built compass is calibrated when the hatchling is first exposed to light as it leaves the nest. In the wild, turtles appear to have an in-built clock, tuned to both the circadian (24-hour) and tidal cycles, by which they regulate their daily activities.

TRACKING TURTLE MOVEMENTS

Almost all the loggerhead turtles of the South Pacific nest on rookeries in the southern Great Barrier Reef. Recapture records of some tagged loggerhead females indicate the complexity of their movements.

An adult female, X38756, was tagged while nesting at Mon Repos Beach in south Queensland and was not seen again for seven years and eight months until she was caught in a shrimp trawl 2,543 kilometers (1,600 miles) away from the rookery in the southern Gulf of Carpentaria on 29 August 1989. Eighty days later she was recaptured laying eggs back at her original nesting beach, and the condition of her ovaries was consistent with her not having bred in the intervening eight years, during which she had traveled a minimum of 5,100 kilometers (3,100 miles). To make the return swim to the rookery she had to average 32 kilometers (20 miles) per day over the 80 days, assuming her migration began the day she was trawled. She would have had to swim firstly northeast to leave the Gulf of Carpentaria, then head generally south after passing through Torres Strait. She would have been exposed to a range of currents throughout the trip, some running with her, some against. It is unlikely that this turtle could have made the return trip so quickly by randomly wandering in search of her nesting beach. The journey would have required purposeful, oriented swimming. As she neared Mon Repos, she would have swum close to, but ignored, other rookeries where loggerhead turtles nest. What recollections of past journeys and associated navigational information are stored in the turtle's memory banks to enable her to make such a circuitous journey to breed?.

Another adult female, X54, was first tagged while nesting on Mon Repos on 15 January 1974, and she laid one clutch for the season. She was recaptured four times at Heron Reef, 158 kilometers (98 miles) from her rookery, between 1975 and 1978. She left Heron Reef on about 26 October 1978, and came ashore to nest at Mon Repos on 2 December 1978 (approximately 37 days later, and four years since her last recorded nesting), eventually laying five clutches for the season. She was recaptured back at Heron Reef once between 1979 and 1981. She returned to Mon Repos on 6 December 1981 (three years after her last recorded nesting) and laid one clutch for the season. Between 1982 and 1985 she was recaptured 29 times back at Heron Reef, and once on neighboring Wistari Reef. Annual internal examination of her reproductive system during this time showed that she did not prepare for breeding in 1982, 1983, and 1984. She did prepare for breeding during 1985, however, and left Heron Reef between 24 and 26 October 1985. She reached Mon Repos on 30 November (about 36 days later, and four years since her last recorded nesting) and laid four clutches for the season. When X54 surfaces for a breath over Heron Reef she is able to see Heron Island, an island where loggerhead turtles come each summer to breed from up to 2,600 kilometers (1,600 miles) away. But she ignores this rookery adjacent to where she lives, and several others nearby, and migrates consistently to lay her eggs at Mon Repos.

HOW DO TURTLES FIND THEIR WAY?

An examination of tag recovery data shows that loggerhead turtles radiate in to the southern Great Barrier Reef rookeries from large distances from the north, south, and east. Some could have found their way by

just following the coast, but for others this is an unsatisfactory explanation. For example, those that migrate in from New Caledonia and from out past the Solomon Islands must cross oceanic waters. Smelling their way home along a trail wafted by the currents also provides an unsatisfactory explanation

David Hughes/Bruce Coleman Ltd.

▲ Pacific Ridleys turtles (*Lepidochelys olivacea*) massing to nest on Nancite Beach in Costa Rica. Human persecution of all marine turtles means that this is now a rare sight in most parts of the world.

▼ Feeding grounds and nesting beaches for loggerhead turtles that migrate to breed on the southern Great Barrier Reef.

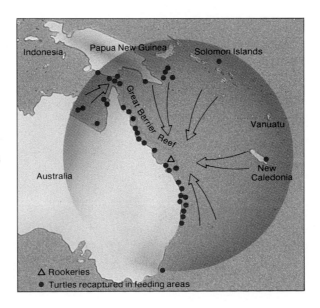

Indonesia
Papua New Guinea
Solomon Islands
Great Barrier Reef
Vanuatu
New Caledonia
Australia

△ Rookeries
● Turtles recaptured in feeding areas

Tom Stack/Tom Stack & Associates

▲ Marine turtles can stay underwater for very long periods but, like any other reptile, they must eventually surface to breathe. Green turtles like this one may reach a length of about 1.2 meters (4 feet) and weigh up to 180 kilograms (400 pounds).

▶ Nesting completed, a green turtle plods its way back to the sea.

of the homing mechanism, for while some turtles would swim with the current, others would have to swim against it. Based on the timing of tag recoveries, made as the turtles return home at the end of a nesting season, it appears that the turtles radiate from a rookery, each one taking its own route home. There appears to be no fixed migratory route that they all follow. To successfully complete a breeding migration, each turtle must be able to perceive its position relative to at least two sites—its nesting beach and its feeding area—and orient its swimming to either of them.

If significant advances are to be made in understanding marine turtle migration and navigation, more information is needed on the precise routes followed by the migrating turtles and several important questions need to be answered. Are the turtles receiving their directional cues while underwater, or when they surface to breathe? Do the turtles swim in relatively direct paths between certain points, or do they swim in some form of search pattern?

There are two separate components to the migrations of the turtles that need to be taken into account. One is the ability of a young adult to return to the natal breeding area from which it drifted some decades before, having traveled perhaps the full ocean gyre in the meantime. The other is the ability of the post-nesting turtle to find its way back to its chosen feeding area.

Currently, the "best guess" assessment is that the turtle is using some broad-scale compass sense, responding to the earth's magnetic field to locate the general area of the rookery. Once in its vicinity, it probably uses a combination of senses, such as hearing, smell, and sight, to locate the nesting beach. If the turtle does not finally choose its original natal beach, but instead chooses one nearby, it must then form a bond with the chosen beach, or the offshore internesting habitat, and be able to recognize it in later breeding seasons. During the migration home, the turtle could use similar processes to locate the feeding area to which it was imprinted during its later years of growth.

144

THE LIFE CYCLE OF THE GREEN TURTLE

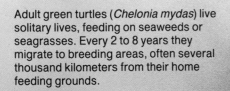

Adult green turtles (*Chelonia mydas*) live solitary lives, feeding on seaweeds or seagrasses. Every 2 to 8 years they migrate to breeding areas, often several thousand kilometers from their home feeding grounds.

Males and females rendezvous at sea to mate near nesting beaches. Copulation takes about six hours. The female mates with several males, storing the sperm and using it to fertilize successive clutches of eggs. Males mate with as many females as they can.

On many beaches, indigenous peoples traditionally dig up nests and take the eggs to eat, and human predation on full-grown adult turtles at sea has greatly reduced many populations. Green turtles are sought for their shells, skin, oil, and meat.

The green turtle is widespread in the warmer oceans of the world, with most populations concentrated at distinct feeding areas in offshore waters throughout the tropics.

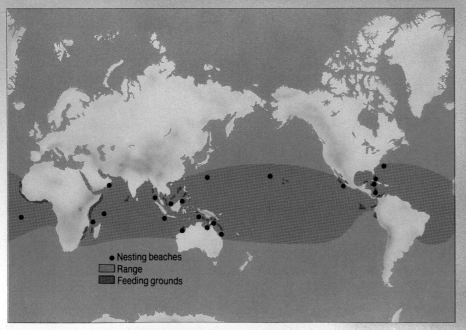

- Nesting beaches
  Range
  Feeding grounds

The young turtle spends several years drifting with the currents of the open ocean, ultimately finding its way to the feeding areas where it will spend the rest of its life, except when breeding.

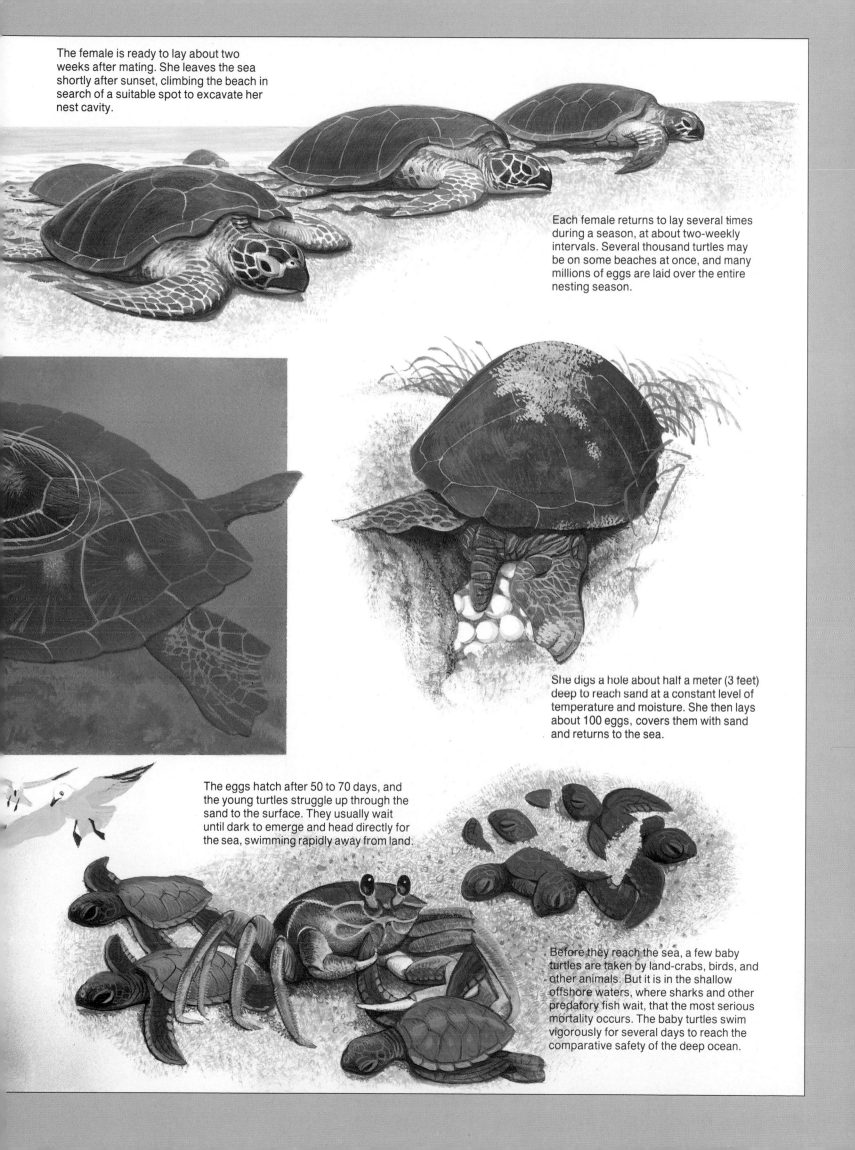

The female is ready to lay about two weeks after mating. She leaves the sea shortly after sunset, climbing the beach in search of a suitable spot to excavate her nest cavity.

Each female returns to lay several times during a season, at about two-weekly intervals. Several thousand turtles may be on some beaches at once, and many millions of eggs are laid over the entire nesting season.

She digs a hole about half a meter (3 feet) deep to reach sand at a constant level of temperature and moisture. She then lays about 100 eggs, covers them with sand and returns to the sea.

The eggs hatch after 50 to 70 days, and the young turtles struggle up through the sand to the surface. They usually wait until dark to emerge and head directly for the sea, swimming rapidly away from land.

Before they reach the sea, a few baby turtles are taken by land-crabs, birds, and other animals. But it is in the shallow offshore waters, where sharks and other predatory fish wait, that the most serious mortality occurs. The baby turtles swim vigorously for several days to reach the comparative safety of the deep ocean.

SEALS, SEA LIONS, AND WALRUSES

M.M. Bryden

Frans Lanting/Minden Pictures

Seals, sea lions, and walruses (known collectively as pinnipeds) are born on land, or in some cases on sea ice, and lead amphibious lives. Although not ranked among the world's great migrators, some of them range widely from their birth place.

Unlike those migrating animals that undergo mass migrations of entire populations, pinnipeds prefer to travel alone or in small groups. Recent studies have revealed that some pinnipeds, for example, male elephant seals, migrate over great distances, returning to their place of origin to molt and breed.

The amount of time spent in the sea and on land varies among families, and to a lesser extent among genera. Some species haul out from the sea quite regularly, particularly in their juvenile years. In general, newborn fur seals and sea lions (otariids) remain tied to the land for longer periods than newborn true seals (phocids). Fur seal and sea lion females leave their pups on land from a few days after birth, making feeding forays that last several days and returning regularly to suckle their young. This continues for weeks or even months. In contrast, true seals remain with and suckle their pups for a relatively short period after birth, in some species only a few days, fasting for most if not all the lactation period. The most extreme example is the hooded seal (*Cystophora cristata*), which weans its pup at only 4 days old.

True seal pups grow very rapidly, usually increasing their birth weight three- or four-fold during this brief suckling period.

The extent to which breeding females are tied to the land because of the need to suckle their pups influences their freedom to travel. In those species in which lactation is protracted, long-distance migration is confined to males, whereas in those with shorter lactation periods, both sexes are equally free to move about. Nonetheless, the females of many true seals do not travel far.

FUR SEALS

Migrations are not regular among most of the fur seals, although they range widely while feeding. Some species, for example the New Zealand fur seal (*Arctocephalus forsteri*) and the Australian fur seal (*A. pusillus*), make seasonal movements between breeding grounds in one region and hauling out areas in another, but these migrations are mainly confined to males. New Zealand fur seals tend to move north in late summer, and south again in late winter, just prior to the spring breeding season.

Among fur seals, the northern fur seal (*Callorhinus ursinus*) has the most distinctive pattern of migration. During winter and spring large numbers of these seals migrate

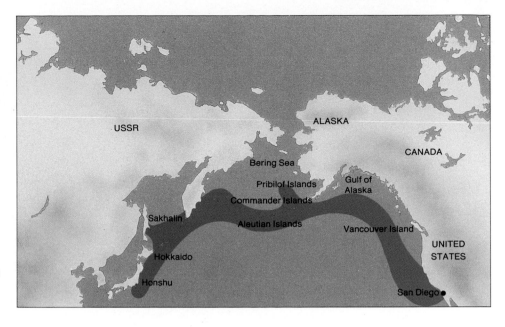

south from breeding grounds on St George and St Paul Islands in the Pribilof group, Copper and Bering Islands of the Commander group, and Robben Island off Sakhalin. Adult bulls do not migrate far, and probably spend the winter in the north, in the Gulf of Alaska. Young seals of both sexes and the adult females range the farthest. The lactation period in this species is shorter than in many other fur seals, which gives the females the freedom to move far from their breeding grounds during winter. The limits of the southward migration are at about latitude 35°N on the western side of the Pacific, and 33°N (at San Diego, California) on the eastern side.

The migration starts from the Pribilof Islands in late September, and the majority of seals have left by December. Most of the animals head southeast, to become widely dispersed between the Aleutian Islands and Vancouver Island. They keep 50 to 100 kilometers (30 to 60 miles) offshore, traveling alone or in small groups of up to about 10 animals. Some move into the deep Alaskan inlets to feed on herring, and occasionally sick animals come ashore between British Columbia and California, or are washed ashore, dead.

Migration northward begins in April and by May there are again large numbers of seals in the Gulf of Alaska. Breeding seals are by this time arriving in the region of the Pribilofs, although the younger animals are still widely scattered.

In the western Pacific, these seals are first seen off Hokkaido, Japan, in October, building in numbers until December, when they are at their most prolific. They then move south, and by April they are present in

▲ During winter and spring, young northern fur seals and adult females migrate southward, while adult males remain in or near the Gulf of Alaska.

◄ (Opposite page, top) The subantarctic fur seal (*Arctocephalus tropicalis*) can be distinguished from other fur seals by the creamy wash over its face and chest.

Jeff Foott/Tom Stack & Associates

◄ Steller's sea lions (*Eumatopias jubatus*) cruising on the surface. These are the largest of the sea lions; some old males approach a tonne (2,200 pounds) in weight. Sea lions are carnivores and feed mainly on fish and squid.

149

▲ A Californian sea lion underwater. This attractive, agile, and tractable animal is the most abundant of the sea lions. Because it is frequently kept in zoos and oceanaria and can readily be trained, it is probably more familiar to people than any other pinniped.

◀ (Preceding pages) A northern fur seal breeding colony, or rookery, on the Pribilof Islands in Alaska. The migration routes and schedules of many species of these animals differ between the sexes.
William M. Smithey, Jr/Planet Earth Pictures

large numbers off northern Honshu. The northward migration starts later than in the eastern Pacific, the last seals still being seen around Hokkaido in July.

There is a certain amount of mixing between the Asian and American herds, especially among the immature seals (3- to 5-year-olds).

SEA LIONS

The best known sea lion is the Californian sea lion (*Zalophus californianus*), a favorite of many zoos and oceanaria. After the breeding season, most adult and juvenile

male sea lions of this species leave their breeding rookeries on islands off southern California and the Pacific coast of Mexico, and move northward. They are regular winter visitors on the coast of southwest Vancouver Island, where their numbers peak in February. They begin to return south in May. Females and young animals either remain on the breeding grounds throughout the year, or move southward.

The only other species of sea lion about which very much is known is the northern, or Steller's sea lion (*Eumatopias jubatus*). Widely distributed in the cooler regions of

◀ In autumn, male Californian sea lions move northward from their breeding rookeries on islands off southern California and Mexico. Some reach Vancouver Island, but others probably do not migrate so far.

Islands, but adult bulls visit the islands during the breeding season only. At other times of the year they move north.

WALRUSES

There is only one species of walrus (*Odobenus rosmarus*), although the walrus that inhabits the North Atlantic is considered to be a different subspecies from the one that is found in the North Pacific.

The Atlantic walrus does not appear to travel far, but Pacific walruses move north in summer and south in winter, in association with movements of the ice edge. They spend the winter (December to April) in the central

▼ Distribution of the Pacific walrus. There is a northward movement through the Bering Strait in summer.

the North Pacific, it ranges from Hokkaido in the western Pacific and from the southern waters of California in the eastern Pacific, northward to the Aleutian and Pribilof Islands, its most northerly breeding area. After the breeding season, males sometimes move further north and reach St Lawrence Island near the Bering Strait.

Although substantial evidence of regular migrations in the species is lacking, seasonal movements do seem to occur, particularly in the case of the males. In southern California, females and young are present throughout the year on San Miguel and Ano Nuevo

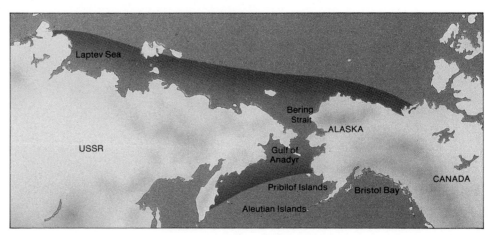

Dominique Braud/Tom Stack & Associates

and southern parts of the Bering Sea, from the Gulf of Anadyr to Bristol Bay. As the ice melts in May and June they move north past Nunivak Island and St Lawrence Island, appearing in the Bering Strait in the first half of June. The females with their newborn calves lead the migration, the males follow later in a separate herd.

The walruses spend the summer in the Chuckchi Sea, as far north as the ice will allow, feeding in the shallow waters. Several thousand bulls, however, remain in the south during the summer, hauling out (coming ashore) on Round Island and other islands in Bristol Bay and in the Gulf of Anadyr.

A general movement south occurs in November, the rate depending on ice and weather conditions. The entire population does not reach the winter quarters until January in some years. It is thought that some males may spend the entire winter north of the Bering Strait.

TRUE SEALS

Migration in true seals remained a mystery until quite recently. Although it was known that some species range outward from their breeding grounds and haul out on land in scattered places, sometimes far from their breeding grounds, evidence for regular and systematic migration was lacking. Recoveries of tagged grey seals (*Halichoerus grypus*) show that they radiate from their breeding areas more or less in random fashion. The habitat of common seals (*Phoca vitulina*) varies somewhat, but local populations do not range far from the breeding areas and no regular seasonal migrations occur.

The Caspian seal (*P. caspica*), which is confined to the Caspian Sea, makes seasonal north–south migrations. The Caspian Sea is shallower in the north than the south, and as a result its northern waters freeze in winter and are warmer in the summer. The seals spend the winter in the northern parts of the sea, moving to the southern regions in April and returning north again in about November. In this way they are always in the coolest water.

In the northern hemisphere the bearded seal (*Erignathus barbatus*), and in the southern hemisphere the Weddell seal (*Leptonychotes weddellii*) and crabeater seal (*Lobodon carcinophagus*), are all found near the polar ice. Bearded seals live around drifting icefloes for much of the year, and crabeater seals live in close association with drifting pack ice. Both species may travel considerable distances north and south, following the seasonal movements of the ice.

Crabeaters move some way south as the ice breaks up in January to March, at which time great numbers can be seen in the coastal waters west of Graham Land, and in the southern part of the Ross Sea.

Weddell seals, the most southerly breeding mammals, are found throughout the year around the coasts of Antarctica. These seals spend the winter beneath the ice, using cracks as breathing holes, keeping them from freezing over with their teeth. They move north with the ice front as the weather becomes colder and the ice becomes too dense for them to keep their breathing holes open. Some seals stay very close to the coast, remaining in the water, where the temperature is more constant, most of the time. The rest move closer to the coast once the ice contracts in spring and summer.

The only true seal of the tropics is the Hawaiian monk seal (*Monachus schauinslandii*), which breeds on a number of atolls of the Leeward Chain, northwest of the main Hawaiian Islands. It ranges widely within and beyond the Hawaiian chain, but regular seasonal movements have not yet been described.

A true seal that has a well-recognized pattern of migration is the harp seal (*Phoca groenlandica*). It is found as far north as the open waters of the Arctic in summer and early autumn, and moves south in late autumn and winter. In the spring, harp seals are found in breeding areas in the White Sea, the Greenland Sea north of Jan Mayen Island, and in the Newfoundland area in two centers known as the Gulf and the Front. The seals disperse after the breeding season, generally moving in a northward direction, although some eastward and westward movement must occur because a very small amount of interchange has been observed between the seals from the main breeding concentrations.

The two species of elephant seal, the southern elephant seal (*Mirounga leonina*) and northern elephant seal (*M. angustirostris*), have been studied in some detail in recent years, and juvenile and adult males have regular seasonal migration patterns. Although some adult females move very great distances from the islands where they breed, they do not all move in the same direction, appearing instead to spread out and cover large areas. Females of the southern species have been seen both north and south of the Antarctic Convergence, the region where cold Antarctic water meets the warmer temperate water.

Evidence from tagged southern elephant

▲ A Weddell seal. This species spends almost all of its time under the sea-ice in winter. In summer it often hauls out, like other pinnipeds, to loaf on shore.

◀ (Opposite page) A herd of walruses ashore. The Atlantic population of this species apparently does not have a seasonal migration, but the Pacific population commutes seasonally to spend the summer in the Arctic Ocean and winter in the Bering Sea.

◀ A Weddell seal surfacing at its breathing hole in the ice. Found farther south than any other pinniped, these seals live at the fringes of the Antarctic ice, periodically surfacing to breath at openings that they keep from freezing over by rasping the edges with their teeth.

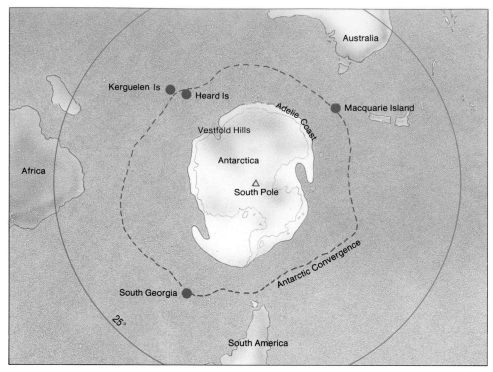

has also been shown that adult males from Macquarie Island swim south to forage in the vicinity of the Adelie Coast, Antarctica, before returning to the island to molt in late summer, and again to breed in the spring. A male elephant seal from Macquarie Island to which a satellite tracking device had been attached was recorded in the Ross Sea after leaving Macquarie Island following the autumn molt. Some adult females venture to waters close to the Antarctic coastline, but they remain offshore, in deeper water than the males. Other females stay in the vicinity of Macquarie Island, foraging just north or south of the Antarctic Convergence, and either to the east or west of the island. The adult males seem to have a preference for feeding on the ocean floor, over the Antarctic continental shelf, whereas the adult females forage in midwater, at depths of up to 1,500 meters (5,000 feet), in regions of very deep ocean.

Sexual differences in foraging have also been recorded in northern elephant seals. Males move from breeding areas in Baja California and southern California, at least as far north as the coast of Washington State, where they appear to bottom-feed over the shelf to a depth of 400 to 500 meters (1,300 to 1,600 feet). Females forage in more open water, and dive to greater depths.

▲ Breeding areas of southern elephant seals (*Mirounga leonina*). Annual migration of some immature males between the Kerguelen-Heard Islands group and the Vestfold Hills has been demonstrated.

seals has shown that a number of juvenile males move annually from Kerguelen Islands to the Vestfold Hills, Antarctica, in late summer. By attaching time-depth-temperature recorders to free-ranging seals, and comparing sea temperature maps with the temperature profiles from the recorders, it

PINNIPED AND GREAT WHALE MIGRATIONS

Among pinnipeds in which migration patterns are known, movements can be somewhat irregular and distances relatively limited. This contrasts significantly with migrations undertaken by the great whales, many of which travel enormous distances between tropical and polar waters.

Crabeater seals and Antarctic fur seals (*Arctocephalus gazella*) share with the great whales the rich krill resources of the Southern Ocean, but whereas the great whales must leave the freezing Antarctic seas to breed in warm tropical waters in the spring, the seals remain in high latitudes, hauling out to breed either on the ice, in the case of the crabeater seal, or on subantarctic islands, in the case of the fur seal.

Heat loss from the body surface is much greater in water than in air at the same temperature, so while newborn seals can survive in these high latitudes because they are born on land, whales, which are born in the water, cannot. The fur of newborn pinnipeds is a most effective insulator when dry, but it has no insulating properties in the water. Whether birth occurs on land or in the water has had a major influence on the evolution of different groups of marine mammals and their patterns of migration.

Even in pinniped species which do show regular seasonal movements, migratory patterns are less clearcut than those of whales. In both the northern fur seal and the elephant seal, the males feed in higher latitudes than females, their larger size (and consequent proportionally smaller body surface area) enabling them to better tolerate low water temperatures, and thereby exploit the extensive food resources of the polar seas. There is a huge disparity in size between adult males and females in these species, males being six to ten times the weight of females. Nevertheless, it appears that not all large males move to higher latitudes to feed. For the last few years an adult male southern elephant seal has hauled out on a farm in New Zealand, where it has defended its chosen area of pasture land against the "intrusion" of resident cattle. Presumably it is a breeding bull or a potential breeding bull from one of the subantarctic islands to the south, which feeds around the Antarctic Convergence with juveniles and adult females.

There is a major contrast in breeding between pinnipeds and whales, and to some extent this is reflected in differences in migration between the two groups. The pinnipeds must return to land or ice to give birth, and this greatly restricts their distribution during the breeding season. Most return to the island or portion of coast of their birth to breed (ice-breeding animals are the exception). Whales, on the other hand, give birth in the ocean, which gives them a far greater range of areas where they can breed, controlled to a great extent only by sea temperature.

Migration of pinnipeds, as in almost all animals, is determined largely by food supplies. Those pinnipeds that breed where the surrounding seas are food-poor must migrate to find sufficient food, whereas those that inhabit food-rich areas have no need to travel far. The most notable of the latter is the Galapagos fur seal (*Arctocephalus galapagoensis*), which breeds on the Galapagos Islands, surrounded by waters in which there are plentiful supplies of food.

Factors other than food such as seasonal changes in water temperature and the drift and changing conditions of sea ice influence the movements of a number of species. However, breeding sites and their relation to food supply are primary factors in determining migration patterns of pinnipeds.

T.S. McCann/Oxford Scientific Films

▲ An Antarctic fur seal (*Arctocephalus gazella*) giving birth on South Georgia. Pregnant fur seals give birth one or two days after they come ashore, and enter estrus and mate about eight days later. They then go to sea to feed, returning after several days to suckle their single pup.

◄ (Opposite page) Southern elephant seals ashore. Males, which often exceed 4 meters (13 feet) in length and weigh up to 4,000 kilograms (8,800 pounds), are the largest of all living pinnipeds. Females are much smaller and average 350 kilograms (770 pounds) in weight.

157

WHALES

M.M. Bryden

Kathie Atkinson

▲ The serrated trailing edge of the tail flukes help to identify this as a humpback whale. Humpbacks often migrate along shallow coastal waters and many can be individually identified by the markings on the underside of their tail flukes.

▶ A humpback whale can leap almost entirely clear of the water in a behavior known as breaching. Even solitary animals breach, apparently just for fun.

▼ Humpback whales commute between extensive summer feeding grounds in polar regions and somewhat more restricted winter breeding grounds in the tropics. They seldom feed while in transit.

Confirmed migrations of whales range from vast annual round-trips from tropical to polar seas and back in some species, to short local movements in others. Sadly, the whales whose behavior is best known are those that have been most hunted.

Whales, along with sirenians (dugongs and manatees), are the only mammals that live their entire lives in water. Dolphins and porpoises belong to the same group and are really small whales.

The whales are divided into the so-called baleen (or whalebone) whales, whose feeding apparatus includes the baleen plates in the mouth for filtering small fish, crustaceans, and the other small creatures that make up zooplankton, and the toothed whales that eat a wide range of fish, squid, cuttlefish, octopus, and in some cases warm-blooded creatures such as seabirds and sea mammals.

Ironically, those species about which we know the most are the ones that have been treated the worst by man. The earliest evidence of whaling comes from Norway in the ninth century. Species hunted since then include the larger baleen whales and, more recently, smaller ones, along with the largest toothed whales.

In the early days of whaling, hunters were land-based and so took advantage of those species that remained close to the coastline during their migration to warm breeding areas. It was not until the twentieth century, with the introduction of improved harpoon guns and factory ships, that large-scale whaling at sea became possible. Some species could then be pursued at a number of different points along their migratory routes.

BALEEN WHALES

The baleen whales include the largest mammals that have ever lived. The largest, the blue whale (*Balaenoptera musculus*) grows to more than 35 meters (115 feet) in length and 130 tonnes (286,500 pounds) in weight, and even the smallest, the pygmy right whale (*Caperea marginata*), grows to 6 meters (20 feet) and almost 5 tonnes (11,000 pounds). The numbers in several species have been reduced drastically, due mainly to developments in the whaling industry. The blue whales were taken first, because the return per catch was greatest. When their numbers were depleted, the whalers concentrated on the next largest, the fin (*B. physalus*), then the sei (*B. borealis*), and most recently the minke (*B. acutorostrata*) whale. In the early days of whaling humpback whales (*Megaptera novaeangliae*) were taken at shore stations. Later they were also killed in Antarctic seas, leading to a severe decrease in their population.

Baleen (or whalebone) is made of the same substance as our own hair and nails, the hoofs of horses, and the horns of cattle. It was used as a flexible reinforcing in corsets and some types of top boot. It was also used in the manufacture of brushes and riding crops, and as a support for the busbies of British and Danish guardsmen. Many other products used to be obtained from whales, the most important of which was oil. Whale oil is primarily a fatty oil, which was used extensively in the manufacture of soap and margarine, and to a lesser degree as a drying oil in paint. Inferior

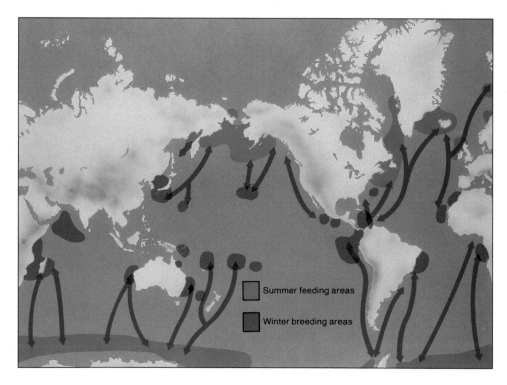

Summer feeding areas

Winter breeding areas

▶ The gray whale (*Eschrichtius robustus*) is the only bottom feeder among the baleen whales. It uses its snout to stir up organisms from the ooze; it then sucks the turbid water into its mouth and uses its tongue to force the liquid back out through the baleen plates, leaving the food behind to be swallowed.

grades were used for tanning, particularly in the manufacture of chamois leather.

For the past 100 years or so there has been circumstantial evidence that baleen whales migrate seasonally over long distances. They are observed in Antarctic and Arctic seas in the summer months, and in the tropics in winter. Investigations of the stomach contents of these whales, even when they are in tropical waters have revealed that ingested food is mainly of Antarctic or Arctic origin, and that the whales' blubber is thinner in the tropics. Certain barnacles and lamprey scars on the skin provide evidence of sojourns in tropical waters, while the film of diatoms found particularly on blue whales (hence the alternative common name, "sulphur-bottom whale") is evidence of a long stay in high latitudes. It was not until about 50 years ago that direct evidence of migrations was obtained by tagging studies.

Most baleen whales breed in warm tropical or subtropical waters, where their calves have a good chance of survival, and migrate to higher latitudes to feed. While we think of the tropics as lush areas with dense rainforests on land, the blue tropical waters tend to be food-poor. Mass concentrations of plankton, and associated concentrations of plankton feeders, are rare in the tropics, where vast areas of ocean form virtual "deserts in the sea." As a consequence these whales have to range far and wide from their breeding areas in search of food, which is usually most plentiful in Antarctic and Arctic summer seas.

There are exceptions. The equatorial waters off the Galapagos Islands, the Caribbean Sea, the Arabian Sea, and a few other places contain literally teeming masses of plankton, fishes, and squids. Large schools of dolphins, sometimes numbering into the thousands, are to be found in these regions and, as is the case with most tropical land animals, they do not migrate far or seasonally because they do not need to.

Amongst baleen whales, Bryde's whales (*Balaenoptera edeni*) are predominantly tropical and subtropical and do not make extensive migrations. Their diet is apparently varied enough to allow them to find areas of high productivity, such as ocean upwellings, to meet their food needs year round. Certain minke whales are also believed to inhabit tropical and temperate waters permanently, while others spend the summer months in the food-rich polar seas.

The journeys of the large, seasonally migrant baleen whales, such as blue, fin, and humpback whales, are quite remarkable. When they leave the plankton-rich polar seas at the end of summer and return to the barren subtropical and tropical waters, only some of them will get any food at all during their long journey. Of nearly 6,000 humpback whales killed at the subtropical land station at Tangalooma, Australia, in the 1950s and early 1960s, only one had food in its stomach. Whalers in the district could easily distinguish the fat northward-migrating humpbacks (that is, those migrating from the summer feeding areas to tropical seas) from the much thinner

▼ Right whales swim more slowly than other whale species and float when dead. In the early days of whaling this made them an easy and profitable target for the harpooners who hunted them to the brink of extinction. Here a southern right whale mother escorts her calf.

Marty Snyderman

southward-migrating ones leaving the tropical breeding areas. In other words, these large baleen whales virtually fast for at least four months of the year, living off their blubber and other body tissues stored during the summer feast. What is even more remarkable, is that they fast while swimming more than 7,000 kilometers (4,300 miles), some of them pregnant as they swim to the breeding areas and suckling a calf on the return journey. And all the while, their body temperature is about the same as that of humans — 37°C (98.6°F).

Little is known about whales' mating behavior. Gestation lasts about 12 months, so a female that mates in one breeding season migrates to feeding areas over the summer months as the fetus is growing, and gives birth when it returns to the breeding area the next year.

Calf births have not been observed with certainty, but the birth process probably occurs rapidly, and close to the surface. The calf, born tail first, must emerge and rise to the surface quickly to take its first breaths, otherwise it will drown. It lives entirely on its mother's milk for some months, probably beginning to take solid food during its first

summer. Growth of the calf, and particularly the deposition of blubber, is rapid as whale milk is rich in fat and protein. This is vital to the young calf because it must accompany its mother to her feeding grounds in freezing polar water.

While we know that almost all baleen whales breed in tropical waters and feed in

▼ Gray whales migrate in shallow coastal waters from their summer feeding grounds in polar seas to calving areas in warm temperate seas.

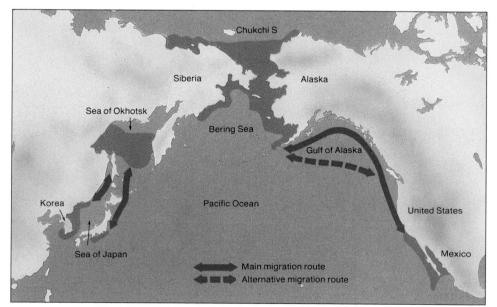

Chukchi S

Siberia   Alaska

Sea of Okhotsk

                    Bering Sea

                              Gulf of Alaska

Korea   Pacific Ocean

                                      United States

Sea of Japan   Mexico

            ➡ Main migration route
            ➡ Alternative migration route

▶ Humpback whales are known for their long and intricate songs, apparently uttered by males only. Songs may last 10 minutes or more and consist of a precise sequence of roaring, moaning, sighing, and chirping sounds, which are repeated unchanged for hours at a time. All males in a given area sing the same song, but it varies gradually over time, so that songs uttered in one year are not identical to those uttered the year before.

Bora Merdsoy/Planet Earth Pictures

the plankton-rich polar seas, we know relatively little about most species' final destinations or routes of migration. In this regard most is known about gray (*Eschrichtius robustus*) and humpback whales, which can be directly observed migrating along shorelines of continents and other landmasses. (They exhibit this behavior possibly because it is desirable for their young to be born in shallow and sheltered waters.) In tropical waters these whales can usually be seen at a depth of 200 meters (650 feet).

The migratory routes of humpback whales are also known quite well from studies of marked individuals. In earlier times the marks were fired from a special gun or modified harpoon gun into the blubber or dorsal musculature of whales, and recovered only when the animals were killed and processed by the whaling companies. Nowadays individual whales are identified by natural marks on the body, particularly the back or the dorsal fin photographed from the side, or the underside of the flukes, photographed from behind as a whale dives. Both methods demand a great deal of effort and resources, and it takes several years to obtain even relatively small data sets.

However, surveys of marked southern humpback whales now show that they occur in five virtually discrete Antarctic populations, and that individuals usually remain within their respective zones, although very occasionally a whale from one zone will migrate to another following seasonal migration. There are similarly isolated populations of northern hemisphere baleen whales.

Blue and fin whales, whose distribution is probably much more dependent on the abundance of food in polar waters, do not form such apparently closed communities and there is a greater interchange of individuals between zones. Even so, most blue and fin whales remain within their separate zones in polar waters, and return there year after year. The migratory routes of these whales do not take them close to mainland coasts and in fact mature individuals, particularly in southern populations, seem to avoid coastal waters altogether. Apparently, calves are born in regions of relatively deep water.

The timing of the seasonal migrations of southern blue, fin, and humpback whales does not coincide exactly. Fin whales migrate to Antarctic seas a little later in the spring than blue whales. It seems that the sexual and reproductive status of whales determines timing. During migration to tropical waters in winter, pregnant

whales now move farther south in summer than they did earlier this century, to feeding areas previously occupied by other baleen whale species that have been drastically reduced in numbers by whaling.

Bowhead whales (*Balaena mysticetus*) are confined to Arctic and subarctic waters between latitudes 55° and 78°N. Migration occurs to the north in spring and summer, and to the south in late autumn. They live mainly in regions with floating ice or icebergs, and are the best adapted of all baleen whales for life among the ice. The bowhead navigates easily through channels in the ice, and can break through thin ice with its head. However, it is not uncommon for individuals to be trapped and frozen in the ice. Although it has been suggested that migration may be influenced by the movements of drift ice, restrictive ice in the Beaufort Sea in 1975 did not seem to prevent bowheads from migrating into traditional feeding areas.

TOOTHED WHALES

Toothed whales occupy a much greater range of habitats than baleen whales, and latitudinal migration occurs in only a few species. Some inhabit rivers and are therefore restricted in their movements, while several marine species that live close to shore show no evidence of regular seasonal migrations.

Less is known about migration and other aspects of the biology of this group because unlike baleen whales, relatively few of them have been harvested. Certainly there is no general pattern of migration among toothed

humpback whales are among the last to leave the Southern Ocean, and cows and calves are the last to migrate to feeding areas in the spring.

It is believed that southern blue, fin, and humpback whales form populations that are distinct from those in the northern hemisphere. Even though they cross the equator, the chances of whales of both hemispheres intermingling are small, because the majority visit tropical waters during their hemisphere's winter. Nevertheless, interchanges are possible. Some baleen whales from southern populations, particularly sexually immature individuals, may remain around latitude 50°S throughout the winter, and there is evidence to suggest that some remain in tropical waters during summer. Whales in southern seas have been observed carrying northern whale lice, and southern hemisphere parasites have been found on blue and fin whales caught off Japan, the Kuril Islands, and Kamchatka.

Sei whales move to higher latitudes in the spring and toward the equator in autumn, but their migrations are more diffuse and irregular than those of the other large baleen whales. Their tendency to follow relatively warm waters, and avoid sea ice, at least partly explains the difference. It has been suggested that southern hemisphere sei

▼ Distribution and movements of white whales (*Delphinapterus leucas*) in Arctic seas. Arrows indicate spring migrations to main feeding areas in summer.

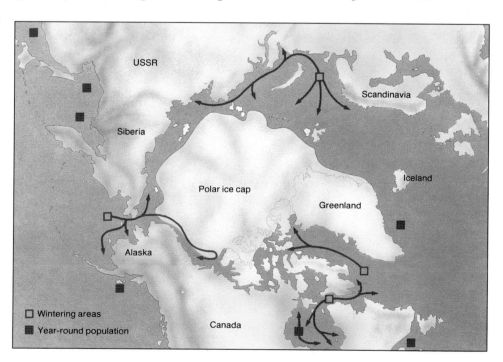

▲ Before the introduction of the explosive harpoon gun in 1846, hunting whales was a bloody and dangerous affair, as portrayed in this lithograph by Currier & Ives.

▼ A pod of white whales idles alongside a bowhead whale (*Balaena mysticetus*). Both species are characteristic of cold Arctic and subarctic waters. They move southward with the margins of pack ice in winter and northward again in summer. White whales often enter river mouths, sometimes moving far upstream.

whales, although migrations of some species seem to be related to seasonal movements of fish and other prey, and water temperature may play a role amongst some of the species that inhabit higher latitudes.

The most important toothed whale, from the commercial point of view, is the sperm whale (*Physeter catodon*). It used to be prized for its oil, which consists of sperm oil and spermaceti; both are liquid waxes. Sperm oil was valued as a lubricant for machinery and was burned for illumination. Spermaceti was used for making candles.

More recently, spermaceti has been used in the manufacture of a detergent used as a scouring agent prior to the dyeing of wool, linen, and synthetic fibers.

As with the baleen whales, the commercial value of sperm whales led to study of their biology. They have been reported from all oceans and, more rarely, in semilandlocked regions such as the Mediterranean Sea. The ranges of adult males and females differ. Females and young males are distributed in the tropical and subtropical waters of each hemisphere, between approximately 40°N and 40°S. Adult males move to higher latitudes in the summer—as far north as the Barents and Bering seas in the northern hemisphere, and south to the edge of the Antarctic pack-ice in the southern hemisphere. The apparent year-round concentration of sperm whales near the equator is believed to represent separate northern and southern populations at the limit of their winter migrations.

In recent years we have begun to learn more about some of the small toothed whales, such as spinner (*Stenella longirostris*) and spotted (*S. attenuata* and *S. frontalis*) dolphins, because millions have been killed in nets set to catch tuna. Systematic examination of the carcasses has led to a greater understanding of their growth, reproduction, and distribution. In each case, however, knowledge has been gained while many whales were killed and some entire populations have been severely depleted.

Other species are being killed by plastic wastes and pollutants in rivers and oceans. The river dolphins are particularly vulnerable to pollution and some species are among the most endangered animals in the world.

Relatively recently, studies of individually recognizable animals (using either tags, freeze bands, or natural marks) have been carried out. Narwhals (*Monodon monoceros*) and white whales (*Delphinapterus leucas*) are widely distributed in the Arctic seas, and show seasonal migration. Narwhals occur in the High Arctic, and occupy the most northerly habitat of any whale species. The most important factor governing their distribution and migrations seems to be fluctuations in the distribution of sea ice. White whales are widely distributed throughout Arctic and subarctic areas, and while some are believed to disperse, converge, and migrate seasonally, others seem to form isolated, year-round populations at low latitudes. Northern bottlenose whales (*Hyperoodon ampullatus*) spend summer months in the North Atlantic, and in winter migrate as far south as Cape Verde and the Mediterranean in the eastern North Atlantic, and New York Bay and Rhode Island on the western side.

Migrations of some inshore dolphins and porpoises, such as harbor porpoises (*Phocoena phocoena*) and some populations of bottlenose dolphins (*Tursiops truncatus*) seem to be related to seasonal movements of food species. Seasonal fluctuations in sea temperature may play a role as well.

HOW WHALES NAVIGATE

The very lengthy migrations of some whales, particularly the journeys of most baleen whales that cross vast tracts of ocean to find quite specific breeding and feeding areas, suggest that whales do have an accurate means of navigating.

Like many animals, both baleen and toothed whales' bodies have been found to possess deposits of magnetite, particularly in the tissues surrounding the brain. It has been suggested that the possession of a magnetic sense, perhaps related to magnetite, permits whales to use the earth's total geomagnetic field to supply them with both a simple map and a timer (in the form of daily magnetic fluctuations), that allow them to monitor their position and progress. To do this, they would need to be capable of detecting small relative differences in total local magnetic field.

It is likely that whales use other senses to navigate locally, but a navigational system such as this one could explain how they can travel very long distances without losing their way.

▲ Common in zoos and oceanaria, the bottlenose dolphin is probably the most widely known cetacean. It is found in temperate and tropical seas, especially in shallow coastal waters, and frequently plays in the surf or rides the bow-wave of boats and ships. Although usually encountered in pods of 5 or 10, it occasionally occurs in much larger groups.

THE MIGRATION CYCLE OF BALEEN WHALES

The distribution and migrations of whales, as of other animals, are governed largely by their food supply. Knowledge of certain characteristics of the Southern Ocean provides us with the answer to why southern baleen whales undergo the great annual migrations from their winter breeding areas in the tropics to freezing Antarctic seas to feed in summer.

In the sea, as on land, all life depends on the presence of plants. They alone can synthesize organic matter from inorganic building blocks, by photosynthesis. Carbonic acid and oxygen, which are the essential ingredients of this process, are more soluble in cold water, while destructive bacteria flourish in warmer seas.

Bottom water rich in nutrients, particularly nitrates, phosphates, and sulphates, moves toward Antarctica, rises to the surface near the continent, and is carried northward in the surface water by ocean currents. The presence of a plentiful supply of oxygen, carbonic acid, and these other nutrients promotes the growth of huge masses of phytoplankton, the tiny plant life that supports the zooplankton feeding on it. Consequently, Antarctic seas are between 10 and 20 times richer in plankton than tropical seas.

Sunlight is essential for photosynthesis, and there is plenty of it in the polar summers as the days are 24 hours long. However, it penetrates only the upper layers of the ocean and phytoplankton is thus found chiefly in the upper 100 meters (330 feet), particularly in the top 10 to 20 meters (33 to 66 feet). Krill feeds on phytoplankton, which explains why krill, though present down to 1,000 meters (3,300 feet), is also most prolific in the top 10 to 20 meters (33 to 66 feet) of the water column. It is in this top water that the krill-eating baleen whales forage.

Whales mate and give birth in warm seas, where their body heat loss to the surroundings is much less than in the freezing polar seas. Newborn calves have virtually no insulating layer of blubber beneath the skin, and if they were born in polar seas they would freeze to death quite quickly. Thus, the "home" of whales, so to speak, is in warm tropical waters, but they must migrate elsewhere, usually to where krill is most plentiful, to obtain the vast amounts of food they require.

One can imagine that the stimulus for whales to leave their breeding areas and go in search of food is simply desire for sustenance. Hunger pangs would not be the immediate stimulus, however, because some weeks elapse between leaving tropical seas and reaching the food-rich polar seas. But loss of body weight in the tropics must trigger physiological changes that are translated to an urge to move to higher latitudes in search of food. There is some evidence that air temperature may play a role as well.

The stimulus to leave feeding areas to migrate to breeding areas is more difficult to imagine. Change in day length is possibly involved, although indirectly, because as the days grow shorter, phytoplankton production decreases and krill descends in the water column. At the same time, ice covers the polar seas and the whales' food supply is cut off.

▼ Throughout the oceans of the world, growth occurs wherever there is sufficient light for photosynthesis and sufficient mineral nutrients in the water to sustain life. Warm, circumpolar, deep water brings vast quantities of inorganic nutrients and dissolved gases to the polar seas. Together with almost continuous sunlight in the summer months, these provide an ideal medium for the growth of the tiny plants that make up phytoplankton and this, in turn, provides prolific supplies of food for krill. By contrast, the subantarctic oceans are relatively poor in nutrients; currents and other oceanographic factors cause the nutrients to sink beneath the surface water, to depths where light cannot penetrate.

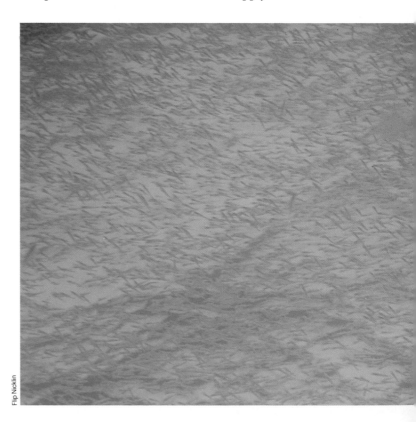

166

Flip Nicklin

▲ The term krill refers to a group of small, semi-transparent, shrimp-like creatures that inhabit polar seas. They are so numerous and congregate in swarms so dense that a baleen whale may take up to three tonnes of them at a single feed.

◄ Related to shrimp, lobsters, and crabs (order Decapoda) but in a different order (Euphausiacea), krill range in size from about 25 to 50 millimeters (1 to 2 inches).

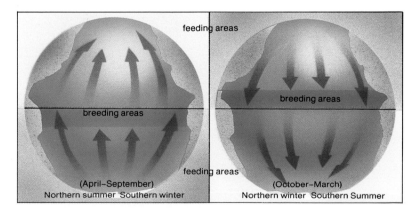

▲ The general form of the migration of baleen whales.

Part 4

CROSS-COUNTRY MARATHONS

Terrestrial animals, large and small, crisscross the continents with their migratory paths. And it should not be forgotten that humans are the most versatile migrants of all.

AMPHIBIANS AND REPTILES

Always vulnerable to predators when migrating, frogs, snakes, and their kin must now also reckon with the hazards of roads and motor traffic.

SMALL MAMMALS

Although mammals such as squirrels travel only short distances to settle, these are massive journeys in relation to their size.

BEARS AND OTHER CARNIVORES

Migration amongst carnivores such as bears is usually related to following their prey or to finding new living areas.

ELEPHANTS

The size of their appetite keeps elephants on the move over considerable distances. But they may soon be left with nowhere to go.

CARIBOU

Traveling vast distances to feed and give birth in the open tundra, caribou thrive in their harsh and often snowbound environment.

WILDEBEEST

Survival for the wildebeest involves an endless search for food and water that has huge herds constantly circling the Serengeti Plains of East Africa.

MIGRANTS OF THE PAST

Some small populations of endangered migrant animals, such as the saiga, have been saved by legislation and their numbers are increasing once more.

HUMANS

The most inveterate and intrepid of migrants, humans have means of adapting to most climatic conditions on earth and have even begun to explore the solar system.

AMPHIBIANS AND REPTILES

A. Ross Kiester

▲ Golden toads (*Bufo periglenes*) mating. As is the case with most toads and frogs, the male fertilizes the eggs as the female lays them. In an embrace known as amplexus, he clasps her tightly around the middle, sometimes for several days, in order to ensure that he is on the spot when she is ready to lay.

Both amphibians and reptiles are particularly vulnerable to predators when migrating to breeding or hibernation sites. More recently, roads and motor traffic have made their journeys even more hazardous and their numbers have decreased dramatically. Efforts to understand and maintain their migratory patterns will be central to protecting these persistent travelers.

HAZARDOUS JOURNEYS

Perhaps the most adventurous migration ever undertaken by a vertebrate was the original trip from water to land by the earliest amphibians. Indeed, the very name "amphibian" implies a migration between the two major realms of life on earth. Today most amphibians, though by no means all, repeat that original journey as part of their life cycle.

Many species undertake an annual migration from their normal land habitats back to a body of water suitable for breeding. Eggs are laid and often fertilized directly in the water. The larvae or tadpoles that hatch then spend from a few weeks to two or three years in the water before metamorphosing into small adults that venture out onto the land. By the standards of many other animals, the distances involved in these annual breeding migrations are not great, a few kilometers at most. But from the point of view of the amphibians the journeys are as dangerous as any.

Although amphibians are the oldest group of terrestrial vertebrates, they seem singularly ill-equipped for travel on land. With their damp unprotected skin and unprepossessing size and body form, the average salamander or frog can die after being exposed to adverse weather conditions such as excessive heat or dryness for only a few minutes. Further, when they leave the habitats in which they were often well hidden, if not actually underground as is the case for many salamanders, they are more exposed to predators than at other times.

A typical example of an amphibian breeding migration is that of newts of the genus *Taricha* from the foothills of the Pacific coast of the United States. In the early spring they change from a rough skin to a smooth skin and grow a keel on their tails. Sporting their new aquatic look, they move down to the small creeks in which they breed at the onset of spring rains. They travel at night or on rainy or overcast days, covering up to 3 kilometers (2 miles). Mature

individuals arrive at breeding sites within a few meters of those they used previously. For many years herpetologists struggled to determine how these salamanders oriented themselves. Blind newts were found to home as well as sighted ones, and after many years of study, Victor Twitty, the leading scientist in the field, demonstrated that the newts use their sense of smell to guide their way during the migration. It is likely that olfaction also plays a key role in the migration of most other amphibians.

Most frogs and toads undertake similar breeding migrations, the most significant difference from salamanders being the males' use of a call to advertise their presence. Each species has a unique call, which is usually employed after arrival at the breeding site. However, some species begin calling during migration. As with calling at

the breeding site, calling during migration is an evolutionary two-edged sword, as it advertises the presence of the male both to potential mates and to predators. Some predators, including bats, are now known to locate their frog prey by following calls.

The difficulties of migration are further demonstrated by the frogs of the genus *Atelopus* in Costa Rica and the wood frog (*Rana sylvatica*) in North America. The males try to circumvent the intense competition for females at the breeding site by clamping onto the back of a female as she is moving toward it. Indeed, an *Atelopus* male may ride on the back of a hapless female for several weeks prior to breeding.

Perhaps partly as a result of such difficulties, a significant number of amphibians have given up such a migratory life and evolved mechanisms for breeding on

▼ The European tree frog (*Hyla arborea*) is only one of hundreds of species of small frogs that live in foliage and not in ponds. Despite their arboreal habits, these frogs must lay their eggs in water, and so once a year they migrate to suitable ponds to mate.

Natural Science Photos

▲ A culvert engineered under a roadway to accommodate migrating European common toads (*Bufo bufo*).

▼ In autumn the marbled salamander (*Ambystoma opacum*) migrates to marshes or ponds to breed. Once laid, the eggs are guarded until they hatch.

land. These newer groups have a dazzling variety of breeding methods that range from carrying the eggs on their backs or in their mouths or stomachs to guarding them under logs. In avoiding the dangers of migration to water, these species represent a new way of life that is no longer really amphibian.

For those that still migrate to water, many objects in the environment—a small downed tree trunk, even a thick clump of grass—may present formidable obstacles to amphibians crawling along toward a breeding site. Yet amphibians have contended with these obstacles for more than 200 million years. Walking or hopping resolutely on their way to a breeding pond or river they sometimes seem like Victorian explorers—underequipped and out of place —but somehow they remain able to get where they want to go.

Today, however, an extraordinary new obstacle lies between the land homes of most amphibians and their breeding sites:

the road. Watching small salamanders of the genus *Ensatina* take five or ten minutes to cross the narrowest country road one realizes that nothing in their evolution has prepared them to cope with oncoming cars. Wherever amphibians still exist interspersed with civilization, a substantial number (thousands or more) are killed each year during migration. It now appears that many local populations have been severely reduced, or actually driven to extinction, by their inability to return to their breeding sites.

Fortunately, in some parts of the world efforts are now being made to help migrating salamanders, frogs, and toads cross roads. The simplest approach is to erect signs to indicate an amphibian crossing and hope that motorists will somehow avoid them. Recently, efforts have been made to guide migratory amphibians along the edge of roads to specially constructed tunnels that lead them safely to the other side.

Zig Leszczynski/Animals Animals

THE LIFE CYCLE OF THE COMMON FROG

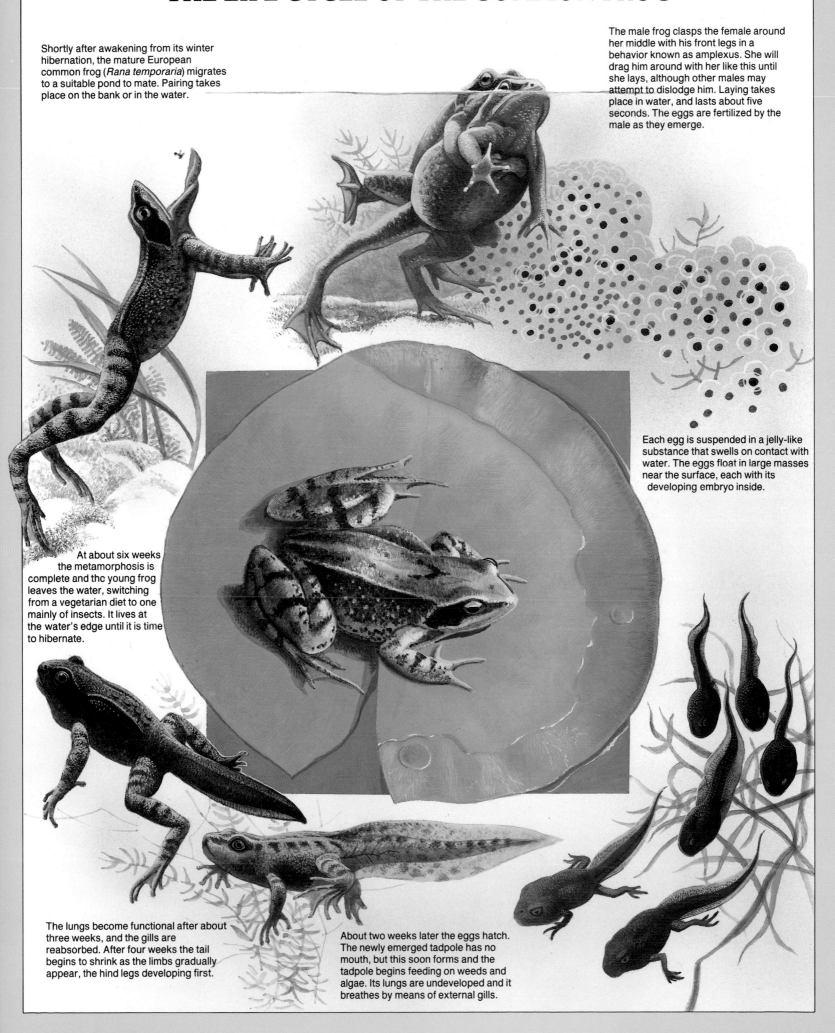

Shortly after awakening from its winter hibernation, the mature European common frog (*Rana temporaria*) migrates to a suitable pond to mate. Pairing takes place on the bank or in the water.

The male frog clasps the female around her middle with his front legs in a behavior known as amplexus. She will drag him around with her like this until she lays, although other males may attempt to dislodge him. Laying takes place in water, and lasts about five seconds. The eggs are fertilized by the male as they emerge.

Each egg is suspended in a jelly-like substance that swells on contact with water. The eggs float in large masses near the surface, each with its developing embryo inside.

At about six weeks the metamorphosis is complete and the young frog leaves the water, switching from a vegetarian diet to one mainly of insects. It lives at the water's edge until it is time to hibernate.

The lungs become functional after about three weeks, and the gills are reabsorbed. After four weeks the tail begins to shrink as the limbs gradually appear, the hind legs developing first.

About two weeks later the eggs hatch. The newly emerged tadpole has no mouth, but this soon forms and the tadpole begins feeding on weeds and algae. Its lungs are undeveloped and it breathes by means of external gills.

Francois Gohier/Ardea London

▲ Snakes such as these North American common garter snakes (*Thamnophis sirtalis*), hibernate communally in caves. While some individuals remain close by in summer, others migrate considerable distances to and from the dens that they use year after year.

▶ The common green iguana is widespread in the tropics of Central and South America. Much of its life is spent in the treetops, but females must periodically descend to the ground in order to lay and bury their eggs.

▼ A baby common green iguana hatching. Though buried in the ground, many eggs are lost to predators. Some female iguanas circumvent this threat and provide a safe nursery for their eggs by migrating to small islands in lakes.

A CAPACITY TO MIGRATE

With the advent of hard-shelled eggs capable of surviving on land, reptiles evolved the freedom from having to return to the water to breed. So for the most part, they have escaped the need for breeding migrations that compel so many amphibians to undertake dangerous annual journeys. Nonetheless, in the course of evolution and radiation into new niches, they have sometimes established lifestyles that include migration for other reasons.

The common green iguana (*Iguana iguana*) lives throughout most of the New World tropics. This large lizard is usually arboreal, although females must come down to the ground and search out open, sunny clearings to lay their eggs in. The eggs are buried in the ground, but they are nonetheless often found and destroyed by a variety of predators such as coati mundis. However, populations of the iguana on Barro Colorado Island in the Panama Canal have developed a way around this problem. During the breeding season the females migrate in large numbers to nearby small islets in the canal that are not large enough to support populations of predators.

Experiments reburying nests on the small islets and the large island have confirmed that predators destroy nests on Barro Colorado but not on the islets. Furthermore, radiotelemetry studies have shown that females can return to the same nest sites. Throughout most of its range, this species of iguana does not normally migrate to nest, but is capable of migrating to take advantage of special local situations where migrating to nesting sites is very advantageous.

Since reptiles depend on their environment to sustain their body temperature, those that live in temperate climates must hibernate to survive winters. Most of the species of reptiles in the United States and Canada do so, and many species of snakes, such as garter snakes of the genus *Thamnophis* and rattlesnakes of the genus *Crotalus*, use communal dens, or hibernacula.

However, in many areas suitable hibernacula are few and scattered. Consequently, annual migration patterns have developed in which individual snakes return from their summer ranges to a den. In Canada, dens of the common garter snake (*Thamnophis sirtalis*) can contain thousands of individuals, some of which summer in the immediate vicinity while others move distances of over 17 kilometers (11 miles) to find suitable summer ranges. Mating in this species is coordinated with the annual cycle of migration. As the snakes emerge from their dens each spring, males have the opportunity of encountering many more females than they would in their dispersed summer ranges.

While these dens provide crucial protection from cold and allow snakes to adaptively radiate into new environments, migratory behavior is now also a serious liability to many species since it exposes them to the same hazards of roads and habitat fragmentation that many amphibians face. An even deadlier situation occurs in the case of rattlesnakes. In parts of the United States they are subject to systematic "rattlesnake roundups" and their need to

A.J. Stevens/Bruce Coleman Ltd

CROCODILIANS

R. Robin Baker

Loren McIntyre

One hundred million years ago, herds of dinosaurs may have migrated across the world's plains in the same way that many mammals do today. Admittedly, the evidence of such migrations is slight. However, at several sites in North America, dinosaur tracks have been found in which the feet of up to 25 individuals all point in the same direction.

Such tracks have been found for a variety of archosaurs (ruling reptiles). Herds were of single species and involved individuals of different sizes and ages. From the stride lengths it can be deduced that they were traveling at a steady pace. (Large mammals use such a pace when traveling over longer distances, compared with the high-speed escape from predators or the slow dawdle when feeding.) Moreover, the herds were not constrained into a common path by topography. The picture, then, is of family groups merging to form small herds and traveling steadily from one part of their range to another.

The only living archosaurs, the crocodilians, cannot provide such a spectacle. Indeed, the popular image of these horizontal predators, lazily floating in the water waiting for a passing meal, is perhaps the absolute antithesis of migration. Yet, surprisingly, the silent vigil of each adult crocodile belies an adolescence of restlessness and exploration.

The spectacled caiman (*Caiman crocodilus*) of Venezuela, for example, spends its life in freshwater lagoons. It is small, compared with other crocodilians, growing only to about 130 centimeters (50 inches). For the first 18 months of their lives the caimans from a clutch of eggs stay together in a "pod," defended by their parents and other adults. Only

▲ The spectacled caiman lives for much of the year in permanent tropical freshwater lagoons, but during the rainy season it often migrates to exploit temporary floodwaters.

when a caiman is about two years old does it set about exploring its neighborhood and fending for itself. During their exploratory phase, adolescent caimans are known to travel distances of at least 1.5 kilometers (1 mile) over land between lagoons. They seem to build up an intimate familiarity with the area over which they travel. Adult caimans captured in one lagoon and released in another 2.5 kilometers (1 1/2 miles) away were found back in their home lagoon just 10 days later. In the dry season, adults keep to permanent stretches of water, but when the rains arrive they migrate to temporary lagoons a kilometer or so distant. It seems that they may know where temporary lagoons form from their explorations as juveniles.

Many crocodilians exploit such freshwater lagoons, but perhaps the longest explorations occur when individuals venture out to sea. A Nile crocodile (*Crocodylus nilolticus*) was once seen 11 kilometers (7 miles) off the Zululand coast and some have crossed to the island of Zanzibar. There is a single record of the African slender-snouted crocodile (*C. cataphractus*) on Bioko Island, 45 kilometers (28 miles) off the coast of Cameroon, and the Indopacific crocodile (*C. porosus*) has colonized the Cocos Islands, nearly 1,000 kilometers (620 miles) from land. It is possible, however, that some of these marine migrations were involuntary, estuarine individuals being swept out to sea by storm waters.

migrate to dens makes them especially vulnerable to this infamous practice. Each autumn the individuals are concentrated in or near a hibernaculum, making it possible to exterminate an entire population. It is now apparent that conservation efforts must work to preserve den sites for any species of snakes that migrate to them. Indeed, the Nature Conservancy in the state of Oregon has one reserve called Rattlesnake Butte that exists specifically to protect a hibernation den. Pioneering efforts such as this must be extended to many other species.

Although most species of reptiles do not have an annual cycle of migration, either for nesting or hibernation, some species that are normally relatively sedentary include individuals that migrate much longer distances. Most three-toed box turtles (*Terrapene carolina triunguis*) in Missouri spend their lives on a home range of 1 to 5 hectares (2 1/2 to 12 1/2 acres). Some may move short distances to find better soil in which to hibernate, but for the most part they remain put, sometimes remaining in the same home range for over 25 years. At the same time, however, an unknown fraction of individuals are true transients—that is, they move continuously (except to stop for hibernation) and more or less in a straight line. One individual was followed by radiotelemetry for 15 months and covered a straight-line distance of over 10 kilometers (6 miles). All the known transients in the box turtle population are males and they have been found mating with females during the course of their movements. These individuals are therefore important in promoting gene flow within the population. The exact nature and evolutionary importance of this variation in lifestyle is not known.

Further variation in migratory patterns has been found in the giant tortoise (*Geochelone gigantea*) that is abundant on the small island of Aldabra in the Indian Ocean. Most individuals within the population are relatively sedentary, but in one area of the island a group of tortoises makes an annual migration to another part in search of food that grows there during the rainy season. The individuals that undertake these migrations are not of any particular age group or sex and, once again, it is not clear why some migrate while others remain steadfastly at home.

From these examples it is clear that, while the majority of terrestrial reptiles do not move far in their lifetime travels, the group as a whole has the evolutionary capacity to do so should an environmental situation call

for this behavior. Because a low frequency of longer distance migrators within a normally sedentary population is very hard to detect, it may be the case that many other species show the varieties of movement patterns that have been detected in turtles. If this is true, then many reptiles may be more migratory than previously thought.

▼ A Galapagos giant tortoise (*Geochelone elephantophus*). Females of this species may have to migrate considerable distances over rough lava to find soil for burying their eggs in.

SMALL MAMMALS

Kay E. Holekamp

John Gerlach/DRK Photo

▲ The Richardson's ground squirrel occupies the western plains of North America, and is very common in sagebrush, prairie, and the eastern foothills of the Rocky Mountains. Its home is a maze of burrows, usually with one main entrance and several inconspicuous emergency exits. This individual is gathering grass and plant stems to take underground to line the breeding chamber.

When they are only a few weeks old, male ground squirrels leave their home burrow and travel up to a kilometer (2/3 mile) before settling. In relation to its size, one of these little creatures covers more ground on such a trip than a wildebeest does on its annual round-trip migration from the southern Serengeti to Kenya and back.

Not long after they are born, many small mammals set off alone, leaving the natal area for good. Such a migration is known as a natal dispersal. Another kind of migration, known as breeding dispersal, occurs when an adult travels from place to place to mate.

Breeding dispersals are less common than natal dispersals and are generally shorter journeys. They may involve both sexes, or only males. Males are far more likely to engage in natal dispersal than females. Even in the relatively few species where both sexes engage in natal dispersal, males tend to move with greater regularity than females, and cover greater distances.

Dispersal movements have been studied in rodents such as mice, rats, and muskrats, in various hares and rabbits, and in a few small marsupials, such as marsupial mice (*Antechinus* species). The most detailed research, however, has been done on several members of the large North American rodent family Sciuridae, to which prairie dogs, marmots (or woodchucks), chipmunks, and squirrels belong.

Ground squirrels are ground-living cousins of tree squirrels. Most of them live in groups on open grassland, where they feed on grasses and seeds. At night they sleep in underground burrows. They are much easier to observe than tree squirrels, and so have been more widely studied.

The dispersal trips taken by these little creatures are, in relation to their size, extraordinarily long. When they are barely 2 months old, and less than half grown, male Belding's ground squirrels (*Spermophilus beldingi*) leave the area in which they were born and never return. At this stage they weigh only 125 grams (4 1/2 ounces), yet they travel a full kilometer (2/3 mile) before settling again. This is the equivalent of a 75 kilogram (165 pound) person walking 600 kilometers (370 miles). To put it another way, relative to its size, the squirrel covers more ground than a wildebeest does on its annual round-trip migration of up to 3,000 kilometers (1,900 miles) from the southern Serengeti to Kenya and back.

D. Parer & E. Parer-Cook/Auscape

178

Some ground squirrels are capable of even more remarkable trips. In one instance a juvenile male Richardson's ground squirrel (*Spermophilus richardsonii*) traveled 9.6 kilometers (6 miles) in only 72 hours! More often, however, dispersals occur gradually, the animal starting off by making a series of short exploratory journeys away from the burrow where it was born.

When a male Belding's ground squirrel first emerges from the burrow, at the age of about 4 weeks, its daily movements are initially restricted to the immediate vicinity of the burrow. It soon begins to move farther afield. The extending boundaries of its home range are influenced by features of the landscape such as streams, forests, and rock outcrops, or the presence of other ground squirrels. By about its fifteenth day above

ground, the juvenile squirrel's home range will be greater than its mother's. It may spend long periods far from the burrow, yet it will still return home at nightfall. Around its twenty-fifth day above ground, when it is roughly seven weeks old, the squirrel will no longer return home at dusk. Instead it will sleep in a vacant burrow, and dispersion will then be complete.

The ideal place for the male ground squirrel to settle at the end of the dispersal movement is an area where there are females around to mate with, yet where there are not already so many other ground squirrels that critical resources like food and burrows are in short supply.

Dispersal can be very dangerous for small mammals. If a ground squirrel makes a poor "spur-of-the-moment" selection of a burrow

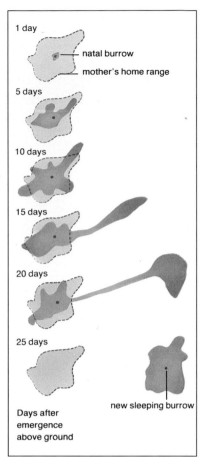

1 day

natal burrow

mother's home range

5 days

10 days

15 days

20 days

25 days

new sleeping burrow

Days after emergence above ground

▲ The process by which male Belding's ground squirrels disperse usually resembles the fissioning of an ameba. When a male first emerges from his natal burrow, at about four weeks, his daily range and movement are restricted to the immediate vicinity of the burrow. He soon enlarges that range into an amorphous shape, the boundaries of which are established by topographic features or the presence of other animals. By about the fifteenth day above ground his range has surpassed the scope of his mother's home range. At this time he may spend long periods far from the natal burrow, yet he will still return home at nightfall. Near the twenty-fifth day, when he is roughly seven weeks old, he will cease returning home at dusk.

◀ A stripe-faced dunnart (*Sminthopsis macroura*) mother with her young. Little is known of the behavior of this widespread inhabitant of arid Australian grasslands, but the rapidity with which it is known to recolonize previously deserted areas after flooding or abundant rainfall is a clear indication of the importance of natal dispersal to its way of life.

because it is new to an area and not yet aware that better burrows are available, it is likely to die of hypothermia. (A burrow must be deep to be warm, and must also be dry.) The squirrel is also likely to be easy prey, as in unfamiliar territory it will be without secure hiding places or escape routes. As dispersals are common to virtually all small mammals, despite such hazards, these movements must be very important for the animals' ability to survive and reproduce.

When male marsupial mice, ground squirrels, and their close relatives disperse, they are not seeking food or vacant burrows. Instead, dispersal in these species has evolved to avoid the effects of inbreeding. By moving away from the home ranges of close female relatives, the males run no risk of breeding with them.

Bannertailed kangaroo rats (*Dipodomys spectabolis*) live in the deserts of the American southwest. They build mounds with numerous tunnels where they shelter and store seeds for eating when fresh food is unavailable. It seems that in this species, dispersal has evolved to enable juveniles to take over vacant mounds. Both males and females migrate, but they travel only as far as the first available mound.

What factors in a small mammal's early

life impel it to make its hazardous journey into unknown territory? If a young male Belding's ground squirrel does not leave home because it is hungry or because it has no burrow, what triggers its departure? Males are no more likely than females to be attacked by other squirrels, so it is not that they are chased away.

The cause of dispersal lies within the squirrels rather than in their environment. Young male ground squirrels are much more inclined to make exploratory trips than females, and are also much bolder, to the point that they behave quite fearlessly in dangerous situations. Male hormones are the reason for these differences. When female ground squirrels are injected with testosterone, the key male hormone, on the day they are born, they behave like males in every way, including dispersal.

A young male ground squirrel is at its most fearless, and is most inclined to explore, when it weighs about 125 grams (4 1/2 ounces). At this point the animal leaves the natal area. The effects of sex hormones, combined with attaining a particular body weight, appear to trigger dispersal in these creatures. Physiological characteristics such as these may very well promote dispersal in other small mammals.

◀ A young Belding's ground squirrel (*Spermophilus beldingi*) pauses for a snack. Very similar in appearance and habits to Richardson's ground squirrel, this species has a more southerly distribution, and is common from Oregon southward. It lives in small social groups and is active during the day.

▼ An Ord's kangaroo rat (*Ordi dipodomys*) in its burrow. So-called because of their long tails, well-developed hindquarters, and hopping gait, kangaroo rats are common and widespread rodents of the American southwest. They are nocturnal, inhabit mainly deserts, and feed mostly on seeds.

J. Cancalosi/Auscape

LEMMINGS—SMALL TRAVELERS OF THE NORTH

William Z. Lidicker, Jr

Aside from the rats and mice that live in the company of humans, lemmings are perhaps the best known of all small mammals, although they are seldom seen. They live only in the inhospitable Arctic and alpine tundra, and their fame rests on their "suicidal marches to the sea."

Spectacular lemming marches are described in Scandinavian legends. The lemmings were supposed to have originated from "foul matter" in the clouds, and caused terror and grief to those whose lands they invaded. It was not until 1878 that the phenomenon of lemming outbreaks was first noted in scientific literature. Then, in 1924, following an expedition to northern Norway, the British ecologist Charles Elton brought the cyclical nature of lemming populations to the attention of ecologists. Since then scientists have struggled to understand the dramatic fluctuations in numbers that characterize lemming

▼ Except in time of mass movements, Norwegian lemmings remain above the timber line, moving seasonally between alpine meadows (summer) and subalpine heath of stunted birch and willows (winter). When outbreaks occur, lemmings travel longer distances in search of uncrowded overwintering sites. They move along paths of least resistance that often take them down the mountains to human habitations, fjords, and even the ocean.

populations, and those of many of their relatives.

Lemmings belong to a family of herbivorous rodents (the Arvicolidae) distributed throughout the northern hemisphere, which includes voles, meadow mice, and the North American muskrat. Except for the latter, they are small, weighing less than 150 grams (5 1/2 ounces), and have short rounded ears, short tails, and a "dumpy" appearance. They generally construct burrows and often make paths through the grass that betray their presence to the numerous predators that consider them delectable, as well as to the biologists who study them.

Strictly speaking, the name "lemming" applies to about 13 species in the genera *Dicrostonyx* and *Lemmus*. The former, commonly known as collared lemmings, do not appear to engage in mass migrations. There are two widespread species of *Lemmus*, plus a few island forms. The Siberian lemming (*L. sibericus*), which inhabits the Siberian tundra from the White Sea to the Bering Strait, is now usually considered to be the same species as the North American brown lemming. The latter occurs across Alaska to Baffin Island. The Norwegian lemming (*L. lemmus*) inhabits the mountains of southern Norway through Lapland to the

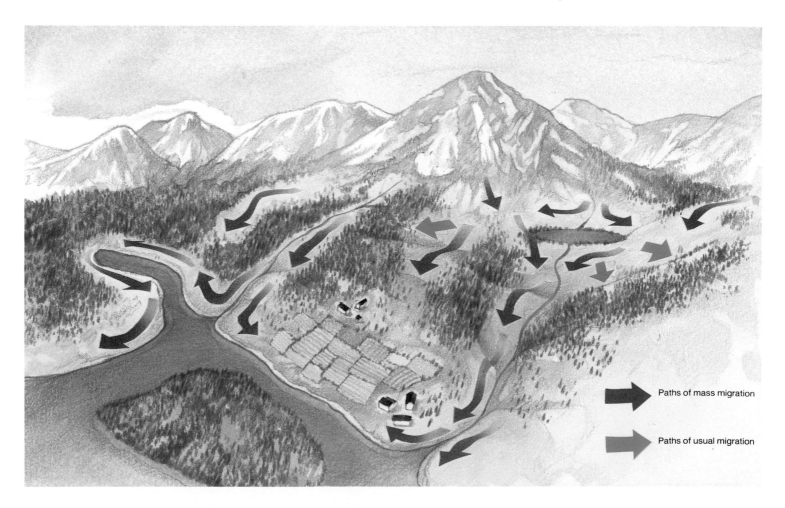

Paths of mass migration

Paths of usual migration

western shores of the White Sea in the Soviet Union. Both species are known to exhibit the quite regular multi-annual fluctuations in numbers that are necessary for the famous mass movements to occur.

To understand the great lemming marches, it is necessary to focus on the Norwegian lemming, as it is from this species that the evidence for mass movements comes. Although a few long-term studies have been done on lemmings in Alaska, Canada, and the Soviet Union, the terrain they inhabit in these countries is flat and movements are much more difficult to detect. In Scandinavia lemmings inhabit a land of gigantic relief, where there are numerous lakes, waterfalls, and spectacular fjords.

Lemmings are seasonally migratory, moving every year from winter habitats to summer habitats and back. In winter they live in dry heathland or on rocky slopes where there is a thick blanket of snow. When the melting snow floods their burrows, they move to summer pastures in moist areas such as alongside streams or bogs. At the end of the breeding season they return to their overwintering sites, a migration that starts as early as July and continues for several months. Adult males leave first, followed by adult females, and finally juveniles. When lemming densities are low, which is most of the time, movements may be fairly short and are only detectable through the tracking of marked individuals.

Every three to four years, however, lemming populations typically increase dramatically from less than 1 to perhaps 200 animals per hectare (2 1/2 acres). Such increases occur when there are few predators, when good conditions in winter allow breeding to occur under the snow, and when a favorable summer follows. Lemmings are capable of producing a litter every three weeks so their reproductive potential is enormous. In the mountains of southern Norway, near the Hardanger Glacier, the lemming population has been studied intensively since 1970, and records dating back to 1870 have been scrutinized to build up an extensive history of this population. Here the average cycle length is 3.6 years.

When peak densities occur, the autumn migration is more noticeable. Lemmings must travel farther to find suitable winter habitats, and become quite aggressive both toward each other and toward any would-be predator or inquisitive biologist interfering with their search.

At the ninth or tenth peak in a series, every 32 to 36 years, a massive outbreak occurs. Numbers reach extraordinary levels, and the subsequent autumn migration is spectacular. Lemmings pour from their breeding grounds in search of a suitable place to spend the winter, and as there is more space downhill, this is the direction they take. They can cover considerable distances, often crossing farmlands. Some even enter towns. They eat whatever plants they can find. They do not move in any socially coordinated way, but are extremely aggressive and try to avoid one another. Some eventually end up on the edges of lakes or fjords and are forced into the water by the vast numbers of their fellows that accumulate along the shores. Lemmings are good swimmers, and they would only enter such large bodies of water with the intention of crossing, but inevitably many of them drown. In fact most of the lemmings in those years are unable to find a suitable wintering habitat and huge numbers die. The few that succeed in overwintering become pioneers and start the process all over again.

Mary Evans Picture Library

▼ ◄ Populations of the Norwegian lemming are subject to two interlocking cycles of abundance, the causes of which remain largely obscure. Every three or four years (on average) the population increases by a factor of about 200, while every 32 to 36 years the population rises even more dramatically and reaches plague proportions. When this happens, lemmings swarm over the countryside in huge numbers. Driven by sheer pressure of numbers behind, they will enter agricultural lands and attempt to cross any body of water they cannot circumvent.

Tom McHugh/Photo Researchers, Inc.

In Finnish Lapland, massive outbreaks occurred in 1902–03, 1938, and 1970. The next one is expected in 2002. Following the 1902–03 peak, lemmings moved out of the mountains and traveled several hundred kilometers during the subsequent few years, even reaching the shores of the Baltic. Successful populations were established in numerous sites along the way, some of which persisted for a decade or more and underwent typical cycles in numbers. Eventually, however, the species' range shrank back to where it had been before the outbreak.

Thus, rather than being bent on suicide, the migrating lemming is simply trying to make the best of an extremely overpopulated habitat. Its propensity to disperse is closely related to its seasonal migrations that take place in a demanding environment. Given their northerly distribution, it may be that as favorable habitats came and went through glacial advances and retreats, natural selection favored those individuals willing to explore over long distances in search of suitable home sites. It may not be coincidental that Norwegian lemmings share a landscape with the likes of Leiv Eiriksson, Roald Amundsen, and Thor Heyerdahl.

BEARS AND OTHER CARNIVORES

Lynn Rogers

The movements of carnivores are governed largely by the movements of their prey, and the need to find living areas away from where they were born. When food supplies fail, certain carnivores, particularly bears, travel great distances in search of nourishment, before returning home.

A young male timber wolf (*Canis lupus*) suddenly moves 886 kilometers (550 miles) away from its lifelong range. A young female lynx (*Lynx canadensis*) moves 483 kilometers (300 miles) away from a place that usually abounds with snowshoe hares. An 11-year-old male black bear (*Ursus americanus*) moves 200 kilometers (125 miles) outside his home area, but returns two months later. These are unusual movements for animals that generally live in areas less than 40 kilometers (25 miles) in diameter, but with the aid of radiotelemetry such movements are being revealed more and more frequently.

Modern studies have given new insights into the travels and capabilities of bears and other carnivores. Their long-range movements usually fall into one of three categories. They are either annual migrations to hunting or feeding areas, unusual movements in years of widespread food failures, or permanent migrations to new living areas.

ANNUAL MIGRATIONS TO HUNTING OR FEEDING AREAS

Annual migration for most animals involves movements to feeding or breeding sites, and is usually tied to changes in season and to the availability of plant or invertebrate animal foods. Most members of the order Carnivora, however, are one step removed from this process, in that their movements are dictated primarily by the movements of their prey. The most common prey of mammalian predators are relatively sedentary mammals, reptiles, amphibians, fish, invertebrates, and ground-dwelling birds, with nesting waterfowl and other seasonally migrant birds sometimes giving a seasonal dietary boost.

Since most prey species do not show seasonal migrations, neither do most carnivores. Exceptions are wolves, lions (*Panthera leo*), and other carnivores whose survival in some locations depends upon seasonally migratory prey like caribou, elk, bison, and African antelopes.

Arctic wolf packs (*Canis lupus tundarum*) follow migrating caribou hundreds of kilometers, and the wolves that formerly occupied the great plains of North America probably followed nomadic herds of bison just as some tribes of Indians did. Lions that live on less mobile prey remain within home ranges of 25 to 400 square kilometers (10 to 155 square miles), but other lions, mostly males, follow migrating herds of wildebeest and other herbivores of the African plains, moving up to 13 kilometers (8 miles) per day. Spotted hyenas (*Crocuta crocuta*) are also flexible in their migratory habits. Of those studied on the Serengeti Plains, some established territories, some followed migratory wildebeest and some commuted up to 80 kilometers (50 miles) from their dens to wherever the main concentrations of game were at the time. In other parts of the world, mountain lions (*Felis concolor*), snow leopards (*Panthera uncia*), and other mountain-dwelling predators follow prey to high elevations in summer and to low elevations in winter.

Carnivores that live in harsh climates are well adapted for the weather. Wolves, foxes, lynxes, Siberian tigers (*Panthera tigris altaica*) and others endure extreme cold by growing thick winter pelts. Some of these animals burrow under the snow for extra protection in the worst weather. Others, like black bears, grizzly bears (*Ursus arctos*), skunks (*Mephitis mephitis*), and badgers (*Taxidea taxus*) reduce their metabolisms to varying degrees and spend their winters mostly underground, hibernating. The same animals withstand summer heat by shedding their underfur and seeking shade, water, or

▲ A young North American black bear. Adult carnivores are, on the whole, less migratory than other large mammals, but youngsters may travel great distances in search of suitable living spaces. In the black bear this post-natal migration is especially marked in males. Young females tend to remain in their mothers' territories, and may ultimately inherit them.

▶ An Alaskan grizzly bear catching salmon as they migrate up river to spawn. The salmon migrate annually in huge numbers and provide a food resource that is temporarily abundant and easy for the bears to catch. Grizzly bears come from great distances to take advantage of this seasonal bonanza.

Stephen J. Krasemann/DRK Photo

▲ Carnivores that rely heavily on a single prey species must keep up with the travels of their prey. Opportunistic predators, on the other hand, rely heavily on an intimate knowledge of their surroundings to ensure a dependable food supply—an advantage that may be lost should the animal leave its home range. The red fox (*Vulpes vulpes*), a versatile predator that includes berries, insects, and carrion in its usual diet of small vertebrates, is a good example of a fairly sedentary predator. There are fox dens that are known to have been in constant use for decades.

cool burrows. In Arctic summers, polar bears (*Thalarctos maritimus*) sometimes burrow down to the permafrost in order to cool off.

Seasonally migrant carnivores must have a sedentary period in which to raise their young. At birth, their offspring have their eyes closed and are unable to walk, and they require several weeks or months of intensive parental protection and feeding before they can travel. In contrast, the mobile animals on which these carnivores prey give birth to young that can follow a herd within a few days of birth. In some species, like the lions of the Serengeti Plains of Africa, it is primarily males without parental responsibilities that follow the herds of migrating herbivores.

Migrations by carnivores tend to be less

predictable than migrations by herbivores and birds because carnivores are less directly tied to the seasonal cycle of plant growth and insect abundance. Black bears are most likely to show regular seasonal migrations because they are omnivorous, feeding on vegetation in spring, berries and nuts in the summer and autumn, and to some extent on flesh and insects. But migrations even by black bears are unpredictable and local, depending upon local food distribution and individual knowledge of distant food sources.

Bear migrations are by individuals, or by mothers and cubs, and not by large groups. Loose gatherings of competing bears may form where there is plenty of food, and in fact the closest associations between black bears are seen where food is most abundant.

HOW FAR WILL CARNIVORES TRAVEL?

How far bears travel in years of food failures is unknown, for the home ranges of bears that show up outside the species' range have not been determined. However, an 11-year-old male provided some insight when drought destroyed the berry crop in his usual range in northeastern Minnesota in 1976.

He moved south, then west, leaving behind the coniferous forests of his home area and traveling though deciduous forests and farmland to an oak area in central Minnesota, 201 kilometers (125 miles) away. There he settled and fattened until mid-October when it was time to return home and enter a den. Instead of retracing his indirect route, however, he turned directly homeward, moving through farmland, skirting residential areas with barking dogs, and passing through somewhat developed areas where bears are seldom seen. He also switched to purely nocturnal travel. He was in unfamiliar land, but he knew his way, moving directly homeward under clear skies or overcast, maintaining a compass-like homeward bearing and ignoring roads and paths that would take him even slightly off course. When he reached his usual range he resumed his normal schedule of daytime travel and began, almost exclusively, to use familiar, easy routes, even though they meandered off course at times. He obviously knew the roads and where they led, and took advantage of them. Finally, he turned off one of the roads, walked over a hill, and entered an old rock den that was just large enough for his 200 kilogram (400 pound) body. His travels were over for the year.

Denver Bryan/Carrstock

▲ A black bear at a deer carcass. Nuts, berries, tubers, eggs, honey, and insect larvae are the staple diet of most bears for much of the year. But they also eat carrion as well as any small mammals and birds they can catch.

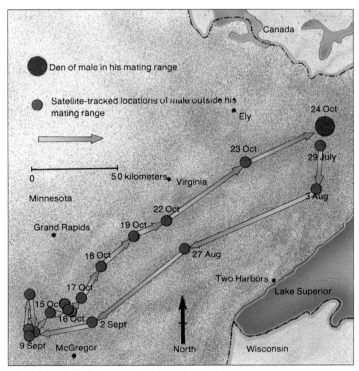

▲ Bears sometimes wander great distances. This individual was tracked for more than 200 kilometers (125 miles) before it finally returned to its home range to den for the winter. At first it meandered by day, but on the return journey it traveled only at night, maintaining a constant compass bearing.

The skills bears use in returning from distant feeding sites are probably some of the same mental "map-and-compass" skills that troublesome bears use in returning home after being transported and released some distance away. Transported black bears have returned home from up to 229 kilometers (142 miles) away. Other transported carnivores have found their way home from equally impressive distances: polar bears, 480 kilometers (298 miles); timber wolves, 282 kilometers (175 miles); grizzly bears, 258 kilometers (160 miles); house cats, 217 kilometers (135 miles); red foxes, 56 kilometers (35 miles); coyotes, 48 kilometers (30 miles); and kit foxes, 32 kilometers (20 miles). Surprisingly, it is the white-tailed deer, an animal which usually stays within a small home range, that holds the record for homing by a land mammal—560 kilometers (348 miles).

▲ Lions (*Panthera leo*) specialize in large prey, such as zebras, which they hunt cooperatively. Their usual hunting technique is a combination of stalking and ambush. The females move quietly into position and wait in long grass, while the male or males spook the prey to within range. The females then charge and bring down the prey, all attacking it at once. When hunting in groups, males are seldom involved in the actual killing.

At garbage dumps bears sometimes feed less than a meter (3 feet) apart and some bears find partners to wrestle and play with. In natural feeding areas, where food is less plentiful, bears usually stay more than 100 meters (330 feet) apart, even in places well known for black bears. One such place is Mukwonago (derived from the Indian words *mukwa*, bear and *onahko*, fat), in Wisconsin, which was famous for the large number of bears that gathered to eat acorns

in the white oak stands of that area in the early 1800s. Indians and white men would converge on the area from considerable distances to hunt the bears—a migration of human predators.

Along the north shore of Lake Superior, food is most plentiful inland in early summer, and near the shore in late summer and autumn. Some of the inland bears were radio-collared and followed to learn whether they explored outside their usual living areas

Stephen J. Krasemann/DRK Photo

and found the richer food supplies near the shore in season. Forty percent of 105 females and 69 percent of 32 males left their usual ranges each year, on the average, and foraged 7 to 92 kilometers (4 to 57 miles) away, sometimes abandoning abundant food at home. Not all the trips were pure exploration. Some of the bears had learned of the food-rich area near the shore from their mothers and returned to it as independent adults. Seventy percent of the trips were to that area. One mother had found an oak stand near the shore, 30 kilometers (18 1/2 miles) outside her territory, and led litter after litter to it over the years. She and her cubs fattened on acorns in years when more sedentary bears were without this food. The cubs returned to the stand in subsequent years and became the fastest growing, earliest maturing bears in the study area, their clan reproducing more rapidly than the sedentary clans.

Sean Avery/Planet Earth Pictures

▲ The spotted hyena (*Crocuta crocuta*) is one of the most abundant large carnivores in Africa. It is essentially a scavenger, but in some areas—especially the Serengeti in East Africa—groups follow the migration of wildebeest, preying heavily on new-born wildebeest calves.

FORCED MOVEMENTS

In years when there has been widespread failure of their normal foods, starving carnivores have made spectacular journeys. Canadian lynxes are noted for their southward migrations during years when snowshoe hare numbers are low in their usual range. Lynxes are seldom seen in the United States, but during these years they become common in northern Minnesota and are seen occasionally as far south as Minneapolis, more than 400 kilometers (250 miles) south of the Canadian border. Lynxes fresh from Canada are seen crossing roads, watching traffic from the roadside, and moving through people's yards. After a year or so the lynxes disappear, either because they have been trapped, shot, or killed on the roads, or they have returned to

the forests of Canada. A young adult female lynx that was ear-tagged in Minnesota on 5 November 1974, during an invasion, moved 483 kilometers (300 miles) northwest into Canada, where she was caught on 20 January 1977. Her movement is the longest on record for a lynx. The next longest movement recorded was for a male that lost a foot and was nursed back to health in captivity. By the time he recovered, another male had moved into his former territory. The homeless lynx then wandered on three legs until he was shot raiding a farmer's poultry an astonishing 164 kilometers (100 miles) away.

Migrating black bears have been making news in eastern North America for more than a century. These migrations differ from the more regular, shorter migrations made by

▲ Black bears (*Ursus americanus*) are found throughout North America wherever there are extensive forests and few people. Migrations by black bears are usually less than 17 kilometers (10 1/2 miles) and occur mostly in late summer or autumn when some bears make traditional movements to rich feeding areas to eat acorns, beechnuts, or other seasonal foods. Bears travel farther, up to 200 kilometers (125 miles), in years when food is scarce. Young males seeking new living areas may also move this far. Biologists estimate that there are between 400,000 and 500,000 black bears in North America.

bears visiting known feeding areas or exploring the region surrounding their territories. In years when there is widespread failure of berry, nut, and acorn crops, starving black bears may leave a region in large numbers and move to an area that is ecologically different. Black bears in northern forests can move into temperate deciduous forest regions or even beyond, to the prairie edge. Today, prairies have mostly been converted into farms and cities, and when a bear moves to the suburbs of Minneapolis it is likely to be killed. The same was true in the 1880s when waves of bears moved through populated areas. In years of mass movements, bears were commonly found along water barriers such as the Atlantic Ocean, the Mississippi River, and the Great Lakes. They moved along the shorelines until they encountered cities, where they were often killed. Bears are still found on a few of these old migration routes. For example, 160 black bears were killed in 1985 on one such route on the outskirts of Duluth and Thunder Bay, both cities on the north shore of Lake Superior.

PERMANENT MOVES TO NEW LIVING AREAS

Many young mammals leave their birthplaces for good before breeding. This movement outward from the maternal range is often called dispersal. The longest movements on record for most species involve adolescent animals seeking places to begin their adult lives. Dispersal is primarily by males in promiscuous or polygamous mammals, but involves both sexes in monogamous mammals, such as the timber wolf and dwarf mongoose (*Helogale parvula*).

◄ The Canadian lynx (*Lynx canadensis*) relies very heavily on the snowshoe hare as its chief prey. This hare is largely sedentary, so that lynxes seldom have occasion to leave their extensive home ranges. However, in a more or less regular cycle spanning some 9 to 10 years the population of snowshoe hares declines abruptly, and lynx are then compelled by hunger to wander far from their normal habitat. They may cover hundreds of kilometers in their wanderings, some even penetrating southward into the United States, where the species is normally rare.

Alan Carey/Photo Researchers Inc.

191

In group-living animals, such as wolves and lions, mating success is achieved primarily by being a member of a group, so dispersal for these species is more a matter of intergroup transfer than simply finding a suitable location in which to establish an adult range. Lone wolves or groups of male lions may roam for months or years before integrating with new packs or prides. Young wolves or lions lucky enough to find mates and space may form new packs or prides of their own.

Dispersal may be voluntary or forced, depending upon social circumstances. In a group of male lions in Tanzania, all left their natal prides before mating. Some left voluntarily to rove in search of new prides to take over. Others were forced out when roving males took over their prides. Subadult females may also be ousted during these takeovers and often become the nuclei of new prides in adjoining areas. Females that reach sexual maturity before their pride is taken over by a new group of males may remain in that pride for life.

Dispersing lions or wolves may settle in adjacent living areas or travel to the limits of the species' range. Of 10 young wolves radio-tracked in northeastern Minnesota, four (two males and two females) took over territories adjacent to their parents' territories, three (two males and one female) moved more than 190 kilometers (120 miles), and three (two males and one female) traveled intermediate distances. Of the last-mentioned, one explored up to

▼ The coyote (*Canis latrans*) is popularly regarded as an animal of the American southwest, but in fact this supremely versatile carnivore is common across much of North America. This may be a recent phenomenon, however. The coyote may have expanded eastward at the expense of the wolf, which has been virtually exterminated in eastern forests since European settlement.

80 kilometers (50 miles) away, returned home, and then settled adjacent to his natal territory. The 886 kilometer (550 mile) movement by one of these wolves—the young male mentioned at the beginning of the chapter—is probably the longest migration on record for a land carnivore. The wolf moved from near International Falls, Minnesota, to near Nipawan, Saskatchewan, in less than 10 months. The second longest movement by a carnivore was also by a young male wolf. He moved 670 kilometers (416 miles) from near Great Slave Lake, Northwest Territories, to near Cold Lake, Alberta, in less than 81 days.

Dispersal by black bears is almost entirely by males. Males travel with their mothers for nearly one and a half years, remain in their mothers' territories for up to two years after that, and leave home when they are 1 1/2 to 3 1/2 years old. The fastest growing males leave home earliest, sometimes soon after they leave their mother's side. Although in this species leaving the mother's territory is voluntary, and occurs whether or not there is ample food, continuing travel outside her territory often takes place because older males and females chase, attack, and sometimes even kill strange bears. This aggression can channel dispersing young bears into suburban areas where they avoid bear trouble but instead get into trouble eating from garbage cans, fruit trees, gardens, bird feeders, and dog food bowls. The bears most often seen during dispersal are young males weighing between 30 and 80 kilograms (66 and 176 pounds).

In northeastern Minnesota, young males settle an average of 61 kilometers (38 miles) away from their birthplaces, with some going no further than 13 kilometers (8 miles) and some traveling as far as 219 kilometers (136 miles). The longer dispersal movements may take more than a year. One male spent a year moving 145 kilometers (90 miles) and then moved another 74 kilometers (46 miles) in the next two weeks. Along the way, he settled briefly near a residential area where there were fruit trees, garbage, and a few other bears. Young males approaching mating age do not settle permanently where there are no females. They begin mating between 3 1/2 and 4 1/2 years of age.

Young females usually stay near their birthplaces, growing to maturity within their mothers' territories. When the young females reach adulthood and require additional space, their mothers shift their own territories away to include new areas. In this way, they both protect their daughters and help them obtain

Stephen J. Krasemann/DRK Photo

living space. Where there is crowding, mothers prefer to battle non-relatives for territory rather than attack their own daughters, whom they continue to recognize.

Dispersal, exploration, and annual migration are similar in that each may involve long movements from the usual living areas. They differ in that dispersal usually involves a one-way migration to a new, more or less permanent, living area, while exploration and annual migrations typically are round trips.

▲ ▼ Polar bears (*Thalarctos maritimus*) sometimes move hundreds of kilometers on drifting ice floes and over seemingly featureless terrain, but somehow they know where they are and do not wander aimlessly. Subpopulations of polar bears maintain fidelity to living areas that are often only 50 to 300 kilometers (30 to 185 miles) in diameter, and females return to traditional denning areas. Polar bears spread out on the ice to hunt seals but aggregate around ice-free channels where hunting is best. Biologists estimate that there are between 20,000 and 40,000 polar bears in the world.

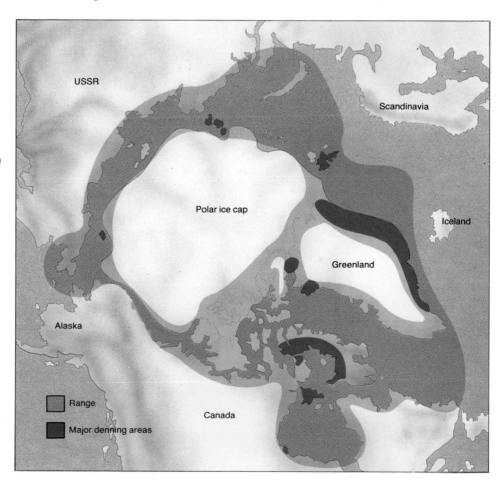

ELEPHANTS

Jeheskel Shoshani

Elephants need to travel to and fro over considerable distances to find the immense amount of food they require, but their habitats are being eroded at such a rate, through the spread of agriculture and human habitation, that they may soon be left with nowhere to go.

The African elephant (*Loxodonta africana*) is now found in 35 countries south of the Sahara Desert, mostly in nature reserves. East African elephant populations are the best known, followed by those in southern Africa, Central, and West Africa. In the Orient, the Asian elephant (*Elephas maximus*) is confined to fragmented habitats in 13 countries. The elephants of Sri Lanka have been the most extensively studied.

Elephant societies are organized along matriarchal lines. The most stable unit is the family, composed of a cow and three to five of her immediate offspring. An association of a few families comprises a bond group, and a concentration of these groups makes up a clan of 50 or more individuals. "Herd" is a general term which applies to any number of associated elephants, of females, mixed males and females, or males alone. The leader of a herd acquires her position through years of observing and learning from her older family members.

Male elephants stay with their families until they reach puberty, at about 13 years of age, and they then are usually driven away by older females of the same herd. These adolescent bulls either join bachelor herds or forage alone. Compared to female or mixed clans and herds, associations of male elephants appear to be short-lived and their composition is continuously changing. Adult sexually active bulls move in search of females in estrus while sexually inactive males may remain together.

PATTERNS OF MIGRATION

Large concentrations of elephants and intermingling herds are most common during the dry season, the animals congregating around waterholes, lakes, riverbeds, and other types of wetland. With the onset of the rains queues of elephants begin to form and the herds spread out, moving toward drier grasslands, zones with mixed habitats, and forested areas.

Mating and calving are closely associated

▲ Elephants at a salt-lick. Like many other large mammals, elephants in some areas suffer a shortage of certain mineral salts in their diet. To remedy this deficiency they habitually visit claypans and similar places where salts are concentrated on the surface, eating the soil to ingest the salts.

▶ Despite its thickness, an elephant's skin is extremely sensitive, and a coating of mud or dust provides a degree of welcome protection from insect bites and sunburn. Elephants often wallow in mud or, like these animals, spray themselves with dust.

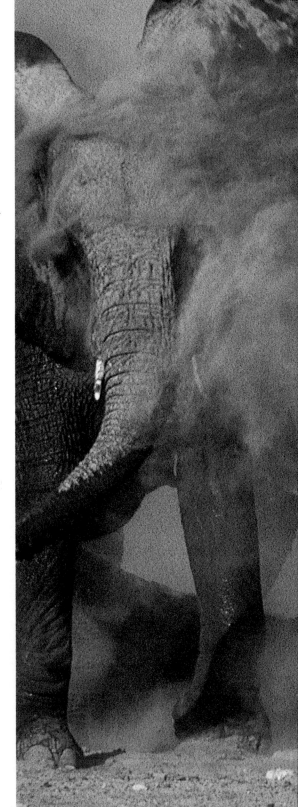

Keith Scholey/Planet Earth Pictures

with the rains. Elephants mate most frequently during the middle of the rainy season. The gestation period for elephants is around 22 months (the longest of any terrestrial mammal), so that births occur in the second wet season following conception, at a time when food is plentiful.

Movements within a home range, or seasonal migrations, are in the form of a loop or a circuit. Home ranges vary in size from 15 to 50 square kilometers (6 to 20 square miles) for females and young, and from 500 to 1,500 square kilometers (195 to 600 square miles) for males. The difference in ranges is due to the wanderings of bull elephants from one female clan to another in search of receptive cows. Seasonal home ranges may also vary; depending on the particular habitat, elephants may have to travel long distances at some times of year in search of food and water. Sometimes home ranges overlap, enabling elephants to mate with animals outside their immediate group. This provides essential genetic

▶ Elephants are strongly social animals and the basic unit is the family, consisting of a female and several of her offspring. This family is on the move in the Amboseli National Park in Kenya.

▼ A simplified diagram showing the relationship between wet and dry seasons, migration, and reproduction in elephants, both African and Asian.

diversity. As they travel, families also explore new niches both within and outside their home ranges.

The overlapping of home ranges and exploration of new habitats sometimes mark the beginning of a one-way migration, for, should a new area prove to be worthwhile, the elephants will probably stay longer than usual, and the area of their home range will shift in the direction of the new habitat. Successive explorations can lead to an overall shift in the home range from one locale to another, which translates into a one-way migration.

WHY DO ELEPHANTS MIGRATE?

One of the main reasons why elephants migrate is to find food. Elephants feed on leaves, bark, fruit, grass, and herbs. With a body mass of 2 to 7 tonnes (4,400 to 15,500 pounds), an adult requires about 75 to 150 kilograms (165 to 330 pounds) of food, and about 150 to 300 liters (40 to 80 gallons) of water per day. As a result elephants spend about 70 to 90 percent of a

24-hour cycle either feeding or moving toward a food source, using the rest of the time for bathing, drinking, resting, and sleeping. They usually stay for a few days in one area before moving on. If they do not move on, they may well destroy the habitat.

Elephants' movements are also tied to the availability of salt-licks. Families sometimes travel tens or even hundreds of kilometers to reach dry ponds or mudholes where the salt content is relatively high. Salts and other minerals available from these sources are essential to the animals' health. Because an elephant's tongue is too short to be used as a licking organ, they have to eat the soil at these salt-licks. At Mount Elgon National Park in Kenya people have been startled to see African bush elephants excavating and eating salt-bearing rocks in the caves.

HOW DO ELEPHANTS NAVIGATE?

It seems that elephants navigate using the sun, the moon, and the stars, and landmarks such as mountains and rivers. Non visual cues such as climatic changes (for example,

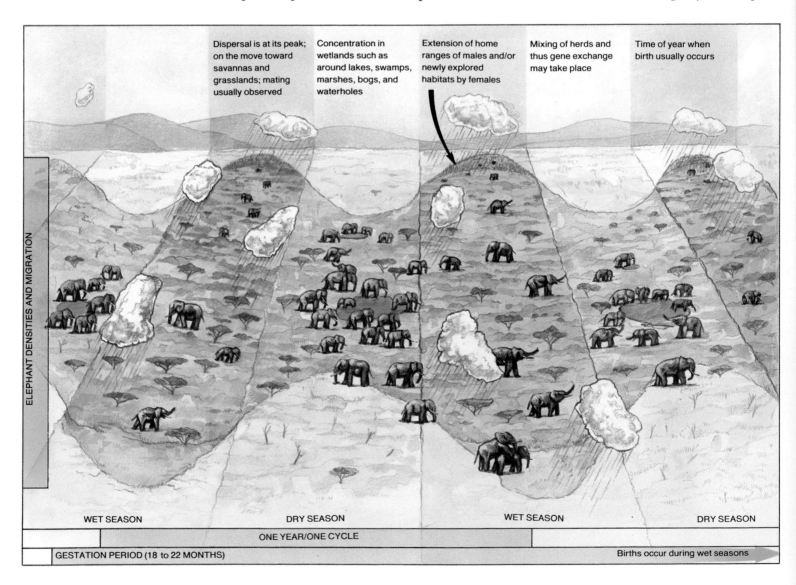

Dispersal is at its peak; on the move toward savannas and grasslands; mating usually observed

Concentration in wetlands such as around lakes, swamps, marshes, bogs, and waterholes

Extension of home ranges of males and/or newly explored habitats by females

Mixing of herds and thus gene exchange may take place

Time of year when birth usually occurs

ELEPHANT DENSITIES AND MIGRATION

WET SEASON   DRY SEASON   WET SEASON   DRY SEASON

ONE YEAR/ONE CYCLE

GESTATION PERIOD (18 to 22 MONTHS)   Births occur during wet seasons

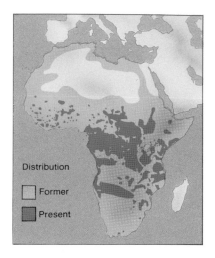

▲ The former (about 5,000 years ago) and present distribution of the African elephant.

Distribution

☐ Former

☐ Present

day length, temperature, wind, and humidity) may also be used, as elephants avoid the heat of the day and most movements take place either in the early morning, or late in the afternoon and during the evening.

Elephant society is a tightly knit one. Daughters, sisters, and aunts remain with their families until death, and may trek the same roads repeatedly on their seasonal migrations. Amongst such groups learning and accumulated experience, coupled with the elephants' legendary memory, play an important role in navigation.

Elephants move along well-established paths, taking routes which require the least expenditure of energy. These paths often follow a river basin, a valley, or a watershed. In the past engineers have used elephant or other big game trails to establish the best baselines for roads along escarpments; an example is the old main road from Nairobi to Nakuru in Kenya.

Recently scientists have discovered that elephants have a "secret" language. Experiments have shown that at a distance of 1.6 to 2.4 kilometers (1 to 1 1/2 miles) elephants seem to be able to recognize signals emitted by other elephants and respond accordingly. Males, for example, move in the direction of a female in estrus, and elephants at different locations seem to synchronize their behavior in response to stress signals. In Zimbabwe field studies showed that, without eye contact, three elephant herds coordinated their movements, moving in a synchronized fashion toward food sources. It is thought that the elephants

Jana Schneider/The Image Bank

◀ An Indian elephant keeping cool in Nepal. This species is most easily distinguished from its African relative by its much smaller ears and rounded back.

are probably communicating in infrasonic, low-frequency sound waves which are inaudible to humans but which scientists are able to detect electronically and observe in sonograms.

The elephant's acute sense of smell and a sensitive skin which enables it to detect wind direction, may also play a part in migratory movements. Early this century scientists in Africa reported that, toward the end of a rainy season, elephants often moved toward swampy areas, sometimes in great numbers, where they would remain during the dry season until the onset of the next rains. How did they know when and in what direction to move? Undoubtedly there is more than a single mechanism involved, but it is probable that certain elephants may be able to detect pollens or chemical cues released from swampy vegetation. They would then share this information with others.

MIGRATION AND SURVIVAL

Today elephants are found in protected areas and in isolated regions far from human activities. In Asia the estimated wild elephant population in 1990 was between 34,000 and 54,000. In Africa the wild elephant population was estimated in 1990 at fewer than 750,000, half the 1980 figure. The sharp decline in Africa is the result of poaching and loss of elephant habitat to agriculture. When herds of elephants can migrate freely in and out of national parks the number of animals in a park at any one time will be in balance with the available food and water. When parks are bordered by dense human populations, however,

imbalances arise, resulting in impaired migration routes. In some areas elephant numbers have been decimated by poachers; in others, there is insufficient space for the animals. When food supplies are limited elephants overgraze the grasslands, destroy trees, and ultimately starve. Under such circumstances park personnel can either simply let nature take its course, or cull. Some governments choose culling, since selling the meat and other by-products raises funds that can be used for the purposes of conservation.

In general, elephant habitats are diminishing. The situation is now critical. For elephants to survive, it is essential that humans, their only natural enemy, work to protect them, and make sure their migratory paths are conserved.

◀ A family of elephants feeding at a baobab tree. African elephants browse more than they graze, and much of their diet consists of the leaves, stems, and bark of trees. In foraging they destroy far more than they eat.

▼ The former (about 6,000 years ago) and present distribution of the Asian elephant.

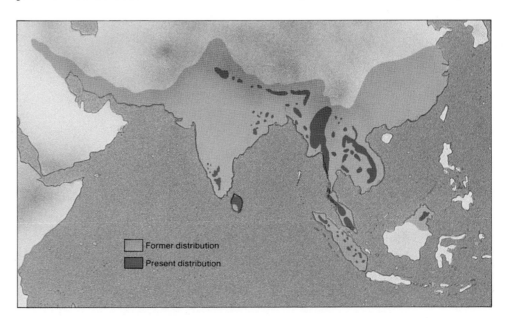

☐ Former distribution

■ Present distribution

CARIBOU

Steven G. Fancy

Michio Hoshino/Animals & Earth

▲ A caribou mother with her calf. Some caribou cover greater distances in their annual migrations than any other land animal.

▼ Members of the Porcupine Herd of caribou on their wintering grounds. These animals are known as "caribou" in North America and "reindeer" in Scandinavia and Siberia, but belong to the same species.

Stephen Krasemann/DRK Photo

Living in a harsh environment that is under snow for much of the year, the caribou thrive. These animals, the world's greatest walkers, travel vast distances to find the food they need, and to give birth in the relative safety of the open tundra.

Barren-ground caribou (*Rangifer tarandus*) are celebrated for their extensive migrations, but the scale of their movements has only recently become known through studies made of the Porcupine Herd in northeastern Alaska and northwestern Canada. Ten adult female caribou from this herd were tracked by satellite an average of 4,350 kilometers (2,700 miles) per year as they migrated between winter ranges in the northern forests and calving grounds on the Arctic coastal plain. One of these cows traveled 5,055 kilometers (3,140 miles) in a year, the greatest distance recorded for any land mammal.

The round-trip distance between the Porcupine Herd's southernmost wintering areas and its calving grounds is less than 1,500 kilometers (930 miles), so the spring and autumn migrations account for only about one-third of the annual distance traveled by some herd members. During the remainder of the year movements are less directed and are made largely in response to environmental stimuli, such as weather, insects, predators, and snow cover.

THE SPRING MIGRATION

The annual cycle of caribou movement begins with the spring migration from wintering areas to the calving grounds. The migration is led by pregnant cows, who begin the journey when the land is still frozen, and often arrive when the calving grounds are still covered by snow and therefore devoid of new green vegetation.

The environmental cues used by caribou to initiate migration, and by which they navigate while they are traveling, are not completely understood. Increasing day length plays a role, through its effects on certain hormones, but even so the start of migration in different years may vary by as much as two months. Snow and weather conditions each spring are important in determining when the animals begin moving north. The snow becomes more compact as the temperature rises and walking conditions become easier.

In terms of energy expended per unit of body weight, caribou are the most efficient travelers of any terrestrial mammal. Studies have shown that the energy cost of walking in snow increases exponentially with the depth that caribou sink into the snow. Traditional migration corridors usually take advantage of windswept ridges, frozen lakes and areas of shallow or crusted snow. If the animals encounter extremely deep snow, or snow with a shallow crust that will not fully support their weight, the migration may stall until snow conditions improve. In deep snow, the caribou travel in single file, the animal at the front of the migration, usually an adult cow, expending the greatest amount of energy breaking a trail. After several kilometers, or only a few hundred meters, another caribou will take the lead.

At the beginning of the migration, small bands of caribou start to come together to form larger groups as they slowly drift toward the calving grounds. The distance traveled each day may vary from only a few kilometers to more than 50 kilometers (30 miles). When walking single file, caribou usually travel 3 to 4 kilometers (2 to 2 1/2 miles) per hour, the speed at which they expend the least amount of energy to travel a given distance. Pregnant cows are

▼ The spring migration of the Porcupine Herd from wintering areas to the calving grounds occurs along three broad corridors: the Chandalar route in Alaska, and the Old Crow and Richardson routes in Canada. The autumn migration is less predictable, but many of the trails used in spring are again followed during autumn.

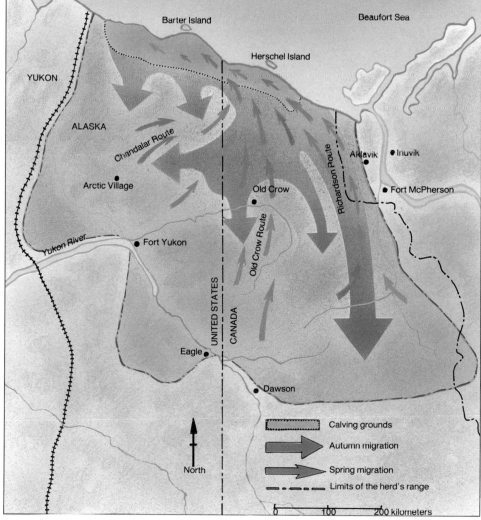

▲ A herd of caribou scattering to feed over the Arctic tundra. The color of the caribous' coat varies widely. Many individuals are spotted and some are very nearly white.

able to adjust their rate of migration so that, whatever conditions they encounter, they arrive on the calving grounds before giving birth. One group of pregnant cows, delayed by deep snows on the winter range, traveled more than 40 kilometers (25 miles) per day for 18 days, arriving on the calving grounds at the same time as another group of cows that had left the winter range one month earlier, but had traveled at a rate of less than 6 kilometers (3 1/2 miles) per day.

Caribou may spend 60 percent of the day feeding when they are migrating, taking regular rest periods. Each active period lasts two to three hours, during which they dig feeding craters to expose lichens and other forage, or graze in areas of shallow snow or on the dried leaves of shrubs. Rest periods last one to two hours, during which the caribou lie and ruminate (chew their cud). If another group of caribou walks by a group that is bedded down, some of the resting animals may stand up and join the group, continuing the journey northward. Caribou

travel both by day and by night, and some can be found walking at any hour.

Once the caribou reach the calving grounds, many of the large groups break up into smaller groups which travel in different directions, and activity patterns become less synchronized. Caribou cows are often alone when they give birth, not because they seek isolation, but because they have to stop moving and the rest of the group continues on. For a period of around seven to ten days, just after calving, the cow and her calf remain in a relatively small area, feeding on the flower buds of cottongrass and on any other available vegetation. This "calving pause" is one of the few times during the year that caribou are relatively sedentary.

Soon after calving, the mother and her calf may join other cow–calf pairs nearby, and small nursery bands form. Several of these nursery bands may gradually drift together and within two weeks of calving caribou may again be traveling an average of 12 to 16 kilometers (7 1/2 to 10 miles) per day, groups continuing to merge and move in a common direction. At this stage groups of bulls and barren females usually join with the cows and calves.

SUMMER MOVEMENTS

Caribou travel farther each day during July and August than at any other time of year. Much of this midsummer movement is to escape harassment by mosquitoes and parasitic flies. By moving to the coast or to mountain ridgetops, areas away from where the mosquitoes breed, and where the breezes and cooler temperatures discourage insects, they gain some relief. They also reduce mosquito harassment by walking into the wind, and by forming huge aggregations, sometimes over 60,000 strong. By early August the mosquitoes cease to be so troublesome and parasitic flies become the dominant insect pest.

During late July and August, the large groups of caribou begin to break up as the animals take advantage of the widespread availability of willow leaves and other food plants. In late summer and autumn, once the insects are less prevalent, the animals can spend more time grazing on the relatively plentiful supplies of fodder and replenish their fat and protein reserves for the coming cold of winter.

Some caribou travel extensively during the late summer. Porcupine Herd cows tracked by satellite have left post-calving aggregation areas on the tundra, traveled more than 500 kilometers (310 miles) south through the Brooks Range and east to the northern Richardson Mountains in the Northwest Territories of Canada, and then returned to tundra habitats along the Arctic coast, all in a period of eight weeks. Studies using computer simulation models have shown that caribou can compensate for the higher energy cost of extensive movements if they can attain even small increases in food intake or digestibility by moving to new feeding areas.

THE AUTUMN MIGRATION

Many caribou have already left the calving grounds before the autumn migration begins, but the first heavy snowfall of the winter often triggers increased movements toward the wintering areas. The autumn migration usually occurs within the same broad movement corridors that are used in spring, but it is much less predictable in terms of timing and the exact routes used. This is partly because the snow cover is much less. During spring the deep snow funnels the caribou into narrow migration corridors and strongly influences the rate of migration.

For most caribou herds, the rutting period occurs during the autumn migration. Mature bulls forego feeding and expend considerable energy establishing their dominance over each other and locating cows in estrus. The rut occurs over a large area, wherever the herd happens to be on the migration route. The rutting period is one of the few times of year that bulls, cows, and younger caribou are all found together. During the rest of the year, the bulls usually travel in separate groups, away from the cows and calves.

John Shaw/Bruce Coleman Ltd.

Although each herd has a traditional winter range that it occupies each year, the use of specific areas within that winter range varies considerably. An individual caribou may spend one winter more than 500 kilometers (310 miles) from the area she used during the previous winter. Snow and weather conditions during the autumn migration and in early winter are thought to have a major effect on which wintering areas are used.

Caribou have been known to move more than 200 kilometers (125 miles) between wintering areas during November and December, but between January and early April they usually remain within a relatively small range. They generally favor areas

▲ A bull caribou on the autumn tundra. Caribou are members of the deer family (Cervidae) and are the only species in which both sexes have antlers, although these are much smaller in females than in males. A large bull may stand about 1.2 meters (4 feet) at the shoulder, and weigh 170 to 180 kilograms (375 to 400 pounds). The spread of its antlers often approximately equals its height.

▶ (Following pages) Caribou are accomplished swimmers, and will frequently swim across a lake rather than walk around it.
Michio Hoschino/Animals & Earth

where the snow is not too deep or is easy to dig through, such as on windblown ridges or in forested areas, so that they can obtain food without too much difficulty. Caribou tracked by satellite traveled less than 5 kilometers (3 miles) per day during February and March. By April, the animals begin to drift toward the calving grounds once more.

WHY DO CARIBOU MIGRATE?

Recent studies of caribou herds in North America and Scandinavia have provided answers to many of the questions concerning caribou migration. A primary factor influencing their movements is the search for food in a seasonal and often harsh environment. Most herds have developed traditional movement patterns between winter and summer ranges as an adaptation to changes in the availability and quality of food, and to variations in snow cover, predator numbers, and insect densities.

During most of the year, slow-growing but highly digestible lichens are the main component of the caribou's diet. Winter ranges are generally areas where lichens grow relatively widely, and where soft or shallow snow makes it possible for caribou to obtain them. However, lichens contain very little of the protein and minerals which caribou need during the summer to grow rapidly and produce milk for the young calves. During the summer months, therefore, the animals move to areas where they can obtain food that will supply these essential requirements. The calving grounds also often have fewer predators than other parts of the range, and their open habitats make it easier for cows to detect and escape predators such as wolves, grizzly bears, and golden eagles.

Forage quality is influenced by factors such as latitude, altitude, and the nature of the land, which in turn influence the length of the plant growing season. The digestibility of most plants at high latitudes, and their protein and mineral content, is highest early in the growth season, decreasing as the summer progresses. Caribou bulls and barren cows frequently follow the progression of snow melt during migration to obtain the most nutritious forage. The pregnant cows, on the other hand, cannot travel at such a leisurely pace. They must reach the calving grounds before their calves are born in order to give them the best chance for survival.

Toward the end of the plant growing season, in August and September, latitudinal and altitudinal patterns of plant quality become less pronounced, and caribou disperse in small groups over large parts of their range to take advantage of local foraging opportunities. As temperatures drop and snow begins to cover the ground, lichens again become the most digestible form of food and the most available source of energy, and caribou therefore begin returning to wintering areas.

In terms of current distribution and numbers, caribou are one of the most successful large mammals on earth, despite the harsh environment in which they live. During their annual cycle, there are only a few short periods during which they pause, for movement is the key to their survival.

▼ Bull caribou fighting in Mount McKinley National Park, Alaska. For much of the year bulls congregate in separate herds away from cows and calves, and the rutting season—in autumn for most herds—is the only time that males, females, and young are found together.

Mark Newman/Auscape

TRACKING CARIBOU BY SATELLITE

Through the use of satellite communication systems it is now possible to chart caribou movements with great accuracy. Biologists are able to locate a caribou wearing a satellite transmitter as often as 10 times a day, and by using sensors within the transmitter package can obtain data about air temperature and the caribou's activities.

Before the introduction of satellites, each caribou could be located only a few times a year, given the absence of roads within most of the caribou's range, and the high cost of aircraft time. Furthermore, poor weather and long periods of darkness make it unsafe and at times impossible to conduct radio-tracking flights during the long Arctic winter.

Caribou are tracked using the Argos Data Collection and Location System, which consists of two polar-orbiting weather satellites and a network of ground tracking stations and data processing centers. Transmitters attached to neck collars on the caribou weigh 1 to 1.5 kilograms (2 to 4 pounds) and have a battery life of one to two years, depending on how often they transmit messages to the satellite. Messages containing an identification number for each transmitter and information from sensors within the transmitter package are received from active transmitters within "view" of each satellite at 60- to 90-second intervals. Differences between the frequency of each message received by the satellite and the transmitted frequency (known as the Doppler shift) are used to calculate the position of the transmitter. With recent advances in transmitter design and computer software, caribou can now be located to within a few hundred meters of their true location.

Since 1984, when the first satellite transmitters were deployed on caribou, more than 100,000 locations have been received for 70 different caribou in Alaska, and the technology is now being used to monitor the movements of at least 12 other species of large mammals around the world.

Satellite telemetry has proven to be an accurate, reliable, and cost-effective approach to monitoring caribou movements in the Arctic environment. The detailed data sets obtained for these animals will greatly assist scientists in their in-depth analyses of the many puzzling questions about caribou ecology and physiology that still remain to be answered.

Steven Fancy

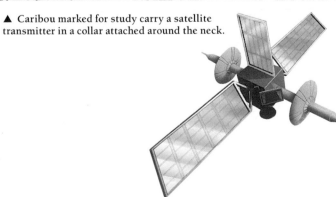

▲ Caribou marked for study carry a satellite transmitter in a collar attached around the neck.

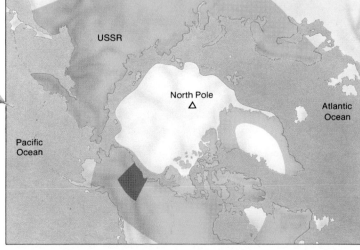

USSR

North Pole
△

Atlantic
Ocean

Pacific
Ocean

▶ World wide caribou distribution. The dark section shows the area over which caribou from the Porcupine Herd have been tracked.

WILDEBEEST

Jonathan Scott

▲ A mother wildebeest and her calf cross a shallow lake bed. Wildebeest have one young each year.

As the wildebeest herds make their way across the Serengeti Plains of East Africa, these great stretches of grassland are literally blackened by their presence. Survival for these animals means an endless search for food and water, a lifestyle to which they are superbly adapted.

Tanzania's Serengeti National Park and Kenya's Masai Mara National Reserve together comprise the most remarkable game viewing region on earth. For years visitors have been drawn to this part of Africa to see the magnificent array of predators, and the great migration of plains game—a spectacle involving the mass movement of thousands upon thousands of zebra (*Equus burchelli*), Thomson's gazelle (*Gazella thomsoni*), and wildebeest (*Connochaetes taurinus*). Vast herds of wildebeest dominate the landscape, conditioning the lives of the other creatures with whom they share the land.

Fossil evidence unearthed at Olduvai Gorge shows that wildebeest seasonally grazed on the Serengeti Plains more than a million years ago. Their ancestors may have done so for millions of years before that. Over the centuries, the wildebeest population has ebbed and flowed, shrinking in the face of disease and drought, expanding in years of good rainfall, the animals' movements dictated by the region's changing mosaic of grass and woodland.

The wildebeest move through a region that extends from the Ngorongoro Crater Highlands in the east almost to the shores of Lake Victoria in the west, and from the Eyasi Escarpment in the south, all the way north to the Mara country in Kenya. This area of 30,000 square kilometers (11,600 square miles) is known as the Serengeti–Mara ecosystem. Their annual journey through this vast region takes the form of a clockwise trek of up to 3,000 kilometers (1,900 miles).

The routes the wildebeest follow are similar to those of the past, yet each year their movements differ to some degree. The extent of the rainfall, and the time of year that it falls, determines the availability of food and thus the animals' movements. Some years it may pour for days on end, from one month to the next, throughout the rainy season. The following year the same area could be a dustbowl.

▶ Nothing deters migrating wildebeest. They sometimes suffer devastating losses at river crossings, especially during times of flood or where the banks are very high. Many plunge in recklessly, only to drown, rendered helpless by broken limbs or injured spines, or trampled in the pandemonium. At particularly dangerous crossings such as this one, a migrating herd may leave behind a river bed littered with hundreds of dead and dying wildebeest.

THE MIGRATION TO THE PLAINS

If the rains are generous in the early part of the rainy season, in November and December, the wildebeest respond by moving from their dry season holding areas among the acacia woodlands in the north and west of their ecosystem out onto the Serengeti's treeless grassy plains. The wildebeest herds form one great mass, cropping the grass as they surge forward. Each animal is always on the move, though by sheer extent of numbers the herd occupies a particular area for a week or more. Migrating wildebeest are the most remarkable sight, with kilometer upon kilometer of the plains blackened by their presence. In amongst them, competing for space, are the other species on the move—zebra, gazelles, and shy parties of eland (*Tragelaphus oryx*), wariest of all the larger antelopes.

The wildebeest cannot stay long in any one part of their range, for there is insufficient grass to feed such vast numbers of animals. The rains arrive and depart in

▶ Some river crossings are used year after year, but changes in water flow and the continual erosion of the river banks sometimes compel migrating herds to seek other crossings.

scattered thunderstorms, some parts of the plains always receiving rain, but the distribution is irregular. At times no more than a few drops wet the dusty soil, while barely a kilometer (2/3 mile) away, dark thunderheads touch the ground, delivering hour after hour of much-needed moisture. The wildebeest respond to these variable conditions by constantly rotating through the grasslands, revisiting areas every few weeks to recrop the grasses when new shoots have grown.

THE TRANSITION FROM WET TO DRY SEASON

As May draws to a close, the herds become restless, as if they can sense that their long journey back to the woodlands is soon to begin. Muddy waterholes begin to shrink as the dry northeasterly winds gust both night and day, whipping the powdery soils into towering dust devils. In June the wildebeest turn their backs on the stinging wind and, like a river in flood, begin to flow northwest off the plains, back toward the woodlands. Dividing then merging again, they pass around the small rocky hills known as kopjes or inselbergs, damming up in clusters to drink wherever they can still find water seeping from the base of granite outcrops.

Groups of lions and solitary leopards look down on the passing herds from their hiding places among rocks and trees: for as long as the widebeest continue to travel through their territories these predators will not be short of food. Spotted hyenas follow the rutted pathways cut by the herds. Hyenas are by far the most numerous and adaptable of all the Serengeti's larger predators. More

than 3,000 of these creatures spend the wet season on the plains, carefully tracking the movements of the wildebeest. Many of the hyenas will soon abandon the barren eastern plains and move northwest to establish dens at the edge of the woodlands, commuting for days at a time from these dens to prey upon the wildebeest herds in the woodlands.

CROSSING THE MARA RIVER

In some years more than a million wildebeest advance across the border into the Masai Mara reserve in Kenya. The Mara and an area in the northwest of the Serengeti known as the Lamai Wedge provide vital dry season pastures for the hungry herds in the northern part of their range. But to reach these rich pastures, the wildebeest must brave the Mara River.

During July or early August, thousands of wildebeest stream from the hillsides of the northern Serengeti to cross the river. Sometimes the animals try to cross at suicidal places, plunging over cliffs and drowning in their hundreds at the foot of insurmountable walls of mud. Older, more experienced animals probably return to where they successfully crossed in the past, and are followed by younger animals, but the contours of the river banks are constantly changing. What might have been a manageable crossing in earlier years can cease to be so in the course of a heavy rainy season.

Whatever factors prompt the wildebeest to cross—and sometimes it is simply the consequence of a build-up of animals wanting to drink—nothing deters them once the urge is established. If motor vehicles or predators prevent them from

▼ A lioness charges a column of migrating wildebeest. The herd provides abundant food for a variety of carnivores, including lions, leopards, hyenas, and hunting dogs.

Mitsuaki Iwago

KEEPING COUNT

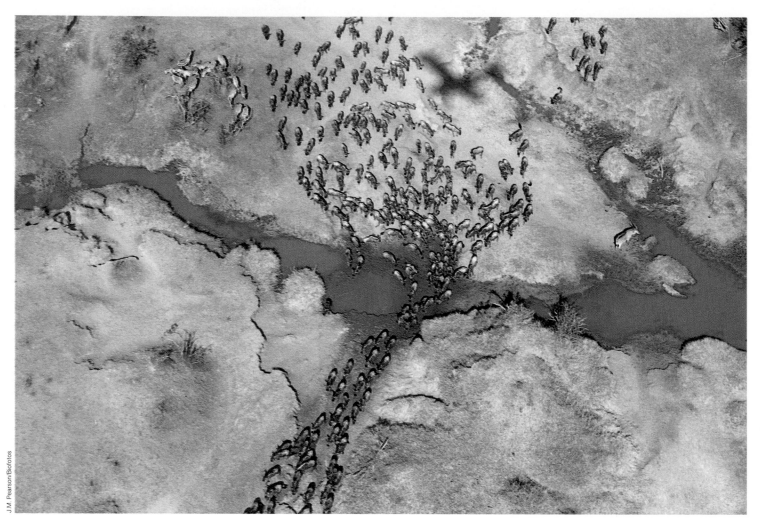

J.M. Pearson/Biofotos

In 1958 Bernhard Grzimek and his son, Michael, conducted the first aerial census of the Serengeti National Park's animals, to determine the migration routes of wildebeest and zebra. Tragically, Michael died when his aircraft collided in midair with a vulture, but by that time the two men had nearly completed their work. The Grzimeks' book, *Serengeti Shall Not Die*, published in 1959, and the subsequent film of the same name, have played a major part in the fight to save African wildlife.

Since the Grzimeks' pioneering efforts, scientists at the Serengeti Wildlife Research Center have refined and computerized their aerial census work. Every two years, during the rainy season, when the wildebeest are massed on the plains, a light aircraft leaves Seronera in the center of the park to begin the daunting task of counting the animals. By the time the pilot has flown parallel aerial transects over the entire herd, approximately 1,000 photographs will have been taken. Individual animals are then counted from the prints using a microscope.

When the first photographic census was completed in 1961, there were found to be 263,362 wildebeest, nearly three times the 99,481 estimated by the Grzimeks. Subsequent counts have charted a sixfold increase in the

▲ An aerial view of migrating wildebeest crossing a river. Wildebeest tend to move in long columns, which spread out to feed whenever the traveling herd encounters an area where recent rain has promoted the growth of the new grass the wildebeest prefer.

population. This dramatic rise is thought to have resulted primarily from the eradication of rinderpest, a highly contagious viral disease of cloven-hoofed animals. The disease first struck the Serengeti toward the end of the last century, having been introduced to Africa by cattle brought from Europe by colonists. The ensuing cattle plague virtually wiped out the livestock of Masai pastoralists, as well as devastating the wild herds of buffalo and wildebeest.

Free from rinderpest and aided by an increase in dry season rainfall during the 1970s, the Serengeti's wildebeest population exploded. When the 1977 aerial count was completed, there were found to be 1.4 million animals. Despite a particularly severe dry season in 1984, and the tens of thousands of wildebeest killed by poachers each year, the great herds continue to prosper. With an increase in rainfall (and subsequent forage) during the last three years the wildebeest population has grown by approximately 200,000. It now numbers 1.6 million animals.

making their way across at a favorite fording place, they simply cross elsewhere, sometimes making their way through thick forest to reach the river.

Calves often become separated from their mothers during the more difficult crossings. As the bulk of the herd heads off, scores of cows and calves gallop to and fro, grunting and bleating, mingling with those still trying to cross, sometimes even re-entering the river in their efforts to find each other.

The height of the river, the place the wildebeest choose to cross, and the number of animals crossing at any one time will determine how many animals die. In a bad year, the Mara claims thousands of victims. Visitors are often shocked by the sight of wildebeest trapped in the mud, and are unwilling to accept these deaths as an inevitable part of the order of life on the plains. But the majority of the victims are weak with exhaustion or have sustained serious injuries—broken legs, damaged spines—and even if they were pulled from the mud they would be unfit to continue their journey. The river soon washes itself clean again. Crocodiles, catfish, hyenas, monitor lizards, and vultures all feed off the carcasses, playing their part in the cycle of life and death.

During late September and October those wildebeest massed in the Mara Triangle (the part of the reserve lying to the west of the Mara River) head back toward the Serengeti. One last river crossing lies ahead of them, where the Mara flows wide and shallow through the northern Serengeti before finally emptying into Lake Victoria. By now the rains have started and the animals follow them south. If the rains falter, the herds wait at the edge of the woodlands; if they continue, the wildebeest continue to move, reaching the short grass plains by December.

ADAPTED FOR SURVIVAL

Wildebeest are superbly adapted to survive in an unpredictable environment. It takes no more energy for wildebeest to run a particular distance than to walk it, thus allowing them to take advantage of the scattered distribution of grass, yet still remain within range of water.

One of the great wonders of the animal world is the mass calving of the wildebeest when 400,000 calves are born. Eighty percent of pregnant cows drop their calves within a few weeks of each other, usually between late January and mid-March. By this time the herds will already be massed on the plains. Rains permitting, the cows will

therefore have been feeding on high quality, calcium-rich forage for a month or so before giving birth.

A seasonal peak in births is beneficial in that young calves are unavailable to predators for much of the year. Instead, they are all vulnerable at the same time, and in the same part of their range. The predators are soon sated by the sheer volume of easy prey. And therein lies each young animal's best chance of survival. Those calves born "out of season" stand out in the herd and are invariably killed. Lions, leopards, cheetahs, hyenas, and wild dogs all compete for their share of the spoils.

A calf's survival also lies in its ability to gain coordination faster than any other hoofed animal (some calves are on their feet within three minutes, most within five), in being constantly on the move, and in being part of the herd. Nevertheless, many still die before their first year's journey has even begun, victims of undernourishment, disease, and predation. Initially a calf is somewhat slower than its mother, and it is these youngsters that the hyenas and wild dogs prefer to hunt. But within a week calves can gallop at 50 kilometers (30 miles) per hour, enabling them to outrun most predators.

The time of day when the calves are born also acts as a form of protection. Some are born at night, and thus cannot be seen by predators. But the majority of births occur around midmorning, when most hyenas are resting in the shade, and the lions are sprawled among the cool granite rocks of the nearby kopjes. The calves have the rest of

▲ Hopelessly mired in the mud at a river crossing, a dead wildebeest symbolizes the costs of migration.

◄ (Preceding pages) Cattle egrets escort a herd of wildebeest as it fords a river. Since the turn of the century the cattle egret has extended its relationship to domestic cattle and is now found around the world, but its symbiosis was originally restricted to the grazing mammals of Africa, like wildebeest and zebra. Cattle egrets accompany large mammals as they graze, feeding on the frogs, grasshoppers, and other insects stirred up by the animals' feet.
Mitsuaki Iwago

THE GRASSES OF THE SERENGETI

The soils of the Serengeti are volcanic, and therefore rich in nutrients, but not far beneath the surface lies a hardpan of calcium carbonate. Impenetrable to all but the shallowest roots, the rock-hard layer prevents trees from taking root. Perennial grasses cover the plains, their shallow roots covered with minute hairs that absorb every drop of condensation that accumulates between the soil particles during the cold nights. Even in the driest weather the grasses survive, sprouting only hours after rain has fallen.

The Serengeti grasses that the wildebeest favor have short stems bearing small fine leaves, a protective response to the thousands of hungry mouths that feed on them throughout the rains. Grazing keeps the grass short, and also keeps it growing. When it is cropped, growth hormones pass from the roots to the shoots, promoting regrowth. The animals' saliva also acts as a growth stimulant.

Small areas of plains grassland have been fenced off by scientists for experimental purposes. Protected in this way from grazing during the rains, the grasses soon mature and flower. The taller grasses grow to heights of 60 centimeters (2 feet) and crowd out the more prostrate forms in the battle for light. This shows that without the grazing herds the composition of grass species on the plains would alter. In a number of ways the wildebeest therefore help to create the short grass conditions they prefer.

The wildebeest never stay long enough in any one place to damage the environment, and as they move from one part of the grasslands to another their excrement constantly enriches the soil. Plants and animals survive in a state of dynamic harmony, allowing both to prosper.

Mitsuaki Iwago

▲ The unique fauna of the Serengeti is maintained by an intimate relationship between grazing mammals, such as wildebeest, and the grasses on which they feed. The animals' dung constantly replenishes the soil, while endless cropping favors palatable, short-stemmed grass species such as this one, and discourages taller, less palatable forms.

▼ Because of the harmony between grass and grazer on the Serengeti, wildebeest prosper there only by remaining endlessly on the move. Wildebeest populations elsewhere in Africa do not migrate as extensively as the Serengeti population, and nor are they so large.

Len Rue, Jr./Photo Researchers, Inc.

◀ A mother wildebeest nurses her calf. Almost all calves are born within a few weeks of each other in February, during the rainy season. Calves are on their feet within minutes of birth and can keep up with their mothers, even at full gallop, after a few days.

the day to gain strength before the predators rouse themselves to hunt again.

Wildebeest unerringly locate areas of good grazing. Rain can fall 50 kilometers (30 miles) from a herd, yet the wildebeest will reach the area in time to feed on the fresh new shoots. Do they hurry over the plains in response to the sight of lightning flickering across the skies, or is it the sound of thunder that draws them? Perhaps they can smell the rain in the distance with their large, sensitive noses. Probably they use a combination of all these senses.

Along with the refined ability to locate food, the wildebeest must learn the easiest way to reach it. A calf accompanies its mother throughout its first year, receiving a guided tour of the current migration route. This provides a broad outline of the path to be followed in years to come: the location of preferred feeding sites, watering places, and river crossings. Whatever instincts the calf is born with are broadened by experience and its natural tendency to follow others.

THE ANNUAL CYCLE OF WILDEBEEST

As they move northward, the columns of wildebeest gather in from all over the plains. Many are killed at river crossings, but the herds move steadily onward.

As May draws to a close on the Serengeti, the plains dry out, the grasses fail, and the wildebeest begin their mass movement northward to the more dependable food supplies in the scrublands and long-grass plains of the Masai-Mara. This is the rutting season.

Mara River

August–October

Kenya

Tanzania

June–July

November–May

Rainfall varies widely on the plains of East Africa, both in quantity and timing, and the wanderings of the wildebeest are seldom the same from one year to the next. Nevertheless, there is an overall pattern of movement between a dry season refuge (July–November) and a wet season range (January–May). The arrows indicate the broad trend of the wildebeest movements.

They spend the rest of the dry season in the woodlands of the Masai-Mara. Eventually rains come again to the Serengeti, bringing a new crop of grass, and the wildebeest begin to move back onto the short-grass plains.

If the rains are generous, by late January the grasses have reached their peak of mineral and nutritional content, enabling females to produce a rich and copious milk supply for their young. Calves are born between late January and mid-March.

By May the rainy season is over, the dry season has begun, and the plains again lose their lush cover of grass. The wildebeest must begin to move northward once again.

Wildebeest are the key member of the Serengeti mammal fauna, but a number of other animals are involved, directly or indirectly, in their wanderings. Zebras and Thompson's gazelles are fellow grazers, and the wildebeest herds provide easy prey for lions, hyenas, hunting dogs, and other predators.

MIGRANTS OF THE PAST

R. Robin Baker

▲ Springbok (*Antidorcas marsupialis*) once migrated in huge numbers across South Africa, but after a century of persecution their remaining populations are now confined to national parks.

▶ The domestication of horses allowed people to keep up with the migrating herds of large mammals on which so many early humans depended for survival. This nineteenth-century engraving depicts a round-up of wild horses in Hungary.

Not long ago, springbok and bison roamed the earth in herds millions strong. The tiny surviving populations of these animals are now confined to reserves, but the saiga continues to travel its traditional migration routes, saved from extinction by legislation.

Go back to the last ice age and picture the frozen tundra and the barren grasslands of Europe and Asia through the eyes of our ancestors. Eking out a living near the northern limits of human existence, humans must have witnessed few more welcome sights than the migratory herds of large mammals. Reindeer, bison, antelope, horses, and even mammoths, would all, from time to time, have wandered past our ancestors' shelters, traveling their prehistoric migration routes. With the arrival of such herds came food and clothing, and thus hope of survival.

On the tundra of Eurasia and North America, caribou (or reindeer) still travel across snow-covered landscapes on their migration circuits. No longer, however, do mammoths (*Mammuthus primigenius*) make such journeys. On their migration to extinction they would have been joined by many other species of large mammal, had it not been for a last-minute change in human behavior from hunter to conserver.

Until recently the grasslands of Eurasia were inhabited by herds of grazing animals that migrated in much the same way as their prehistoric ancestors. However, farmers and pastoralists do not welcome migratory herds the way that hunters once did, and modern weapons can kill faster than mammals can breed. Many species, such as the European bison (*Bison bonasus*), and Przewalski's horse (*Equus przewalskii*), are now dangerously near extinction. The only sizeable herds left are those of the saiga (*Saiga tatarica*), found on the southern Asiatic steppes, stretching from the Caspian Sea into Mongolia.

The ancestry of the strange-looking saiga, with its long neck and bulbous nostrils, is obscure. Although classified as an antelope, the saiga has many characteristics in

common with sheep and goats. The almost trunk-like nose is designed to exclude dust and to warm the air before it reaches the lungs. Saiga are unable to withstand extreme cold, or to feed where there is more than 20 centimeters (8 inches) of snow covering the ground.

For centuries, humans hunted the saiga without serious consequences. With the introduction of firearms, however, and the discovery of a lucrative market for saiga horns in China, their numbers dropped to dangerously low levels. By 1918, out of herds that had previously numbered millions, scarcely 1,000 animals were left. Only last-minute legislation to control hunting saved the species from extinction. In 1960 saiga were estimated to number 1.3 million, and their numbers are now thought to be well over 2 million.

In spring the saiga migrate from the Caspian region northward to their calving grounds 300 to 350 kilometers (190 to

▲▼ The plains Amerindians relied on vast herds of migrating bison for much of their food, clothing, and shelter. Perhaps 60 million strong, bison roamed much of North America (below), but with the coming of the Europeans they were slaughtered in vast numbers. There are now about 30,000 left, all in reserves.

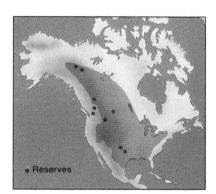

Reserves

221

▲ Saiga (*Saiga tatarica*) once migrated in millions across the steppes of Asia. The species was reduced by hunting to less than 1,000 by 1918, but was rescued from the brink of extinction and is now thought to number about two million individuals.

220 miles) away. Here the females give birth. Depending on weather conditions, this leg of the annual migration circuit takes about 14 days. Extensive snow cover and frequent storms slow progress. The saiga travel either in small groups or large herds, sometimes up to 60,000 or 100,000 strong. After the breeding season, the herds migrate 200 to 250 kilometers (125 to 155 miles) southwest to summer feeding grounds, traveling farther west in drier years to where the rainfall is higher. Between the end of August and the beginning of October, the herds migrate eastward back to the Caspian lowlands. Finally, with the arrival of the snows at the end of November, they head south to their winter quarters in the lowlands around the Caspian Sea.

The modern herds of saiga are a heartening reminder of what can be done to conserve large mammals. In East Africa the designation of conservation areas spanning

national boundaries has largely kept intact the migrant herds and traditional migration routes of zebra, wildebeest, and other antelopes. It remains to be seen, however, how well even these areas resist the pressure of future development, particularly if the tsetse fly is brought under further control, allowing cattle ranching to become firmly established on the plains.

Until the late nineteenth century, springbok (*Antidorcas marsupialis*) were numerous in many parts of South Africa. But these small, graceful antelopes competed with the settlers' domestic grazing animals for food, and so were ruthlessly persecuted. Before human settlement the springbok migrated between humid upland areas in the southwest of the country and the semi-arid grasslands in the northeast. Apart from this seasonal pattern, mass migrations occurred every three or four years in response to drought or population pressure. Herds of springbok all moving in the same direction merged into massive hordes, thousands strong, trampling everything in their path. One such horde, witnessed in 1896, took several days to pass an observer. It was 220 kilometers (137 miles) long and 20 kilometers (12 1/2 miles) wide, and was estimated to contain about a million animals. During these episodes crop damage was so extensive that at times the South African government issued firearms to the local population with instructions to shoot as many springbok as possible. The tiny surviving population is now confined almost entirely to nature reserves.

Before Europeans arrived in North America, American bison (*Bison bison*) were found from southern Canada to northern Mexico and were estimated to number more than 60 million. They migrated up to 500 kilometers (310 miles) between summer and winter ranges along roughly circular routes. Early eyewitness accounts of migrating bison describe vast herds, millions strong, covering hundreds of square kilometers. One herd crossing the Arkansas River in 1871, was 80 kilometers (50 miles) long and 40 kilometers (25 miles) wide.

From the middle of the nineteenth century, bison were slaughtered by European settlers in quite staggering numbers. Between 1870 and 1875 alone, more than 12.5 million

animals were shot. Sometimes they were killed just for the tongue, which was considered a delicacy. At other times, they were massacred purely to deprive the local Amerindians of their sole means of support. By 1880 there were no herds left south of the Arkansas River, and a census conducted in 1889 could find only 1,091 individuals remaining from the once vast herds. From this remnant, the current population of over 30,000 has been re-established within the protection of national parks.

The vanished migrant herds of springbok and bison are now as difficult to imagine as a herd of mammoths, those few animals that remain bearing witness to the human propensity for destruction.

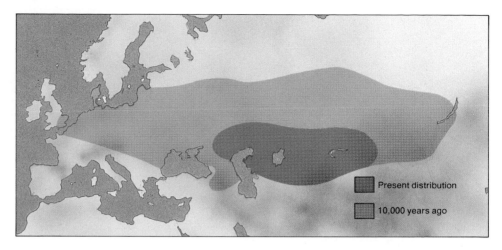

▲ Hunting and climatic deterioration have reduced the distribution of the saiga to its present size.

Present distribution

10,000 years ago

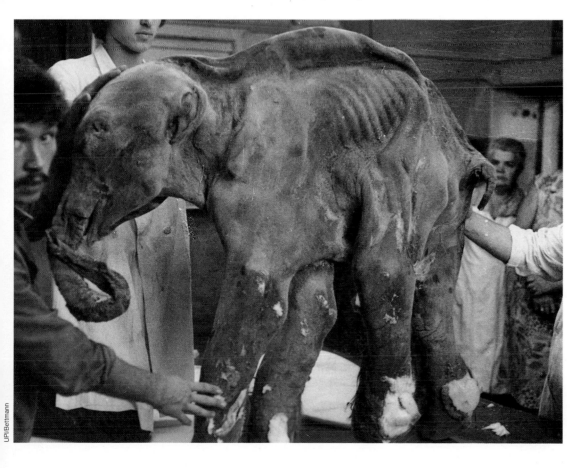

◄ Early humans were witness to the extinction of a range of large mammals, including the mammoths (*Mammuthus primigenius*) that roamed the grasslands of Eurasia and North America before the last ice age. Mammoths resembled elephants, but had long shaggy hair. This nine-year-old baby died about 10,000 years ago, and was found frozen in permafrost in northeastern Siberia in 1977.

HUMANS

R. Robin Baker

▲ A bright handful symbolizes the early heritage of the human species as a nomadic hunter-gatherer. The discovery of agriculture tied later humans more closely to the land, but the rise of technology has freed them to wander once again.

Driven by the same instincts as their primate ancestors, humans are perhaps the most migratory species of all. There is scarcely a centimeter of the earth's surface over which they have not traveled, or an area of ocean they have not crossed.

It is April in Norwegian Lapland. The winter snow is disappearing and the reindeer herds are becoming restless. Laplanders are preparing to leave their winter home among the sheltered inland forests near the Finnish border. By the end of the month they and their reindeer will have set off on a 10- to 12-day northward trek to their summer home 400 kilometers (250 miles) away on the coast of the Arctic Ocean, and they will not return south until the end of September or beginning of October. Their annual to and fro migration follows a traditional route that has been used for at least 400 years.

Migrations of this kind are common among pastoral nomads. The cattle-herding Fulani of west Africa travel about 200 kilometers (125 miles) between dry and wet season homes, while the Bedouin of the Arabian peninsula migrate around circuits over 1,000 kilometers (620 miles) long, taking advantage of shifting rainfall and pasture.

Few people, other than nomads, would think of themselves as migratory, yet, since they first evolved, humans have traveled more than any other species. Humans first appeared several million years ago, on the savanna grasslands of Africa, but they did not leave this region until a few hundred thousand years ago. Thereafter, they spread rapidly northwest through southern, western, and central Europe, and east through southern Asia to central China. This spread coincided with periods of glacial advance, when bitterly cold weather prevailed across northern Europe and Asia. Humans managed to live at the very edge of the frost line, probably because they could use fire.

By 40,000 years ago, humans had colonized as far north as Japan and as far south as Indonesia, and were poised for two further migrations. To the south, they island-hopped to Australia; to the north, they gradually worked their way across Beringia, the tundra land-bridge that existed at the current site of the Bering Sea. Ancestors of modern Amerindians and Inuits crossed Beringia in at least two waves. The Amerindians arrived first and, once on the North American landmass, spread rapidly. Central America was reached about 20,000 years ago, and the southern tip of South America 12,000 years ago. Later—10,000 to 8,000 years ago— Inuits crossed Beringia to arrive in Alaska and the Aleutian Islands. They then migrated eastward to arrive in the eastern Canadian Arctic about 5,000 years ago, and northern Greenland about 4,000 years ago.

The colonization of virgin land has only been one aspect of human migration, however. There have also been wholesale movements of people into particular regions. These invaders have killed, displaced, or simply genetically infiltrated the existing human occupants. In the past 2,000 years, such migrations have included Angles, Saxons, and Vikings moving to western Europe at the expense of the indigenous Celts; Negroids moving south through Africa at the expense of indigenous Bushmen; Caucasoids moving to southern Africa and Australia at the expense of the indigenous Negroids and Aborigines; and Caucasoids and Negroids moving to North and South America at the expense of the indigenous Amerindians.

Throughout most of his existence, *Homo sapiens* has been a hunter-gatherer, and it was as a hunter-gatherer that he colonized all the continents, except Antarctica. Agriculture and animal husbandry evolved in the Middle East some 12,000 years ago, resulting in many people living a more settled existence. Industrialization in western Europe in the last few hundred years has brought vastly changed ways of life, which have spread to many parts of the world. Genetically, however, humans probably remain hunter-gatherers.

Hunter-gatherers live by collecting fruit and vegetables and hunting animals.

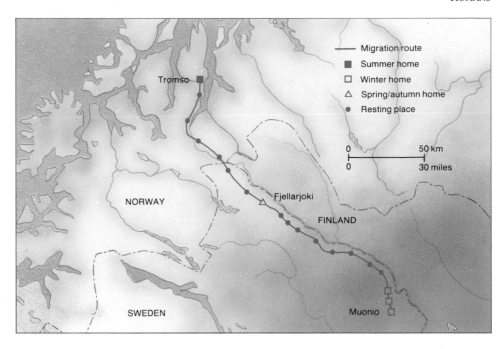

▲ ▼ For generations, Lapps have accompanied reindeer on their annual migrations. The Lapps have fixed residences at each end of the route and also at the point where the reindeers rut in autumn and calve in spring.

▲ The nomadic Fulani of West Africa milk their cows, a habit otherwise rare in Africa, and exchange surplus milk for other foods.

▼ Persecuted in their own country, the Pilgrim Fathers crossed the Atlantic in 1620 in search of a place which allowed freedom of religious belief.

(*Papio cynocephalus*). In common with chimpanzees and baboons, humans also show a sexual division of labor. Whereas vegetable food is collected largely by females, the hunting for large and small animals is carried out mainly by males, either alone or in small, strategic groups.

Human migration patterns have evolved from the way their primate ancestors used space. Primates, like most mammals, live in home ranges—areas of land that they know intimately. At any time, they know the best place to go, whether for food, drink, sleep, or to find a mate, and they know the best route to take. Individuals develop this familiarity through their travels and explorations when young, and through continual awareness of what is taking place in their environment.

All mammals show sexual differences in their movement patterns. Males are much more exploratory and travel longer distances than females. Male primates tend to undertake their explorations alone. Female primates do not travel as far from their home base as males, and when they do

Fundamentally, the way of life of humans differs little from that of other primates, except that they supplement their vegetable diet with significant amounts of animal protein, a characteristic they share only with chimpanzees (*Pan troglodytes*) and baboons

V. Englebert/Photo Researchers, inc.

explore they invariably do so in groups. Male gorillas (*Gorilla gorilla*) and chimpanzees, for example, once they reach adolescence, may travel alone for several years, exploring large areas of forest and turning up tens of kilometers away from their nearest known habitat. From time to time, these males associate with other families or social groups, and may even revisit their parental group. Eventually, they find a new group to join and settle down to reproduce.

Humans are typical primates. Adolescent males are much more likely to go on long-distance, solitary explorations to new places. Females do not travel as far, and when they do leave home they are usually accompanied by other females or a male partner. Unlike most primates, however, when the male finds a mate the pair tend to return to the male's home area. Perhaps the best known of these adolescent phases of exploration is the "walkabout" of young

▲ A Tuareg encampment in the Ahaggar Mountains of southern Algeria. The Tuareg are of Berber ancestry and their name is said to have its origins in an Arab word meaning "God-forsaken." For centuries they have lived a nomadic and fiercely independent existence in the central and southern Sahara, relying on their camels, goats, and cattle.

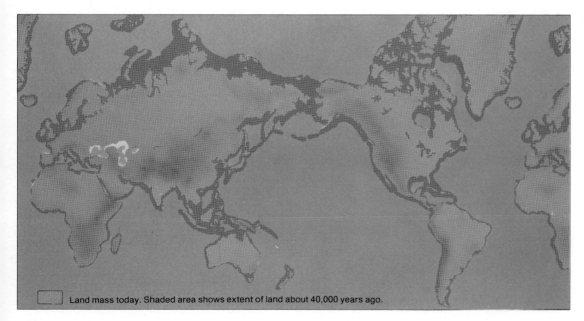

Land mass today. Shaded area shows extent of land about 40,000 years ago.

◄ Several hundred thousand years ago, early humans left their original home on the savannas of East Africa and spread across Europe and southern Asia. Approximately 40,000 years ago the sea level was much lower than it is today, and several continents, now separated by sea, were connected by land. About this time, humans used the land of bridges thus formed to cross southward to Australia, and westward to North America.

▶ (Following pages) The peoples of the southern highlands of New Guinea are mainly subsistence farmers. They slash out small gardens in the rainforest in which to grow their crops of taro, sweet potato, and bananas. This means that their staple diet is rich in complex carbohydrates but low in protein. When a pig is butchered the occasion is one of great festivity.

Brian J. Coates/Bruce Coleman Ltd.

227

▲ Over much of Africa, indigenous peoples are dependent on their cattle, and have evolved a nomadic existence commuting between dry and rainy season quarters in search of water and good grazing. Families and their herds scatter widely during the rains, but congregate at the few sources of permanent water during the dry season.

male Australian Aborigines. Around puberty, the young Aborigine goes off for several years on an exploration that takes him far from where he was born. Gradually he goes farther and farther from home and builds up a detailed and intimate knowledge of the surrounding country and people around his home. Equivalent explorations by young men can be found in most human cultures, not least among modern city-dwellers.

Exploration involves traveling to places never previously visited, while retaining the option of returning to the place where the journey began. Such a return requires navigational ability. From the explorations of bush-living tribes in Africa and Australia, to the oceanic travels of the Vikings, Polynesians, and modern mariners, humans have always used the sun, the stars, and the

earth's magnetic field to help them find their way. Experiments over the past two decades, mainly on students, have shown that even modern city-dwellers can navigate intuitively using these clues.

In experiments that attempted to mimic walkabouts, people were taken on explorations through unfamiliar woodlands, then asked the direction of and distance to the start of their journey. In such tests, both males and females showed a subconscious ability to use the sun as a navigational aid. In addition, like almost all animals that have been studied, humans are able to obtain directional information from the earth's magnetic field. As in birds, experiments suggest that the sense organ involved, the magnetoreceptor, is located at the back of the eyes, in the retina.

Human males and females in walkabout experiments use navigational information differently. Females have a more intuitive system, based primarily on the use of magnetoreception to judge direction and the twists and turns of the journey. Males place more reliance on the sun and stars. As a result, under overcast skies, males and females can judge the direction of home with equal accuracy, whereas under clear skies males are more accurate than females.

Throughout human history, the urge to explore and to settle in new and distant places has been a principle cause of human traveling. These migratory urges, and the ability to navigate, have carried humans across virtually every centimeter of the planet on which they evolved, and even out into the solar system.

N.A.S.A. Photo/Planet Earth Pictures

◄ In many ways, humankind is the most migratory of animals. Having traveled the entire surface of the earth, the species has performed the first migrations of exploration out into the solar system.

NOTES ON CONTRIBUTORS

CLIFF ASHALL

Cliff Ashall was born in Lancashire, England, completed two undergraduate science degrees in zoology at Sheffield University, and served with the Royal Engineers during World War II. Research Officer and Control Adviser with the Desert Locust Survey in East Africa from 1949 to 1962, he was subsequently Assistant Director and Head of the Field Division at the UK Ministry of Overseas Development's Anti-Locust Research Centre (later, Centre for Overseas Pest Research). Mr Ashall has carried out field research on locusts in Arabia, eastern Africa, and Australia, and has acted as a consultant to various national and international locust research and control organizations.

R. ROBIN BAKER

Robin Baker received his BSc and PhD (on "Evolution of Butterfly Migration") from the University of Bristol, UK, where he later became a postdoctoral fellow. Between 1970 and 1974 he worked at the University of Newcastle-Upon-Tyne, then at the University of Manchester, where he was promoted to Reader in Zoology in 1980. Dr Baker is best known for his pioneering works on human navigation and magnetoreception, and human sperm competition, and is author of over 70 scientific papers and five books including, *The Evolutionary Ecology of Animal Migration, Human Navigation,* and *Migration: Paths through Time and Space.*

PETER BERTHOLD

Peter Berthold was educated at the University of Tübingen, Germany, where he completed his PhD in 1964. A former president of the German Ornithological Society, Professor Berthold is Director at the Max-Planck Institute for Behavioral Physiology, where he has served as a staff member since 1967. His areas of interest and expertise include avian migration, annual cycles, genetics, behavioral physiology, and conservation. He has conducted long-term research projects on bird migration in Scandinavia, several Mediterranean countries, and Africa, and has written approximately 160 scientific papers and three books.

VERNER P. BINGMAN

Verner Bingman obtained his BSc at the University of Wisconsin, and his MSc and doctorate at the State University of New York, Albany. Currently Assistant Professor of the Department of Psychology at Bowling Green State University, Ohio, Professor Bingman's areas of specific interest include brain mechanisms that control homing pigeons' navigational behavior, the development of migratory behavior in birds, and comparative neuroanatomy.

MICHAEL BRYDEN

Michael Bryden, Professor of Veterinary Anatomy at the University of Sydney, Australia, has spent the past 26 years dedicated to the study of marine mammals. He has held academic posts at various universities around the world.

Since the mid-1970s, Professor Bryden has supervized surveys of bottlenose dolphins and humpback whales, and in 1988 he began a project to study humpback whales in Hervey Bay, Queensland. He is joint editor of three books and author/joint author of eight government reports and more than 80 research papers.

HUGH DINGLE

Hugh Dingle received his PhD from the University of Michigan and began his studies in migration at the University of Cambridge while a postdoctoral fellow. He worked at the University of Iowa from 1964 to 1982, before moving to the University of California at Davis in 1982, where he is presently Professor of Insect Behavior. He has studied migration in marine and terrestrial organisms in North America, Europe, Thailand, East Africa, the Caribbean, and Central America. Professor Dingle is the author of over 100 articles on migration and life history evolution.

STEVEN G. FANCY

Steven Fancy received his MSc from Humboldt State University, California, and his PhD from the University of Alaska. He has conducted research on the use of satellites and radio telemetry to monitor animal movements, and on energy intake and expenditure amongst caribou herds in Alaska and Canada. Dr Fancy now works as a wildlife biologist with the Pataxent Wildlife Research Center of the US Fish and Wildlife Service, where he is engaged in research on endangered forest birds in Hawaii, while continuing his studies on caribou populations and other large mammals in Alaska.

M. BROCK FENTON

M.B. Fenton is Professor and Chairman in the Department of Biology at York University, Ontario, Canada. After receiving his PhD in 1969, he worked for 17 years in the Department of Biology at Carleton University, Ottawa, before moving to his present appointment in 1986. He has contributed extensively to the scientific literature on the behavior and ecology of bats, and is the author of two books: *Just Bats* and *Communication in the Chiroptera.*

PETER J. FULLAGAR

P.J. Fullagar was born in Sussex, England, and received his PhD from the University of London, but his lifelong dedication to the study of small mammals and birds has taken him all over the world as an adviser and consultant to a number of wildlife organizations and as a co-organizer of the Australasian Seabird Group. In addition to his field experience and knowlege of the reproductive physiology, ecology, and social behavior of small mammals and birds, he has expertise in wildlife sound recording and sound spectrography. Dr Fullagar now lives in Australia, where he works as a Senior Research Scientist with the CSIRO (Commonwealth Scientific & Industrial Research Organization).

ANN M. GRONELL

An experienced marine biologist who has worked mainly in the tropics, specializing in the reproductive behavior of fishes, their social organization, and ecology, Dr Gronell is currently doing environmental work with the CSIRO Division of Fisheries in Hobart, Australia. Her interests range from social behavior and physiology to evolution, and the interaction of these fields through natural selection processes. She is also interested in making science understandable to non-scientists, and this is reflected in publications she has contributed to the non-technical literature.

MARK S. HARVEY

Mark Harvey obtained his PhD, on the systematics of pseudoscorpions, from Monash University, Australia. He continued his studies on arachnid systematics at the CSIRO, Canberra, and the Museum of Victoria, Melbourne, before his appointment as the Curator of Arachnids at the Western Australian Museum. Extensive field work in Australia, as well as a brief stint on Krakatau, Indonesia, has resulted in the collection of many arachnids and other invertebrates. The author of many research articles, he also co-authored the book *Worms to Wasps*, and recently had published *Catalogue of the Pseudoscorpionida*.

WILLIAM F. HERRNKIND

Professor of Biological Science at Florida State University and Director of its Marine Laboratory, Bill Herrnkind is interested in the migrations, orientation abilities, and other behavioral specializations of marine animals. Much of his research has been conducted using scuba and undersea tracking telemetry; he has also manned undersea habitats to study the behavior and ecology of the spiny lobster. Along with some 50 research publications, Professor Herrnkind has written for *National Geographic*, acted as field consultant for Jacques Cousteau and for various BBC television programs, and has been an adviser to state and federal fisheries agencies.

KAY E. HOLEKAMP

Kay Holekamp received her PhD from the University of California, Berkeley, for a dissertation on the natal dispersal in wild Belding's ground squirrels. She then pursued postdoctoral work in behavioral endocrinology at the University of California at Santa Cruz. At present, Dr Holekamp works for the Department of Ornithology and Mammalogy at the California Academy of Sciences in San Francisco. However, her home is in the bush in Kenya, where she is conducting a long-term study of behavioral development and dispersal amongst spotted hyenas.

Frans Lanting/Minden Pictures

Stephen Dalton/NHPA

A. ROSS KIESTER

Ross Kiester received his PhD from Harvard University, USA, but grew up in southern California in the days when it was a wonderful place to learn about amphibians and reptiles. His research has taken him to much of Latin America, the Caribbean, and the Pacific, mostly in search of lizards or turtles. In addition to his long-time interest in natural history and the evolution of biological diversity in particular, he has developed a strong interest in mathematical models in evolution and ecology. Currently, both these interests are focused toward conservation biology and the management of natural systems.

MICHAEL J. KINGSFORD

A lecturer in Animal Biology at the University of Sydney, Dr Kingsford's major research interests include the influence of oceanographic features on zooplankton and ecological problem-solving. Research for his MSc and PhD projects (the recruitment and spawning of damsel fish, and the early life history stages of fish) was based at the University of Auckland's Leigh Marine Laboratory. Thereafter, he carried out contract work for the New Zealand Ministry of Agriculture and Fisheries before taking up a fellowship at the University of Sydney. Dr Kingsford has written 15 research articles on fish and plankton.

WILLIAM Z. LIDICKER, JR.

William Lidicker is Professor of Integrative Biology and Curator of Mammals at the University of California. He has served as President of the American Society of Mammalogists (1976–78), and in 1986 received the Society's C. H. Merriam Award for "outstanding service to mammalogy." He was elected Fellow of the American Association for the Advancement of Science in 1968, and Fellow of the California Academy of Sciences in 1969. From 1980 to 1989 he acted as chairman of the Rodent Specialist Group, Species Survival Commission, International Union for the Conservation of Nature (IUCN). Professor Lidicker has had about 85 scientific papers published, including several books and monographs.

COLIN J. LIMPUS

Colin J. Limpus grew up in Bundaberg, Queensland, where his lifelong fascination with reptiles developed during his regular visits to nearby turtle nesting beaches. A graduate in physics and mathematics, he taught in schools for several years and was an amateur herpetologist before retraining in zoology, eventually completing an MSc in sea snake toxicology and a PhD on sea turtle ecology. Leader of the Queensland Turtle Research Project, Dr Limpus is now a Senior Conservation Officer with the Queensland National

Parks and Wildlife Service, where he has worked for 16 years, researching freshwater crocodile and marine turtle biology.

TERENCE LINDSEY

Terence Lindsey was born in England but raised and educated in Canada. Six consecutive Arctic winters defeated him and he set off in search of any place where the birds are interesting and the climate warm enough for water to be liquid. He settled in Australia in 1968. He has traveled widely in Australasia and the southwest Pacific, written several books on birds, and acted as editor, contributor, consultant, researcher, or illustrator on many others. Active in several ornithological societies, he is an Associate of the Australian Museum, and a part-time teacher with the Department of Continuing Education, University of Sydney.

G. V. T. MATTHEWS

After completing his PhD at Cambridge University, G. V. T. Matthews spent five years researching bird navigation, which led to a book of that name in 1955. Based at Slimbridge, UK, he was, before his retirement in 1988, Director of Research and Conservation and Deputy-Director of the Wildfowl Trust, as well as Director of the International Waterfowl and Wetlands Research Bureau. Dr Matthews has been Honorary Professor at the University College, Cardiff, and Special Lecturer at Bristol University, served on many committees devoted to conservation and research, and published numerous papers on bird migration and on wetland and waterfowl conservation.

CHRIS MEAD

Chris Mead is a failed mathematician who got hooked on birds at Cambridge University 30 years ago and has worked for the British Trust for Ornithology ever since, where he is now in charge of the National Bird Ringing Scheme. He has written numerous papers and several books, and has banded possibly 250,000 birds. Mr Mead's analyses deal with the migration and also the survival and longevity of ringed birds. After almost three decades at Tring, Hertfordshire, he is settling to live in Norfolk (which he considers to be Britain's best birding area) where the Trust has its new headquarters.

DUNCAN PARISH

Chosen British Young Ornithologist of the Year in 1976, Duncan Parish was active in amateur surveys of migratory birds before commencing his biology degree at Durham University, where he eventually graduated with honors. In 1981 and 1982 he organized undergraduate expeditions to cross the Great Sandy Desert in northwestern Australia and to survey the slopes around Lake Victoria. Mr Parish now coordinates the activities and development of the Asian Wetland Bureau, one of the largest conservation organizations in the world, which he established in Malaysia in 1987.

THOMAS P. QUINN

Thomas Quinn is a New Yorker whose interest in fishes led to a PhD from the University of Washington, his dissertation focusing on the use of the earth's magnetic field for orientation by juvenile sockeye salmon. In 1985, he left Seattle for four years with the Canadian Department of Fisheries and Oceans' Pacific Biological Station in Nanaimo, British Columbia. An Associate Professor in the School of Fisheries at the University of Washington, Dr Quinn is currently researching the patterns, mechanisms, and evolution of migration and homing in salmon, their reproductive behavior, and the effects of forest practices on salmon in streams.

LYNN L. ROGERS

A wildlife research biologist employed by the US Forest Service's North Central Forest Experiment Station, Lynn Rogers has spent the past 24 years studying carnivores—especially black bears—in the forests of northern Minnesota. He has developed a "Dian Fossey approach" in which he gains the confidence of black bears and spends up to 24 hours with them as they travel, nap, nurse cubs, and sleep through the night with little attention to their observer a few meters away. Dr Rogers has written scientific papers on carnivore dispersal, migration, navigation, social organization, habitat use, food habits, and other aspects of carnivore biology.

JONATHAN SCOTT

Jonathan Scott has spent most of the last 15 years in Africa pursuing his lifelong passion for wildlife by studying animal behavior. He has frequently appeared in television documentaries and has produced six books, most recently, *Painted Wolves: Wild Dogs of the Serengeti-Mara*. In 1987 he won the BBC Wildlife Photographer of the Year award, and in 1989 was one of the presenters of "Africa Watch" a BBC television series transmitted via satellite from the Masai-Mara in Kenya. At present, he is working on a new book on the Masai-Mara from his base at Kichwa Tembo Camp.

JEHESKEL (HEZY) SHOSHANI

Dr Shoshani's interest in the natural sciences began when he was a shepherd living in a kibbutz. He worked in zoos in Israel and England, and later moved to the USA where he trained in mammalian comparative anatomy, ecology, and evolution, and progressed to studying elephants. The initiator of the Elephant Interest Group and editor of its publication, *Elephant*, he has been a consultant to the National Geographic Society on several elephant-related projects, conducted research in natural history museums, and participated in several paleontological/archaeological excavations. He is the author of 75 publications and is currently consulting editor for a popular book on elephants.

RONALD E. THRESHER

Principal Research Scientist at Australia's CSIRO Marine Laboratories, Ronald Thresher has a particular interest in the population dynamics (including migrations) of southern Australian marine fishes. Awarded his MSc and PhD at the University of Miami, he has since held positions at Cornell University, USA, and the Tanaka Memorial Biological Station, Japan, and has been a Contributing Editor with the International Oceanographic Foundation, Florida. Dr Thresher has received postdoctoral fellowships from the Australian government and the National Science Foundation, and has published close to 40 technical papers on fish behavior and ecology, as well as two books.

INDEX

ACKNOWLEDGMENTS

Every effort has been made to acknowledge copyright holders of all material published in this book, but in the event of any omission, please contact Weldon Owen.

THE RIDDLE OF PATHFINDING
Page 31: adapted from an illustration by R. Wehner (1971) in *Animal Orientation and Navigation*; S. Galler, K. Schmidt-Koenig, G. Jacobs and R. Belleville (Eds.); NASA, Washington, D.C.
Page 32: adapted from A. Hasler and A. Scholz, *Olfactory Imprinting and Homing in Salmon*; Springer-Verlag, Berlin (1983).

LOCUSTS
Page 56: adapted from an illustration by R. C. Rainey (1963).

BUTTERFLIES AND MOTHS
Page 71: adapted from an original concept by Frederick C. Lincoln in *The Mystery of Migration*, R. Robin Baker (Ed.); MacDonald Futura Books, London (1980).

OCEANIC FISHES
Page 113: adapted from W. N. McFarland and Z. M. Hillis (1982), "Observations of agonistic behavior between members of juvenile french and white grunts" in *Bulletin of Marine Science*, Vol. 32, No. 1, 1982.
Page 118: adapted from a map from CSIRO Division of Fisheries, Hobart, Australia.
Page 119: adapted from Tesch, F. W. (1979), "Migratory performance and environmental evidence of orientation" in *Environmental Physiology of Fishes*, M.A. Ali (Ed.); Plenum Press, New York.

EELS
Page 129: adapted from Harden Jones, F. R. (1969), *Fish Migration*; Edward Arnold, London.

SALMON
Page 130: adapted from R. M. McDowall, *Diadromy in Fishes*; Timber Press, Portland, Oregon.

SMALL MAMMALS
Page 179: adapted from a diagram in *American Scientist*, May/June edition, 1989.

ELEPHANTS
Page 196: adapted from an original idea by J. Shoshani, with drawings by J. S. Grimes and G. H. Marchant.